DECISION IN AFRICA

Decision in Africa

Sources of Conflict

by W. ALPHAEUS HUNTON

With forewords by W. E. B. DU BOIS
and
TIMOTHY JOHNSON

*Revised Edition
With a Postscript by the author and a
Afterword by David H. Anthony*

NEW YORK
INTERNATIONAL PUBLISHERS

Revised Edition

Library of Congress Catalog Number: 57-13393

© INTERNATIONAL PUBLISHERS CO., INC. 2021

PRINTED IN THE U.S.A.

ISBN-10: 0-7178-0859-9 ISBN-13: 978-0-7178-0859-5
Typeset by Amnet Systems, Chennai, India

CONTENTS

	Page
Johnson Foreword	ix
Du Bois Foreword	xi

PART ONE: *SOURCES OF CONFLICT*

1. THE PRESENT IS CHILD OF THE PAST — 13
   African Heritage, 14; A Chronicle of Plunder, 16

2. LAND AND LABOR — 24
   The Two Africas, 23; Patterns of Government, 26; Land Is Life, 27; "We Must Make Them Work," 29; Farm Peonage, 31; Levels of African Farm Production, 34; "Like a Colossus"—UAC and Others, 37

3. MINE BOY — 42
   Origins of the Cheap Labor System, 41; Grievances and Strikes, 45; "Many of Us Die for 22 *s.* 6 *d.*," 47

4. WHITE CITIES AND BLACK WORKERS — 52
   Shanty Towns, 51; Bus Boycott, 52; "He Must Obey the Laws of the White Man," 53; Prison Labor for Hire, 56

PART TWO: *AFRICAN AIMS AND AMERICAN INTERESTS*

5. WORLD WAR II: THE CONFLICT GROWS — 61
   Europe Rediscovers Africa, 64; The War and African Raw Materials, 65; Cross Currents, 67

6. LOOT—AND MORE LOOT — 70
   Twenty Billion Dollars Worth—Plus, 68; Africans and Mining Rights, 71; Profits and Poverty, 73; The Postwar Drive for Strategic Materials, 74

7. DOLLARS AND EMPIRE — 82
   Government Cooperates with Private Enterprise, 81; Stockpile Bonanza, 83; The Main Objective—Investment and Control, 84; Attractive Investment Climates, 87

8. BASES AND OIL · 93
    Claimants in Ethiopia, 93; The "Great White Hope" in North Africa, 94; Oil Concessions and War Bases, 96

9. LIBERIA'S OPEN DOOR · 102
    The Fruits of American-Liberian War-Time Relations, 102; Making It Eeasy for the Concessionaires, 104; Adding Up the Results, 107; American Boasts and Liberian Facts, 109; Political "Stability" or Democracy? 112

10. URANIUM AND OTHER SOUTH AFRICAN ATTRACTIONS · · 117
    American Business in South Africa, 116; The Diamond Monopoly, 119; The Uranium Deal, 120; The African's Share, 125

11. BOOM IN RHODESIA · 129
    Federation: Prerequsite for Large-Scale Investment, 127; American Corporations in Rhodesia, 130; More Copper—with Washington Help, 132; Copper Profits, 134; "We Have Had Enough of Slave Wages," 136

12. SOME OTHER AMERICAN INTERESTS · · · · · · · · · · · · · 145
    North African Lead and West African Bauxite, 143; Uganda and Congo Attractions, 147; A Summary of U.S. Postwar Trade and Investment in Africa, 152

PART THREE: *ISSUES AND PROSPECTS*

13. DESIGN FOR EURAFRICA · 158
    The Economic Squeeze-Play, 157; The Role of the United States, 159; The Colonial Pattern of Production, 161; European Immigration Schemes, 162; More Europeans Require More Land, 167; The Question of Political Control, 171

14. THEY WON'T STAND FOR IT! · · · · · · · · · · · · · · · · · · 178
    South African and Rhodesian Tinder Boxes, 177; The Fight for a Living Wage, 182; Tired of Being Cheated, 186; To Determine Their Own Destiny, 190

15. FREEDOM ROAD · 194
    One Man—One Vote, 193; African Self-Government and Non-African Minorities, 197; After Political Independence—What? 204; Some Problems of the Emergent African States, 206; After Suez—What? 212

16. NEW HORIZONS: THE WORLDS OF BANDUNG
AND SOCIALISM   220
    The Alternative of Socialist Assistance, 218; The Cold War
    vs. African Self-Determination, 220; The Meaning of Bandung, 226

17. "WHO IS ON MY SIDE?"   232
    Wanted: a Policy of Coexistence and Cooperation, 232;
    Questions for Americans, 235

POSTSCRIPT   241
AFTERWORD   255
REFERENCES   259
INDEX   273

LIST OF TABLES

1. Main Areas of European Population in Africa   26
2. Comparative Land Held by Africans and Europeans   28
3. Yearly Income of Workers on the Large Gold Mines in South Africa   46
4. Average Monthly Cash Wages, Northern Rhodesia Copper Mines   50
5. Convictions of Africans under Pass and Allied Laws in South Africa   57
6. The Value of Principal Minerals Produced in South Africa   71
7. Eximbank and World Bank Loans in Africa   89
8. Rubber Exports, Firestone Profits, and Government Revenue in Liberia   113
9. South African Uranium and Gold: Production and Gross Profits   125
10. Net Profits, Copperbelt Mines, 1949-1956   137
11. Income and Expenditure, Northern Rhodesia Copper Industry   138
12. U. S. Share in African Exports and Imports   154
13. Direct Private U. S. Investments in Africa   155

MAPS

General Map of Africa   viii
Political Map of Africa   27
Africa's Raw Material Resources   80

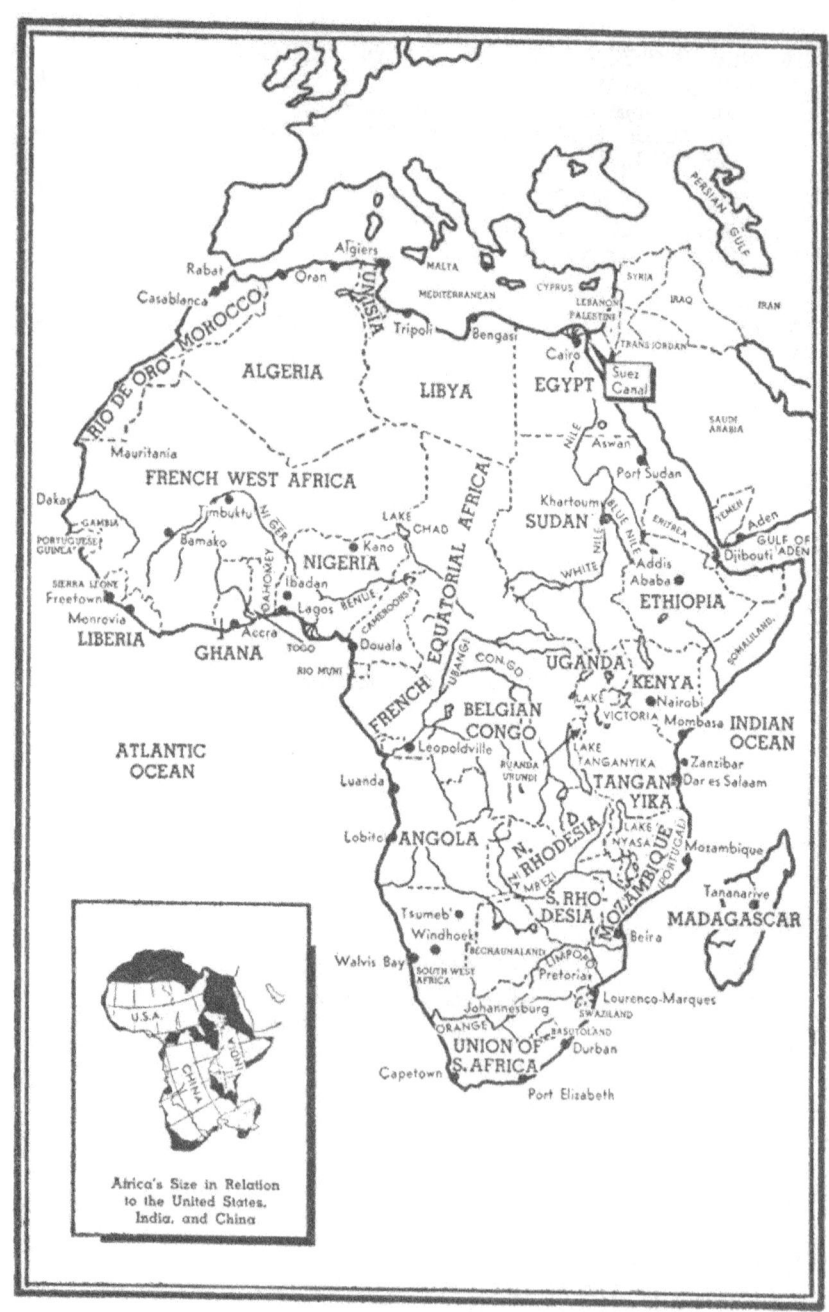

GENERAL MAP OF AFRICA

Timothy V Johnson

Foreword: In search of an alternative to capitalist development

In 1960, International Publishers released W. Alphaeus Hunton's *Decision in Africa: Sources of Current Conflict*. At the time of publication, most African countries were only a few years into (nominal) independence from their former European colonizers; several were still under Portuguese colonization; and at least three were under native-born white, racist domination.

Hunton was no stranger to Africa's problems. After playing a leading role in the struggle for equality for African Americans through his activities in the Southern Negro Youth Congress and the National Negro Congress, Hunton joined Paul Robeson in his work with the Council on African Affairs (CAA). He later served as the executive director and edited its publication, *New Africa*. Hunton helped lead the CAA from its founding in 1943 until its dissolution, as a result of McCarthyite repression, in 1955. He spent the remaining years of his life in Africa, living in Guinea, Ghana and Zambia, where he died in 1970.

In this under-recognized work of economic and political scholarship, Hunton examined the history of the economic exploitation of Africa, the contributions of this exploitation to the economic development of Europe and North America, and potential paths for economic development for the newly liberated countries. Most importantly, he documented the emerging anti-imperialist and class struggles within the colonized countries which led to independence.

Much has changed in the ensuing years since Hunton's book was first published, but the key question he posed is still germane. That is, how does Africa develop given the context of its past exploitation?

Hunton argued that the newly independent countries must search for an alternative to capitalist development and base theirpolitical development on the working class of each country. He looked to countries such as Guinea (which had sharply broken economic ties with France, its former colonizer) as a possible example. He also stressed the significance of joining the non-aligned movement or directly aligning with socialist nations. History has dramatically reduced these potential opportunities. The dissolution of the "socialist camp" has left a constricted space for this sort of economic development on a non-capitalist path - although there are examples from the experiences of Cuba and Viet Nam, from which some lessons can be drawn.

Ironically, Hunton's postscript does leave open an alternative. He demands that progressive forces in the dominant capitalist countries, especially African Americans in the U.S., play a major role in demanding that their own ruling classes be more forceful about ending the economic exploitation of Africa. He concludes the book with the cry: "Africans regard the freedom of all oppressed people of African descent, wherever they may be, as their responsibility...Let us not be fools! Let us not be cowards! Let us at last say it is so that all the world can hear, 'Yes, brother, we will stand together with you!'"

Timothy V Johnson
Editor, *American Communist History*

June 2021

Du Bois
Foreword

Dr. Alphaeus Hunton has spent most of his working time during the last fourteen years in a study of the development of Africa. I know of no one today who has a more thorough knowledge and understanding of that continent. I have been trying to point out since my first little book on Africa, brought out in 1915 for the Home University Library, the importance of that continent's role in the progress of the human race during the Twentieth Century. To be sure, Africa has long meant much to humanity. Egypt is historically African, and not, as many writers assume, Asian or even European. Egyptian culture came north from central Africa and not south from Europe or west from Asia. Greece looked toward Africa for inspiration; Rome saw Africa as a main part of her empire. There was a period during the early Middle Ages when Africa led the world, and in Africa the Catholic Church was born. The European Renaissance had some of its roots in Africa. A main center of the Moslem empire when it spread west was Africa, and later the black kingdoms of the Sudan were of prime significance to modern culture. The African slave trade built up the American world and later established capitalism in Europe, while modern art is built on African foundations.

Today, after colonial imperialism has flourished two centuries in Asia and Africa, the recoil of the peoples of these continents against European aggression is the beginning of a new world development. However, our American attitude toward Black People is leading us to neglect and forget the great uprisings of the African peoples. This book, then, with its broad sweep and deep knowledge of what is now happening in Africa and the development of present conditions from the recent past, is invaluable. In a day when facts about Africa are habitually distorted or even concealed, this book presents a wealth of figures available nowhere else and invaluable

Du Bois Foreword

not only for understanding Africa but for understanding Europe and America, which are becoming increasingly dependent on Africa for their future development.

Moreover and fortunately, Dr. Hunton from heredity and long association can see Africans as human beings and not merely as means of making money or sources of entertainment for the idle rich or current fools. He is not misled by the show and power of the capitalistic age, and European self-worship and self-praise. He knows and appreciates the rise of socialism and sees in it the coming emancipation of the darker world from the exploitation of the White World. He has carefully studied the steps of this emancipation and presents the innumerable facts which foretell the rise of socialized states which will supplant the poverty and ignorance which Europe and America, through trader, merchant, investor, and missionary, have forced upon helpless peoples and today are trying desperately to retain and replant. The British Empire is today seeking desperately to rebuild its power and prestige on domination of Black Africa, while France is centering her hope of survival on the Dark Continent. Africa, then, is shown by this book to be destined to stand with Asia in the new free world of the future, and to be readying itself to learn from the Socialism of the Soviet Union and its allied states; to be helping to redeem South America and the islands of the seas from the crass materialism, cruel theft, and heartless degradation which are characteristic of current white supremacy.

In all this, Dr. Hunton is fair and objective. He seeks his facts with the unprejudiced fairness of the scholar; he does not try to foretell the economic path to happiness and justice for particular groups or states. He does insist, however, that social welfare and not private profit must be the goal of all people, and that black Africans are people. This thesis his book supports with a wealth of material, and for this reason it is a notable contribution to African freedom.

W. E. B. Du Bois

Part One: Sources of Conflict

1. The Present is Child of the Past

Two MIGHTY CROSS currents sweep Africa. They have ebbed and flowed for as long as the white man has been in that continent. Struck by the gales of the Second World War the currents swelled to full tide. In one place, then another, their massive waves clash.

On one side is an aggregation of the continent's colonizers and exploiters who conceive it to be proper and necessary that *their* interests should have priority in Africa. On the other side is the forward thrust of many millions of people in every area of the continent who are determined to win their freedom and reclaim what is theirs.

Over a century ago, in 1843, an English writer described the great British Empire of that day—Africa was still to come—and concluded: "If we could be assured that our starving millions had resolved quietly to lie down and die, there would be nothing to dread, save the slumbering botts of divine vengeance . . . but no such determination has yet been announced by the sufferers, and divine retribution assumes some tangibility of shape, when we see human instruments ready prepared to work."[1]

"Listen to this," said Pierre Mendès-France, addressing the French National Assembly, February 4, 1955. "We found, in a prison of Morocco, a child of eight who had been there for more than a year, and Mr. Schuman is my witness that I am not telling you the worst, for there are some things that one does not dare to say from a public platform. . . ."

An English woman, writing of what she saw in Kenya's Mau Mau detention camps, tells of a women's prison at Kamiti where there were 17 young girls serving life sentences and a number of prisoners under 14 years of age; and of a juvenile compound where the guards had "carried out a mass beating up of the inmates including two boys . . . aged approximately four and seven [who] had no relatives in the camp, the father being detained elsewhere and the mother's whereabouts unknown."[2]

"I drew my revolver and pointed it in the direction of the children," a white detective sergeant testified in Johannesburg, South Africa, during the prosecution of four young African men and women charged with running an illegal school. He said he had led 16 other armed police in a raid on an open field where five or six hundred children were gathered. Why did he draw his gun? What was he afraid of? "The children. They afterwards started attacking us with stones. . . . It was like a hail storm."[3]

"I met children in the bombed-out houses and among the ruins searching for their parents. I saw parents; they, too, were searching with bleeding hands in the wreckage . . . of their homes to find their killed children," writes a Swedish press photographer who was in Port Said, Egypt, when it was attacked and occupied by British forces in early November, 1956. The horror and terror against civilians, he said, went beyond anything in his long experience as a war photographer.[4]

Can police, jails and bombs rob Africa's children of their tomorrow?

To preserve the sanctity of the White Highlands and other privileges of the white settlers of Kenya it became necessary to enlist the aid of five regular battalions of the British Army to reinforce the large locally recruited forces, together with artillery, bombing planes, and even 60 police dogs alleged to have been "instrumental in making 734 arrests" in 1955. To hold Algeria the French used troops evacuated from Indo-China, called up additional reservists, and transferred their NATO troops from Europe there along with American-made military equipment. In a desperate attempt to regain control of the Suez Canal and all that goes with such control, the British and French resorted to deliberate and flagrant aggression against Egypt, coordinating their attack on that country with Israel's.

In one place, then another, the waves clash. . . .

The demand for status, the revolt against overlordship, is everywhere in Africa. The levels and forms of struggle are varied and yet have certain common characteristics, like the topography of the vast continent. The people's expression is fashioned in one way or another by what they were, the kind of social institutions they had, before the European came; by the form of European governmental control; and, perhaps most decisively, by how they provide for their needs or earn their living.

This book is primarily concerned with the last-mentioned facet of African life. It is our purpose to trace the evolution of the African's relation to capitalist enterprise in his land, seeing how it has influenced and is today determining the content and form of his striving toward a better, freer life.

There is no lack of information as to how much of this or that metal or crop Africa produces for the world market. But seldom are we told *how* it is produced. There are some who point to the notable increases recently achieved in the production of a number of Africa's exports as evidence that everything is working out all right in this best of all possible worlds. All right for whom? That is the question.

Increased production is the aim always emphasized in an assortment of five-year plans and other schemes of economic development devised and implemented or in process of implementation by those who rule Africa or control its economy. How do these development schemes look to African eyes? Who benefits from them? Who pays for them? What are the already apparent and probable future consequences of these schemes?

These are questions to be weighed by Americans as well as others. For their government and American industry have more than a finger in the pie of Africa's resources. It was not only as Eisenhower's diplomatic representative that Vice President Nixon toured eight African countries on the occasion of Ghana's achievement of independence; he was also, in effect, acting as the representative of those American business executives who regard the further development of African sources of supply as "mandatory to the booming U.S.A. economy."

About a year prior to Mr. Nixon's African junket a white Rhodesian industrialist visited the United States. He came on a mission to recruit three or four thousand young American couples (white) to settle in Rhodesia, "Americans who will bring the spirit of enterprise and American knowledge of production methods."[5] Why Americans? Because over $60 million in direct United States grants and loans, which means taxpayers' money, has gone to Rhodesia to promote production, and American corporations have invested a larger sum there.

Likewise in other African territories the fact of United States investment or of economic-strategic interest is indisputable. Mr. and Mrs. America have hardly begun to realize that they are *involved* in the Africans' freedom struggle and not merely side-line spectators of it.

African Heritage

It has been said that "So long as the African is regarded as a man without a history and without a culture, doubts concerning his ability to govern himself will find credence." The racist and the imperialist speak to millions, the student of African history to mere hundreds, and so the myth and the doubts persist. The first task is to set the record of history straight. Any honest appraisal of what is going on in Africa today must begin with that.

"The point is not that Africans have no history," says the historian Dr. K. Onwuka Diké of Nigeria, "but that there is profound ignorance concerning it, and an almost pathological unwillingness to believe the evidence of it when presented."

Was Pre-European African society merely a "multi-cellular tissue of tribalism" as a well-known English scholar, Miss Margery Perham, asserts? Dr. Diké answers:

> Certainly many areas of West Africa have remained isolated and there is a rational explanation for the absence of certain external manifestations of civilization in them. The forest belt produced a restrictive environment. . . . In contrast the open park-land of the Western Sudan made movement easy. Here the Arab civilization of the Middle Ages met Mandingo culture and the two were united by trade and a common religion for centuries; here throve the Negro empires of Ghana (300-1270) and Mali (1285-1468) and along the 1,000 miles of the Niger that is continuously navigable, Songay (1355-1591). It is by the intermingling of cultures that civilization develops and where suitable conditions existed West Africans evolved empires and wide confederacies.[6]

In the Congo basin there flourished such states as that of the Bushongo, the Balunda Empire, and the Kingdom of Congo. In the area of Central-East Africa now consisting of southern Uganda, Tanganyika and Ruanda-Urundi the present ruling dynasties of the Buganda, Bunyoro, Ankole, Ruanda and Karagwe states have an unbroken continuity of some 500 years, and sites of recently found capitals date back a thousand years or more.

We cannot go further into this historical background here. The few facts cited may help toward understanding that the concept of nationhood has roots in the African's own heritage and that he has reason for impatiently rejecting the European's political "tutelage."

Recalling the efforts of the great Zulu leader, Chaka, to create a strong and united African empire, a South African writes:

> We do not owe African Nationalism to the oppressor. Even long before we of Africa had met the white man, we had already set ourselves on the road to a greater nationhood. We were already conscious of a certain destiny of our own. Oppression merely intensified and accelerated this movement towards the goal which we as a people had already set ourselves.[7]

In a petition to London in 1920 it was stated that

> in the demand for the franchise by the people of British West Africa it is not to be supposed that they are asking to be allowed to copy a foreign institution. On the contrary, it is important to notice that . . . according to the African system no Headman, Chief or Paramount Ruler has an inherent right to exercise jurisdiction unless he is duly elected by the people to so represent them.[8]

One of Nigeria's great nationalist leaders of the recent past, Herbert Macaulay, reminds us of another point from pre-European African history that should be remembered today:

> The fact is indisputable that the people of this country owned their mines beneath the surface of their lands centuries before the advent into Nigeria of the white man. . . . They dug out such minerals as iron, chalk copper, tin, and they utilized these minerals in the local manufacture of their poisoned arrows for battle, their hoes, their copper vessels and tinware, the bronze used in the ancient works of art of life and Benin.

The rich copper deposits of Central Africa, now the property of Belgian, British and American corporations, were originally owned and worked by Africans. One Gasper Velloso in 1514 sent a letter to the King of Portugal telling of African extraction of copper in what is now known as the Copperbelt of Northern Rhodesia. In the present Messina district of the Northern Transvaal, South Africa, the Bavenda carried on extensive shaft-mining and smelting of copper ore. And in South West Africa copper ore dug by the

Herero was carried northward by caravans from Tsumeb to Ondangua to be smelted and worked by the Ovambo coppersmiths. Today the Tsumeb mines are owned by New York corporations and the Herero and Ovambo are brought to the mines to work as unskilled laborers.

Finely wrought terra-cotta figurines have been found near the village of Nok in Southern Zaria, Nigeria, buried under stratified deposits 42 feet deep. From this fact it is deduced that they represent a culture in existence in that area some 2,000 years ago. The antiquity of the culture of the Nile Valley is more widely known. How old is the civilization of Europe, whose conquest of the "backward" continents of Asia and Africa, so most of us have been taught, was a normal and natural development? History has a way of correcting misconceptions, and the fast-paced tempo of change in Asia and Africa during the past ten years is there for all to see. But there remain some people who won't see or can't see. They cling to their comforting illusions even as reality is breathing down their necks.

A Chronicle of Plunder

In the beginning there were only the European trading posts and settlements at various points along Africa's perimeter. The early Dutch settlement at South Africa's Cape was, like others, merely incidental to the search for routes to the wealth of the East. Then came the traffic in slaves. Then the merchant traders, seeking other profitable wares. Penetration inland, the staking out of territorial claims, and political conquest were accomplished during the last quarter of the last century. Then came the first stage of economic conquest: the building of railroads, capital investments—some from the United States—in mining and agricultural enterprises, and the promotion of European migration to the main areas of investment.

The final step in this process, in the aftermath of World War II, has aimed at carrying the economic conquest to completion, systematizing and accelerating the extraction of the continent's resources, with government investment playing an important part and the United States assuming the role of general overseer.

Let us review briefly the pre-twentieth century part of this chronicle. What were the motivations? What were the results?

In his *Capital and Slavery* Dr. Eric Williams has shown in documented detail how the eighteenth century slave trade, centered in Liverpool, provided the foundation of nineteenth century British capitalism. "It was . . . the capital accumulation of Liverpool which called the population of Lancashire into existence and stimulated the manufactures of Manchester." A Liverpool writer in 1893 put it this way: "It was the price of human flesh and blood that gave us a start."[9]

The benefits of this traffic were fully shared, of course, on the other side of the Atlantic by the Southern planters and slave dealers and by New England's rum distillers and slave runners. "The Americans," says one writer, "may take some comfort in the fact that, generally speaking, their vessels were not quite as tightly packed as those under the Union Jack. British slavers averaged 285 captives, those of Rhode Island only 139¾."[10] The elder of a Newport church, each Sunday following the arrival of a slaver, was accustomed to thank God that "another cargo of benighted beings had been brought to a land where they could have the benefit of gospel dispensation."[11]

The slave trade, Dr. W. E. B. Du Bois has written, was

continent-wide and centuries long and an economic, social, and political catastrophe probably unparalleled in human history . . . at least 10,000,000 Negroes were expatriated. Probably every slave imported represented on the average five corpses in Africa or on the high seas. The American slave trade, therefore, meant the elimination of at least 60,000,000 Negroes from their fatherland. The Mohammedan slave trade meant the expatriation or forcible migration in Africa of nearly as many more. It would be conservative, then, to say that the slave trade cost Negro Africa 100,000,000 souls. And yet people ask today the cause of the stagnation of culture in that land since 1600![12]

The justifications of the slave trade were numerous and varied. So with the rest of the chronicle. In 1876 Leopold II, King of the Belgians, called together a "geographic conference." The news of Stanley's successful exploration of the Congo basin had just been received in Europe. Said Leopold, "To open to civilization the only part of our globe where it has not yet penetrated, to pierce the darkness which envelops whole populations, is a crusade, if I may say so, a crusade worthy of this century of progress."

Later, when the scramble for territory all over Africa was nearing a crisis of conflicting claims, a conference of the interested powers, with United States representatives participating, met in Berlin. Out of the horse-trading deals and double-deals came finally, in February, 1885, the General Act of Berlin, a gentlemen's agreement for the partition of Africa. In the document's 38 articles, two were included (VI and IX)—added as an afterthought, it has been said—having to do with the people of Africa. "All the Powers," it was pledged, "undertake to watch over the preservation of the native races, and the amelioration of the moral and material conditions of their existence. . . ."

The "treaties" which hundreds of African rulers were bribed, tricked or coerced into "signing" with a cross read that they ceded their territory—a concept meaningless to a people for whom the land was a sacred communal heritage—"with the view to the betterment of the conditions of our country and people."

The pattern continues with the entrance of private enterprise. For example, Harvey S. Firestone, negotiating his rubber plantations concession in 1925, declares, "We are interested in any undertaking for the betterment of Liberian life." Harry F. Sinclair twenty years later announces that in return for the exclusive oil concession granted by Emperor Haile Selassie, the Sinclair Oil Corporation has obligated itself to "promote the general welfare" of Ethiopia. And in the present period it has been officially explained again and again that while the African economic development projected in the Marshall Plan program was "designed to strengthen the economies of the countries participating"—that is, the Western European colonial powers—"the interests of the African peoples are given first consideration."[13]

Now let us glance for a moment underneath the humanitarian sugar-coating at the reasons for the partitioning of Africa. Up to the end of the slave trade, coastal trading stations and settlements sufficed for what Europe wanted. Access to such things as palm oil or rubber, however, required penetrating inland to the supply-source if they were to be secured in sufficient quantity and at the most profit.

Thus, for instance, in the Gold Coast,* as Sir Hugh Clifford, prior to becoming Governor of Nigeria (1919-1925), explained:

> For many decades after 1815 . . . the maintenance of uninterrupted trade routes to and from the interior represented the highest ambition of the British Government on the Coast, and it was in order to secure this object that little by little jurisdiction was extended . . . the assumption of responsibility for the welfare of the natives, whose world our coming had turned topsy-turvey, was shirked and evaded as much as possible. . . . Thus the history of British relations with the peoples of the Gold Coast and Ashanti, rightly

---

* The former designation of the West African state is used in this book interchangeably with Ghana (see p. 14), the name officially adopted on the achievement of independence, March 6, 1957.

viewed, is the story of an attempt to secure our merchants' profits at the least possible cost to ourselves, and the gradual assumption of extended responsibilities undertaken in pursuance of that object.[14]

Meanwhile in Europe itself the mid-nineteenth century advances of industrial production had by the 1870's outgrown the home markets and the limited external ones. Africa was "discovered" when Europe needed it. Said Jules Ferry, addressing the French Chamber of Deputies in 1885, "It was a question of having outlets for our industries, exports and capital. That was an absolute necessity; that was why France had to expand in West Africa, on the Congo, in Madagascar."[15]

As with France, so with Britain, Germany, Belgium and Portugal. In each country, during the last two decades of the nineteenth century, investment capital was organized in various companies, some of which were granted blanket charters to open up, seize, and control what lands they could, while others received long-term concessions over vast areas in the new colonies.

Leopold, having created the Congo Free State in 1885, decreed a royal monopoly on all rubber and ivory in the land and a forced labor tax on its inhabitants. Overseers and a conscript army enforced the decrees with fiendish brutality. From his personal domain and the receipts from concessionaires it is thought that, all told, Leopold's civilizing crusade netted him $20 million.[16] It cost the life of every second inhabitant. The world-wide outcry of horror finally led the Belgian Parliament in 1908 to assume direct control of the territory and inaugurate some reforms. The big concession companies, however, still remain.

Of the British joint-stock companies chartered from 1885 to 1889 to extend Queen Victoria's realm in Africa, by far the most spectacular and profitable was the British South Africa Co. In 1949 the sixtieth anniversary of its incorporation was celebrated. The occasion was noted by a dinner in London at which the assemblage of British worthies heard the Company's president, Sir Dougal Malcolm, declaim:

> How much the British Empire—I prefer that old title—owes to the enterprise and efforts of the merchant adventurers, including the chartered companies, of the City of London! . . . the spirit of adventurous romance . . . was reinforced by the invaluable spirit of private enterprise and of profit-making, one of the most respectable motives in the world.[17]

It may be debated how much of the spirit of adventurous romance there was in Cecil John Rhodes, who created the BSA

Co., but no one will dispute his zeal for profit and power. Having fought or bought his way to control of South Africa's developing gold and diamond industries with the formation of his first two companies, Consolidated Gold Fields (1887) and DeBeers Consolidated Mines (1888), Rhodes turned his eyes northward. There had come rumors of great mineral riches to be found in the land of the Matabele across the Limpopo River.

So Rhodes in 1889 secured a royal charter for his BSA Co., called by Sir John Swinburne "the most monstrous concession to private individuals that Parliament ever heard of." The Company was authorized "to àcquire by any concession, agreement, grant or treaty, all or any rights, interests, authorities, jurisdiction and powers of any kind or nature whatever, including powers necessary for the purpose of government and the preservation of public order." No need to repeat here the sordid story of the treaty-signing trickery whereby Lobengula, King of the Matabele, was alleged to have surrendered his lands; or his vain appeals to Victoria—"The white people are troubling me much about gold. If the Queen hears that I have given away the whole country it is not so." At the battle of the Imhembesi River the Matabele warriors, with a heroism yet unsung, made a desperate last stand against the invaders' blazing Maxim guns.

London newspapers hailed the acquisition of 150,000 square miles of the land of the Mashona and Matabele, to become known as Southern Rhodesia, and noted the simultaneous rise in the shares of the BSA Co. Exclusive mineral rights in parts of Nyasaland and Bechuanaland and throughout Northern as well as Southern Rhodesia were claimed by Rhodes' company. It retained direct administration of Rhodesia until 1923; as landlord of the Rhodesian copper belt it continues to pay dividends to this day.

There was an American who had empire-visions, too, back in the 'nineties when Rhodes was busy in South Africa. It was Henry M. Stanley. Back in New York from his African explorations, he tried to interest friends and Wall Street men in financing an American East Africa Co. He wanted to buy up land in the area which the British were soon to stake off and call Kenya. "My plan contemplates an organization of American capitalists, the purchase of vast tracts of territory . . . in short, the control by American capital of the richest part of Central Africa, and the possession of a power not surpassed by that once held by the East India Company."[18] He was unsuccessful in raising the needed capital; there were other investment interests nearer home at the time. Soon after the turn of the century, however, United States investment capital began entering the African market, one of the first centers of interest being Leopold's Congo Free State, a portent.

Only in South Africa's Boer War did white men shoot other white men in the grab for the African's land. But in every section of the continent Africans died resisting the European invaders. Colonization was not accomplished by partitioning agreements, or through "treaties" which were invariably followed by revolts once the meaning of the European's contract became understood. No, the colonization of Africa was brought about only by armed force. It is maintained today only by the same armed force.

The years 1880 to 1900 marked the most sweeping seizure of property in the world's history. By the latter year an area larger than that of China, India and the United States combined had been all but completely overrun and brought under the control of the European powers. In all of Africa there remained outside such control only Morocco, occupied by France in 1912; Libya, taken by Italy in the same year; Ethiopia, which had decisively repulsed an Italian invasion at the battle of Adowa in 1896; and Liberia, saved perhaps by its foreign loan obligations and European fears of provoking American displeasure.

The end was not yet. Following World War I, defeated Germany's colonies were divided among Britain, France, Belgium, and the Union of South Africa in the form of League of Nations "mandates" to be held by them as "a trust" and to be governed—naturally—with primary concern for the welfare of the inhabitants.

In the town of Douala in that part of the German Cameroons, West Africa, that went to France, the Africans in their independent church used to sing a hymn:

> This is what our life is like here below. Why bewail our lot? The Germans have gone. The French have come in their place. They in turn will go. If the English or the Americans come in their place, it will be just the same, until the day when we have our freedom. Meanwhile, take my corpse, put it in the sepulchre; freedom is on the way, and in spite of all sing Alleluia![19]

2. Land and Labor

Eighty-three-year-old Colonel Ewart S. Grogan is one of the last of that group of Englishmen who first acquired titles to the land of Kenya. During a half century of prominence in the affairs of the British East African colony he has consistently exhibited a rare and unabashed bluntness of expression, scorning such hypocrisy as "the mawkish euphemisms in which we wrap our land-grabbing schemes." He was himself the recipient of a 200,000-acre forest concession in the 1903-4 parcelling out of land in Kenya.

In a book published at the beginning of the century, when European settlement of the newly opened continent was in the air, Mr. Grogan had this to say:

> There are two distinct standpoints from which I view the African. As a spectator and student of social evolution, I see a people infinitely more wise, infinitely more decent, infinitely more sane than we. The absolute logic of their life bewilders our distorted minds. We can never learn to understand them. They soon see through us. . . .
> The other point of view is that of the man in their midst with work to do. We are dependent upon their aid. To assist us they must be moulded in our ways. But they do not want to be, and yet they must. Either we give up the country commercially or we must make them work. . . .
> I have small sympathy with the capitalist regime. . . . But it is the regime in which we live as yet, and till it top-heavy crumbles to the ground the native too must fall in line. We have stolen his land. Now we must steal his limbs. . . . Compulsory labor is the corollary of our occupation of the country.[1]

Compulsion is necessary to secure the Africans' "cooperation," he says again, "because where negroes (*sic*) are, white men will not do manual work. And the negroes will not disappear, as have savages of other lands."[2]

There is the crux of the difficulty, of course. The African does not see why he should remain someone's manual or menial slave, and neither will he quietly lie down and die or otherwise disappear.

LAND AND LABOR 25

And so compulsion finally reaches the point of shooting and bombing uncooperative "terrorists."

"Hang the rascals for treason, confiscate all the land of the Kikuyu" demanded the Honorable Mr. Grogan in the early days of the undeclared Kenya war against the Mau Mau.[3] More than a thousand Kenya Africans were indeed executed for various offenses, and the plots of land belonging to Jomo Kenyatta and a long list of other alleged conspirators were in fact declared forfeited.

The Two Africas

In the United States, it has been observed, resistance to accepting and implementing the Supreme Court decision on desegregation in the schools increased in direct ratio to the size of the Negro population in relation to the whites. In Africa resistance to the black man's economic and political advancement rises in direct ratio to the size of the white population and the power it wields.

Historically, it is true, the Sahara divided the Mediterranean countries of Africa from the rest of the continent, Black Africa. But from Mussolini's invasion of Ethiopia to Bandung and the French and British military operations in North Africa, Kenya and Egypt, much has happened to erase the former significance of that natural barrier. There is also the important link represented by the predominantly Moslem belt of Black Africa extending across the northern parts of French West Africa, Nigeria, the Cameroons, French Equatorial Africa, the Sudan and along the east coast. Today it is not so much the Great Desert but rather white settlement that divides Africa.

In 1835, according to Dr. R. R. Kuczynski, there were 135,000 whites in the whole of Africa; a century later the number was four million. Today it is close to six million, about half in the Union of South Africa, out of a total population of over 220 million.

Listed on page 24 are the countries of Africa which now have a white population of 40,000 or more (Egypt is omitted here, because its 250,000 whites are not in the category of settlers possessing either political power or any major land holdings).

The countries listed constitute one Africa. The other Africa consists of territories with negligible white populations: notably Nigeria with 35 million inhabitants, Ghana with close to five million, the Republic of the Sudan (over ten million), and Uganda (six million)—to name only the more populous ones. In these the resident whites range from fewer than 5,000 to a maximum of 15,000. There are, in addition, marginal countries such as Tanganyika with 25,000 whites and eight million Africans.

TABLE 1. MAIN AREAS OF EUROPEAN POPULATION IN AFRICA[4]
(in thousands)

	European Population in Previous Years			Current Estimate of Total Population			
	1921	1935-36	1946	European	African	Other	
Union of South Africa	1,422	2,004	2,336	2,907	9,306	1,281	Colored [a]
						421	Asian [b]
South West Africa	19	31	39	50	370		
Southern Rhodesia	34	55	84	176	2,300	13	Asian, Colored
Northern Rhodesia	3	10	22	65	2,100	5	Asian
Kenya	10	18	23	58	5,902	152	Asian
						33	Arab
Algeria	791	946	1,040	1,200	8,600	140	Jews
Morocco	81	203	293	400	8,000	250	Jews
Tunisia	156	213	239	250	3,500	145	Jews
French West Africa	8	25	32	82	19,000		
Madagascar	17	25	28	60	4,628	17	Asian
Belgian Congo	7	20	50('48)	93	12,600		
Angola	°	°	44('40)	110	4,200	30	Colored
Mozambique	°	°	31('45)	68	6,000	30	Colored
						17	Asian

[a] Persons of mixed parentage. [b] Mainly or entirely Indian.
°Data unavailable.

What led to the concentration of the Europeans in certain areas and not in others? There was, of course, the proximity and convenience of the North African territories, though they were by no means easily conquered. There was the lure of diamonds and gold in South Africa, leading on from there into Rhodesia and South West Africa. There was the attraction of the beautiful high plateau country in Kenya and Southern Angola. There were government-sponsored settlement schemes for strategic or economic objectives. On the other hand, in West Africa, the Sudan and Uganda, the existing well-established African states and the bitter resistance to conquest on the part of the Ashanti, Sudanese, and others discouraged a policy of outright European settlement. Furthermore, neither the resources nor the climate of these

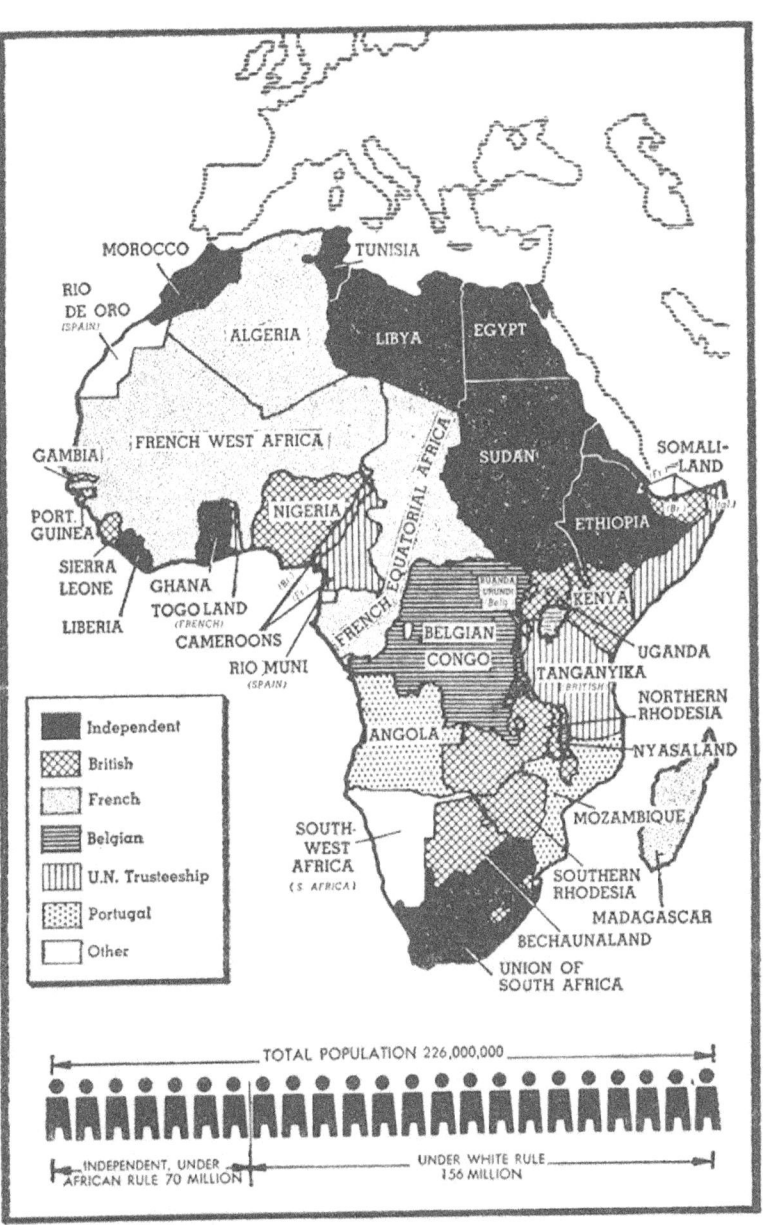

POLITICAL MAP OF AFRICA

countries—not to mention the deadly mosquito—appeared too inviting. In any event, a more tactful indirect rule system was employed in these areas and the people's land, for the most part, remained theirs.

Patterns of Government

Since how people live and earn their living depends in part on how they are governed, we should pause here for a moment to consider the general forms of political control in Africa. The pattern in basic terms is this:

		Total Area (millions of sq. miles)	Total population (millions)
I.	Politically independent and governed by Africans	2.8	70
II.	In transition to political independence under African government	0.6	51
III.	Independent or semi-independent and governed by resident whites	1.5	27
IV.	Colonies ruled directly and entirely from European capitals	1.8	31
V.	Colonies where local political responsibility is shared by the central governments in varying degrees with the colonial inhabitants	4.8	47

Group I includes Egypt, Ethiopia, Liberia (governed mainly by the descendants of black settlers from the United States), Libya, the Sudan, Tunisia, Morocco, Ghana, and Guinea.

Group II includes (a) countries for which formal commitments toward early independence have been made: Nigeria (1960) and Somalia (scheduled by the United Nations to graduate from Italian trusteeship to freedom also in 1960); and (b) countries in which current events point to approaching sovereignty: Algeria and Uganda are examples.

Group III includes the independent Dominion of the Union of South Africa and South West Africa, in effect annexed to it; Southern Rhodesia, Northern Rhodesia and Nyasaland, together comprising the Central African Federation, established by the white residents in 1953 with British sanction; and Kenya, where the white settlers have long been accustomed to running their own affairs with little hindrance from London, even though the territory still remains a British colony.

Group IV includes the Belgian Congo and the colonies belonging to Portugal and Spain. These are ruled directly from Brussels, Lisbon and Madrid through local administrators as though they were part of the metropolitan countries. Except in the Belgian Congo, where a limited franchise has lately been introduced, there are no representative political institutions in these territories.

Group V comprises the territories of Britain and France (UN trusteeship territories included) which are outside categories II and III—Sierra Leone, Tanganyika and French West Africa, for example, though pressure for independence is rapidly mounting in the first two countries.

An important point to be noted in this analysis is that most of the countries in Groups III and IV (excepting the Spanish territories) have large white populations, and that circumstance and the form of political control exercised represent the most formidable road-blocks on the path to freedom for close to 60 million Africans. That is why much of our attention in this book will be focused on these particular territories.

This is, of course, only a preliminary bird's-eye view of the subject. The relation between political and economic factors in the various countries will unfold as we proceed, and it will be observed that while political self-determination is the basic and primary prerequisite for all of Africa, it is only democratic self-government *coupled with their own control of the land and its resources* that will enable Africans to secure the maximum good for themselves from their labor.

Land Is Life

Though marketing and trade, village industries and specialized crafts of various kinds existed in many sections of pre-European Africa, the dominant feature of the economy was agricultural and pastoral production for self-subsistence. In all but a few societies in which domestic slavery was practiced, the land was regarded as the common property of the group—the family, clan, tribe or nation. A representative example of this is found among the Ibo of Nigeria, for whom

land tenure is based on three cardinal principles: that the land ultimately belongs to the community and cannot be alienated from it without its consent; that within the community the individual shall have security of tenure for the land he requires for his cattle compounds, his gardens, and his farms; and that no member of the community shall be without land.[5]

The land still remains the basis of life for the great majority of the people of Africa, including the most industrialized section of the continent, South Africa. But the old security of tenure was doomed by the advent of the European, who set before the African a new standard of money values which he was expected to accept at cut-rate befitting his inferior status, and who taught the African about individual ownership of property while robbing him of his most prized possession.

In Algeria, South Africa, Kenya, Rhodesia, or Mozambique, it was the same story over and over again, of the original inhabitants pushed back, back by the newcomers, who took the choicest areas for themselves and marked off what they did not require of what was left for the "exclusive" habitation of the "natives." Vast areas were sequestered against future contingencies or out of sheer greedy speculation: in Kenya, for example, in 1938, 1,890 Europeans were in possession of 5,053,448 acres of land of which only 546,602 were under cultivation, while some 600,000 or more Kikuyu were crowded into a "Native Reserve" measuring 3,936,640 acres.[6]

The Belgians in the Congo and the French in Equatorial and West Africa preferred not to designate any areas reserved for Africans, thus enjoying greater freedom in allocating land for settlement or to concessions. Moroccan-owned land was expropriated in 1914 (again in 1927) so that, as General Lyautey later said, the administration might encourage "a horde of Frenchmen to stake out land and take possession, creating titles to this land without inquiring too closely into their legal rights to it." South Africa's 1913 Land Act made many thousands of Africans homeless and landless; they were forced to move to the "Native Reserves" conceded by the whites for African residence, an area representing 7.3 percent of the country. The record of land expropriation as of 1957 in some of the territories is shown in Table 2.

TABLE 2. COMPARATIVE LAND HELD BY AFRICANS AND EUROPEANS IN RELATION TO TOTAL AREA OF ALLOCATED LAND[7]

	Africans			Europeans		
	% of Pop.[a]	% of Land	Acres per capita	Acres per capita	No. of Holdings	Acres in Average Holding
Algeria	87	63	1.1	4.3	25,000	204
Morocco	95	80	1.3	6.3	6,000	417
Tunisia	93	78	2.1	8	6,000	333
Kenya	99.9	76	5.8	195	3,000	3,400
Southern Rhodesia	93	44	17	278	6,000	8,200
Union of So. Africa	75	12	3.8	92	120,000	2,200

[a] European and African only. Population figures cited in Table 1.

The white man's "Native problem" in Africa had its origin in his expropriation of the land. It was this which gave rise to repeated revolts in the Mediterranean colonies, and in Eastern and Southern Africa. It was this that led to the founding of organizations such as the African National Congress in South Africa in 1913 and the Kikuyu Central Association in Kenya in 1922.

Kenya Africans addressed numerous protests to London and to the Parliamentary commissions that were sent again and again to look into the land question. "Had our land been thus robbed by any other native tribes," they said, "the Kikuyu would have certainly given their lives for their property, but confronted by a people with the latest and most formidable weapons of precision and destruction such an idea was and is unthinkable."[8]

The commissions, one after another, came, saw and issued their reports, but the 999 year leases to Europeans and the prohibition of any "non-European" (African or Asian) from management, occupation or control of any land in the "White Highlands" remained. The robbery of African lands continued. "What Africans want now is not commissions but the restitution of their land," said Jomo Kenyatta in 1932 when he was general secretary of the Kikuyu Central Association.

"We Must Make Them Work"

An official of the Kenya Government's Agricultural Department in 1945 made a survey in the South Nyeri District of the colony to determine how much land was needed to maintain an African family of six and provide an annual income of £20 (about $98 at that time) for purchase of essentials and payment of taxes. He found that 11.5 acres would be needed. This meant that 48 per cent of the families would have to disappear to enable the remaining 52 per cent to subsist.[9]

That, of course, was one of the prime objectives of driving the Africans off the land into restricted areas: to force as many as possible to work *outside* the land available to them. Land alienation transformed self-supporting peasants into squatters, tenant farmers or migrant laborers on the settlers' farms, or drove them to the mines and cities—to France itself in North Africa—in search of work.

Further, where the land was taken or where it wasn't, a tax was levied on every male African who appeared to have reached his sixteenth or eighteenth birthday (whites become liable for taxation when twenty-one). Such taxation, reinforced by automatic fines or imprisonment—50 per cent of the tax or two months in jail in Nyasaland, for example—served effectively in increasing the labor supply. Except, that is, when the people joined together and refused to pay, as has often happened since Bambata's rebellion in 1906 rocked Natal, South Africa.

In making this system work, the chain of command extends from the top officials of government through their district commissioners in the rural areas to the tribal chiefs. Making these rulers dependent upon themselves for the maintenance of their station and income, the colonial officials and settlers used them as instruments for insuring the collection of taxes (from which they often received a rebate) and for the requisitioning of labor. Where the African society had had no such ruler but was governed by a body of elders or an elected council, as in the case of the Kikuyu, the Europeans appointed and installed their own chiefs (who accordingly were normally dealt with as enemies by the Mau Mau). Exploiting and degrading the traditional practice of communal labor, the authorities converted the chiefs into recruiting agents to supply workers for road-building and other "public works," or for the plantations and mines.[10]

Not all the chiefs, by any means, are to be regarded as mere servants of the overlords. There have been numberless African rulers who defended their people's interests and were made to suffer for it. The Nyasa chiefs rose as one in opposition to the Central African Federation plan. A Zulu chief, rather than obey a government order for his tribe to move, gave his last command to his people—to scatter themselves to the four winds. The president general of the African National Congress in South Africa, Albert John Luthuli, is a deposed chief. There still remain, however, those African rulers who consider it the better part of wisdom to remain loyal to those who maintain them in authority. But judgments alter with events and the colonial rulers sometimes are dismayed by sudden and unexpected defections like that of the late El Glaoui, Pasha of Marrakesh, Morocco.

To return to our subject of getting the African's labor, let us illustrate its operation. In 1919 the Kenya settlers were experiencing a labor shortage. Besides ordering up Africans to expend their labor on state projects, the colonial officials sent a circular of instructions to district commissioners, calling upon them to "exercise every possible lawful influence to induce able-bodied male natives" and women and children as well to hire themselves out to white farmers.

The news reached London and there was a noise made about it. To the charge that this represented a policy of forced labor for the benefit of the European settlers, the Acting Governor of the colony made a categorical and indignant denial. Addressing the colony's Legislative Council, he not only defended the procedure of securing African labor but said, "It even appears to me that, if persuasive measures fail to achieve that object, it would be our duty to take legal powers to prevent the natives from remaining idle, with the attendant risks of lawlessness and disorder in the Reserves."[11]

That was in May, 1920. A year later the settlers moved to cut the wages of their farm labor from ten shillings a month to six or seven. A memorandum of protest addressed by leaders of the Young Kikuyu Association, forerunner of the Kikuyu Central Association, to the Acting Chief Native Commissioner led to a conference on June 24, 1921. An English writer who was present has described the meeting:

Senior Government officials . . . District Officers, missionaries, Kikuyu chiefs and attendants, natives in red paint, mission boys and members of the Young Kikuyu Association in imported clothing—the old order and the new in the native world; the Government insistent upon respect for the recognized (and salaried) chiefs and headmen; younger men, acting *in combination,* thrusting themselves in between the paid chiefs and the Government. . . .

The young men acted and spoke with a composure and self-confidence that grated upon the paid chiefs. . . . They complained of forced labor of girls and young women. . . . Their wages were going to be reduced. Their hut tax was too high. . . . There was no Government education for their children.

"When we went to do war work" (as porters in the Carriers Corps in World War I) "we were told by His Excellency the Governor that we should be rewarded," they said. "But is our reward to have our tax raised and to have registration papers given us and for our ownership of land to be called into question . . . ?"[12]

What followed is reminiscent of events thirty years later. The young men toured the countryside holding meetings which became larger and larger, three thousand, five thousand, and more and more militant. They sent cablegrams to the Colonial Office and members of Parliament. There was a proposal made to collect all the registration certificates and dump them in front of Government House in Nairobi. Then the Government struck without warning. The

Association's leader, Harry Thuku, and his brother were arrested and jailed in Nairobi on March 15, 1922. A crowd of supporters—several hundreds—gathered and remained all through the night. Next morning the city awoke to a general strike. The crowd in front of the jail swelled to thousands. A shot went off, followed by general firing by the police. The square cleared. Over a score lay dead or wounded on the ground. Thuku and others were exiled to the north country, and their organization was declared illegal.

"But the idea of union had taken hold of the people's imagination," says Jomo Kenyatta, writing of this period, "and instead of being killed the Association was driven underground. . . . The Africans of Kenya had their Maquis long before Hitler appeared on the European scene."[13] The end of the sequel to that meeting in June, 1921, has yet to come.

Farm Peonage

How fares the African farm laborer? Conditions vary according to the employer and place of employment. In general, however, it may be said that his existence is precarious, his status in many areas borders on slavery, and his earnings are negligible—sometimes little more than the rations received or the food he can grow. Such conditions explain the universal drift of work-seekers toward the towns. Mine operators in South Africa are able to recruit workers, meager though the mine wages are, from a thousand miles away in Nyasaland because there the general wage for most of the 100,000 laborers employed on the tea estates, tobacco plantations, and other farms is 17s.6d ($2.45), exclusive of food allowance, for every thirty days worked.[14] A work week may be up to sixty hours, which comes to less than one cent an hour.

Or take the case of Mr. Blundell's farm hands in Kenya. Mr. Michael Blundell is one of the most prominent political figures in the colony. The Yorkshire-born country gentleman owns a relatively small 1,200-acre farm in the heart of the "White Highlands." It so happened that during a debate in the House of Commons, December 16, 1952, on Kenya's Mau Mau troubles, Mr. Leslie Hale, a Labor M.P. who had recently visited Kenya, held up a piece of paper and said:

I have in my hand a contract in printed form . . . dated July 21, 1952. It is a contract for three years which cannot be terminated by the worker.

It provides that he shall have a piece of land not more than two and a half acres in extent. It does not provide any home, but does provide that the occupier shall supply him with building materials. . . . It does not provide him with any food; it specifically says 'No posho' [corn flour]. It restricts the crops he can grow on his land to maize [corn], potatoes and other vegetables. It refuses to allow him to own any cattle. . . . If he has a lad who has reached 16, that lad must work for the employer or go elsewhere. The name of the employer is Mr. Michael Blundell.

The contract was for 3s. (42¢) a week, seven days a week, labor of women and children included.[15]

Hired farm labor is most commonly used on the large estates and farms of white settlers and on the foreign-owned agricultural concessions. On African-owned cocoa farms in Ghana and Nigeria or cotton and sugar plantations in Uganda, except when held as investments by wealthy owners, the size of the farm and value of the crop determine whether workers other than the owner's family are needed. Such workers are seasonal, migrant day-laborers, in the main, employed especially at harvest-time; they number approximately 250,000 in Ghana, 100,000 in Uganda, according to United Nations estimates. In addition to the migrant farm laborers there are in many areas tenant farmers or resident laborers like Mr. Blundell's man, and sharecroppers like the *khammés* in Algeria, who receive one-fifth of the harvest, or like some of those on the larger West African cocoa farms.

Both agricultural and industrial workers in most of Africa are bound by a legal code which sets them apart from and below free workers in other countries. This is the labor service contract whereby the African is imprisoned or fined for quitting a job short of his term of employment, losing or damaging the property of his employer, or other misdeeds. The labor service contract may range from a month to three years and the penalty for breaking it is usually two or three months in jail or a fine equivalent to six months' or a year's wages. The terms of these contracts are most restrictive and the penal sanctions are heaviest and most rigidly enforced in areas of European settlement.

By the terms of South Africa's Native Service Contract Act of 1932, for example, an African living on his employer's farm cannot leave it, except to go to his home, without a document of identification signed by his master. He cannot secure other employment unless he can produce a labor contract or a statement signed by the same master indicating that he is under no obligation to render any service during the period in question. The Act of 1932 further makes the African's labor service contract automatically applicable to his children aged ten to eighteen without their consent, and the legal penalties, including flogging, apply to the entire family. The whole family may be evicted if one member fails to render required labor service.[16] Such are the legal trappings in which South African peonage is garbed.

But that's only a fraction of it. One cannot talk about South Africa without mention of the Pass Laws. Their true nature and purpose can be seen in their genesis. This goes back to the regulations first imposed by the Dutch East India Company in 1760 to control the movement of slaves in the Cape Province, and to the Earl of Caledon's Proclamation of 1809. The latter aimed at converting Hottentot nomads into farm laborers by authorizing local authorities to treat as vagrants any of them found without passes (documents of identification and employment record), contracting them out to work for whomever they pleased and on the employers' own terms. From this it was only a step to broaden the application of the pass system to the restriction of Africans in general to certain areas. In the Transvaal and Orange Free State, the upper regions of South Africa, the pass system was found useful in supplying labor for the Boer farms and keeping it there. The development of gold mining and the "problem" of the increasing number of Africans in the cities, as we shall see, led to its still wider application.

The unremitting struggle of the people against this hated yoke of serfdom extends back to the period before the Union of South Africa was established (1910). The Free State Government ordered African women to carry passes. They refused, rejected the passes, paid their fines and went to jail in one of the earliest demonstrations of passive resistance in the country.

Levels of African Farm Production

Let us now try to get a final over-all picture of the African's place in agricultural production. This, it should be re-emphasized, is the means by which the great majority of the people in every part of the continent yet live or earn their living, even though the number of non-agricultural wage-earners in such areas as South Africa and Rhodesia is on the rise. The proportion of the total population engaged in both subsistence and market agriculture, as estimated for the year 1952, ranged from 68 per cent in Tunisia and 70 in the Gold Coast to 89 per cent in Nyasaland and 98 in Uganda.[17]

Of the adult male population engaged in agriculture, an average of between 50 and 60 per cent in the continent as a whole (77 per cent in French West Africa, for example) is said to be still growing food simply for self-subsistence,[18] scratching the earth with primitive tools as their fathers did before them—with the difference that they have far less land than their forebears, and what is left is overworked.

Of those outside the subsistence production sector, some derive their income directly from their own production for the market—from cocoa in Ghana; cocoa, peanuts, palm oil in Nigeria; cotton and coffee in Uganda, and so on. Others derive their income as wage-earners, most often on European-owned farms and estates. At this point we need to recall our discussion of the two Africas. For it is in those countries where Africans have retained the land that they are, for the most part, direct producers for the market and accordingly derive a greater share of the total money income. Thus in 1950 the portion of such income received by Africans, not counting the profits of government marketing boards held in trust for them, ranged from about half in Uganda ($68 million) to two-thirds ($266 million) in the Gold Coast and three-quarters ($627 million) in Nigeria, according to United Nations studies.[19]

On the other hand, where the land has been alienated and agricultural production is European-controlled, the great majority of the Africans in non-subsistence agriculture are simply wage-workers and the Africans' share of the total money income in such territories is relatively small. In Kenya, for example, only five per cent of the adult males in agriculture were engaged in *African* market production in 1950 (compared with 64 per cent in the Gold Coast), and Africans in that territory received less than one-fourth ($45 million) of the total money income.

Still more revealing is the contrast in per capita annual incomes. For the African these came to $8.20 in Kenya, $21.20 in Nigeria, and $68.20 in the Gold Coast in 1950. The difference here is due not only to the greater proportion of white-employed wage-workers in Kenya, but also to the fact that 70 per cent of the farmers there were engaged simply in subsistence production and received no money income, whereas those so engaged in Nigeria numbered 57 per cent and in the Gold Coast only 21 per cent. Income of course varies also according to farming methods. In Uganda, where the African per capita income came to only $13, the peasant with a small plot of land may combine or alternate market crops with subsistence crops, using antiquated techniques and tools and consequently getting a low yield. In the Gold Coast, by way of contrast, cocoa involves developed and specialized full-time farming; the income of the larger producers is substantial.

The essential difference between the African-controlled and settler-controlled agricultural systems has been aptly characterized as follows:

> The wealth of [the West African] colonies is largely due to the fact that they are cultivated by the people of the soil working in their own interests. . . . It is not an accident that colonies where the land remains in African hands pay their way. Where the land is given to settlers, agriculture has to be subsidized in one way or another. Even in South Africa the white farmer will not do a man's job, and farming there survives by the crushing exploitation of the African, and by differential taxation, and special concessions on the railway, which have to be paid by other users.[20]

In 1955 in the Province of Buganda, Uganda, African coffee growers received about $38 million for their crop, and in Tanganyika Africans accounted for 7,000 out of a total of 10,000 tons of coffee produced, despite an extra tax on the African's coffee for "local development expenditure." But in Kenya coffee-growing was until lately almost the exclusive privilege of the white settlers. African cash-crop farming has been prevented or discouraged in countries like Kenya partly to guarantee the European farmer's dominance, and more especially to insure a ready supply of black labor for him. The African like anyone else would naturally prefer working his own land, if he can, to working someone else's land.

Speaking of the problems of his country at a missionary conference on Africa held in Ohio in 1952, a young Kenya African told his audience:

> The argument that few African farmers [in Kenya] are ready to handle export crops does not hold water. It is true that African farmers have no adequate resources to buy farm machinery, have no government subsidy programs such as those afforded European farmers, and lack the training necessary for proper land utilization. But if the red tape and political pressures from European settlers were removed, there is no reason why Kenya farmers could not follow the footsteps of Uganda's and Tanganyika's African farmers. . . . It is about time that we started helping the African communities so that they can ultimately help themselves.[21]

"Like a Colossus"—UAC and Others

West Africans kept their land, save for plantation and mining concessions granted here and there, but they had and still have another yoke to bear. Out of virtually every shilling or franc earned a kind of imperial tribute is exacted. This particular levy goes not to the government's tax-collectors but to the all-powerful trading companies which from the time before colonial rule was fully established have been exploiting the land's people and resources going and coming.

Of the Royal Niger Company, chartered in 1886 and a contemporary of Rhodes' British South Africa Company, an official report from Nigeria to the British Foreign Secretary in 1889 stated: "They can open and shut any given market at will, which means subsistence or starvation to the Native inhabitants of the place. They can offer any price they like to the producers and the latter must take it or starve. The reason why, is the Company's dividends."²²

The Company gave up its charter in 1899, receiving over $4 million and retaining a 99-year right to half the royalties on all minerals mined. Lever Bros. bought out the Niger Company in 1920, royalty rights and all, bestowing them upon its subsidiary, the United Africa Company (UAC), established in 1929. UAC soon developed into the colossus of West Africa's import-export trade. In 1956 it bought in all African territories produce valued at $272 million and sold $512 million worth of merchandise.

The bosses changed; the business remained the same. But not quite. Through experience and organization the people of the Gold Coast and Nigeria learned how to boycott the over-priced imported merchandise and hold back their own produce for a fair offer. The UAC combined with other trading companies to fix prices; the peasant farmers combined to resist them, as in the six-months cocoa strike of 1937-38.

As a wartime measure, but still retained, government marketing boards were established in the British West African colonies to expedite exports to Britain and set the price for the peasants' palm oil and palm kernels, peanuts, cocoa and cotton. As one of the licensed buying agents for the boards, UAC plays a major role in the collection, purchase and sale of these products along with others like hides and skins, rubber, bananas and copra. If the boards stabilize the farmers' income, they also give UAC an accurate measure of how much money they have to spend. And Africans protest that price increases for their produce are invariably cancelled out by price increases on the things they have to buy. "The local Governments," it was charged in 1945, "were either in the deal with the European firms or were too weak to keep a check on the growing arrogance and unbridled rapacity of the combines."[23]

This opinion is no doubt shared by the thousands of UAC's African employees who have struck time and again for a living wage and found the Government playing strikebreaker. For example, in Lagos, Nigeria, August, 1950: "Nearly seventy steel helmeted policemen armed with batons kept up a goose trot at the Marina and around Kingsway [UAC] Stores awaiting the arrival of the picketers. The police were out to picket the picketers and as the strikers arrived in large bodies, police batons swung furiously at them. . . . Five strikers were arrested on the spot."[24]

From its African and global empire of peasant producers and laborers and plantations (nearly two million acres in the Belgian Congo alone) come the fats and oils that go into Lever Bros., products like Good Luck margarine, Spry, and Lux, Rinso, Lifebuoy, Sunlight and Surf. These, together with a wide assortment of other products including chemicals, paper, cosmetics, toilet preparations and food (such as Lipton's teas and Birds Eye frozen foods), add up to an annual sales volume of about $4 billion—yes, *billion*—for the mammoth British-Dutch Unilever organizations, of which Lever Bros. and UAC are important components.

Sales operations in the United States and management of the fourteen plants around this country are directed from Lever House on New York's fashionable Park Avenue. You look at this tall, striking glass-and-steel structure and you wonder how many hours of underpaid black labor and how many thousands of tons of underpriced palm oil and peanuts and cocoa it cost to build it.

UAC, though the biggest, is of course not the only one. Among others that dominate most of West Africa's trade and commerce are John Holt, Oliphants, Paterson Zochonis, and Leventis. And then there are the two big French trading companies: *the Société Commerciale de l'Ouest Africain* and the *Compagnie Francaise de l'Afrique Occidentale* do business all along the African West Coast from Senegal to Angola, including the British territories. With

UAC they control three-fourths of the trade of French West Africa.

In the last century there were men like King Ja Ja of the Opobo River, Nigeria, who strove desperately to prevent the European traders from gaining control of the inland sources of produce. The chiefs of the Cameroons in a treaty with the German colonizers dated July 12, 1884, declared their wish "that white men should not go up and trade with the Bushmen, [and should have] nothing to do with our markets. . . ."

Is it to be believed or expected that in the present period the big trading companies can continue to stand astride West Africa and, in the interest of their shareholders, dictate the terms of trade, labor and life for many millions of people under their domination? And what of the foreign concessionaires with their private empires, hundreds of thousands of acres in Algeria, Liberia, the Congo and elsewhere? And what of the European settlers whose special privileges and prosperity are the Africans' slavery and hunger?

How long? The honorable Mr. Grogan, as we have seen, thought that the African must stay in line until "the capitalist regime. . . . top-heavy crumbles to the ground." But the peoples of Asia, suffering under similar disabilities, did not wait on that event.

Let us turn now to another side of the African economy where the conflict of black and white interests is equally acute and explosive.

3. Mine Boy

AN AMERICAN, ONE of many who took part in the diamond rush in South Africa over eighty years ago, has left us a picture of it. The newly-arrived prospector at the mining camp had three things to do: get his license from the local authorities, buy his tools and gear, and obtain his "boy" from one of the white "labor agents." There was the usual raw life of such get-rich-quick locales. It was raw particularly for the African.

    The police seldom had many whites in the "trouk" (jail). Drunkenness was no crime there, and consequently the police fraternized with the drinking community. The principal offenders were the Caffres,* who at the hour of 9 P.M. were supposed to leave the streets and keep in their tents or enclosures. Now a Caffre thinks himself as good as a white man, and he never understood the reason why a "boss" could stay out all night, get drunk, fight, and behave as he liked, while he was so mercilessly kept under. Numbers were continually evading this law, and every morning a long row of trembling natives stood out in front of the "trouk" to receive from 10 to 25 lashes each. . . .
    I saw one young boy receive 35 lashes for stealing diamonds. He stood up bravely, while strips of flesh hung down from his back and great drops of blood coursed down his legs. Whir, whir, the cat crossed his shoulders until his large eyes were blood-shot, his lips quivering, his hands working in agony; but he kept silence until the thirtieth time the lash descended, when, with a deep groan, full of the misery of physical torture, he fainted.
    At such scenes as these the black spectators would become much excited. They would grind their teeth, and with menacing looks gaze upon the officers of justice. I often thought they only waited for some favorable opportunity to wreak vengeance on their masters.[1]

    * More commonly "Kaffirs," an Arabic word meaning "pagan" and applied to any and all Africans by the 18th century Dutch settlers in South Africa. Though offensive to the African, the term is still widely used in the country.

The 9 P.M. curfew for Africans, the daily police round-up, and the penalty of the lash for various "native offenses" remain characteristic features of today's South Africa.

Origins of the Cheap Labor System

The discovery of gold in 1886 followed about twenty years after the discovery of diamonds in South Africa. The scene of the second rush was the Transvaal's Rand (Witwatersrand: Ridge of the White Waters). Hundreds of Americans joined the stream of prospectors to the new Eldorado. The very first hotel in Johannesburg, it is said, belonged to the United States consul, one Sam Height, of Luka, Mississippi. American engineers and technicians had a prominent part in opening and running the mines, and some United States citizens like John Hays Hammond figured in Rhodes' empire-building adventures which culminated in the outbreak of the Boer War, 1899. At that time there were over a thousand Americans with considerable property interests in the Transvaal.

The labor problems of the developing gold mining industry were aired by company spokesmen at a government hearing in 1897. There were general complaints about the high cost of African laborers and the fact that large numbers worked for only a few days and then deserted their jobs and could not be found because of the ineffective operation of the Pass Law. "If every kaffir could be traced; if it could be told whether they have been registered before, or been in the service of a company, then we would have control over them."[2]

The consensus of testimony was that "A constant and ample supply of native laborers is necessary to fix and adhere to a low standard of native wages."[3] The general manager of the Crown Reef Gold Mining Co., Mr. Sidney J. Jennings, testified that in 1896 the wage-bill for his company's African employees had amounted to 24 per cent of the total cost of operation, 2s.10d. (about 70¢ at that time) per worker per shift (day's work) including cost of food rations. This could be reduced to 1s.6d., he said, if the laws, particularly the Pass Law, were properly enforced. This Mr. Jennings was something of a genius in his line:

> If we had complete control over the native labor, [he continued] we would teach the kaffirs to do all lower forms of work that are now done by white men. By these reductions other mines would be brought into operation, and more white men of greater skill would come into the country. The lower classes

of labor, mostly unskilled, would be done by kaffirs. This would be a permanent benefit to the country in many ways. You would have more mines at work . . . and the man who had invested his money in the mines would receive greater dividends.[4]

A half century later the Transvaal Chamber of Mines was answering critics of its labor policy by declaring, "The allocation of skilled work to Europeans and unskilled work to Natives is . . . an established feature of the labor structure of the mines. Any attempt to expand the classes of work open to competent Natives would meet with strenuous and bitter opposition from the European employees and their trade unions. In addition, the Native employee is restricted by law and by custom from undertaking skilled labor."[5] The creators of the Jim Crow mine labor system have with seeming coyness passed the responsibility for it to the white workers, to government, and to society in general.

How were "complete control" and the "constant and ample supply" of black workers obtained? The company spokesmen in 1897 asked for tightening up of the Pass Law which had been enacted two years earlier at their own behest. This was done. They asked for increased taxation on the African peasant to force him to work.[6] That was done. They urged government assistance and cooperation in getting and holding their labor supply. Government responded with appropriate legislation like the Native Regulation Act of 1911 which imposed a ten pound ($50) fine or two months imprisonment upon the African for deserting his job, not fulfilling his contract of employment, or other offenses such as committing "a breach of any rules prescribed for good order, discipline, or health on mines or works."

Above all, however, the continuous flow of cheap labor to the mines was guaranteed by the companies' elaborate and efficient recruiting network covering an immense area of southern and central Africa. Said the Chamber of Mines President in 1930, "The truth is that little of the gold mining industry as we know it would ever have been initiated, or if started, could ever have been continued, except upon the basis of utilizing the great Native labor supplies that are available in southern Africa."[7]

Since 1936 over 300,000 Africans and close to 40,000 whites have normally been employed each year in South Africa's gold mines. All but two or three (used as "boss boys" or in clerical posts) out of every hundred Africans employed are classified as "tribal natives." That means that they have had little or no previous wage-earning experience, or else that they worked in the mines before, returned to their tribal communities, and have come back for another contract period. They are migrant workers, contracted for by the hundreds of agents of the mines' two recruiting organizations (each with its own geographical assignment). The recruiting agents work through the usual channels from governmental authorities to tribal chiefs in arranging for the quota of men to be hired. The recruit puts his "x" mark on the service contract as directed, leaves his home and family behind, and goes off to work on the mines.

The contract calls for him to stay there from nine to 18 months. He lives in a jail-like compound or barracks in the company of others of his tribe, duly protected from trade union organizers and such "alien interests . . . that would undermine his tribal customs and allegiances and his own conception of values." Having thus provided that neither the length nor environment of employment shall be such as to "spoil" the "tribal natives," the mine operators are then, of course, in a position to say that their African employees "are not yet sufficiently advanced for trade unionism, nor do they want it." It is generally conceded that it is primarily the powerful influence of the gold mining companies that explains why the most industrially advanced country in Africa has continued to deny legal recognition of *any* African trade unions, mine workers or otherwise.

Back in the 1870's the owners of the diamond mines got together and agreed to cut the wages of their black workers from ten to seven shillings a week. But it didn't work. The Africans simply quit, and it was necessary to pay them 15 shillings and more to get them back to work.[8] The owners of the gold mines soon learned how to succeed where their predecessors had failed. They had the advantage of a continuous and ample supply of workers, thanks to their recruiting system and the Government's cooperation. The first of a series of agreements among the companies for freezing African wages in the gold mines, reducing them about a third, was made in May, 1897. By 1914 the rate for underground workers had been further cut from 2s.6d. to a flat two shillings for a day's work.[9]

Table 3 shows the snail's pace advance of African wages (accelerated slightly in the last few years by the opening of the new Orange Free State mines). The widening gap between the African's income and that of the white worker (salaries and allowances of managers, engineers, etc. are included) will be discussed at another point.

Management has made no secret of its cheap labor policy. It pleads the necessity of keeping working costs to an absolute minimum because the price of gold remains normally fixed over long periods (though when it did rise, wages still remained unaffected).

TABLE 3. YEARLY INCOME OF WORKERS ON THE LARGE GOLD MINES IN SOUTH AFRICA[10]

	African		White	
	Number Employed	Per Capita Income*	Number Employed	Per Capita Income*
1911	184,229	$ 97	25,248	$ 941
1921	171,227	110	19,534	1,529
1931	220,416	92	20,968	1,162
1941	376,327	111	38,402	1,472
1945	313,401	124	32,923	1,803
1950	311,972	147	39,242	2,369
1953	294,598	171	40,708	2,910

* Amounts in pounds sterling for all years converted at the rate of 1 pound = $2.80.

Moreover, runs the argument, that is the only way to keep the poorer-yield mines operating (paying dividends, that is). Thus it is that now and again someone in the South African Parliament rises to ask "whether the Government was doing its best to see that the mines received cheap labor and as much labor as they needed from the [Native] reserves. The price of production must be kept as low as possible so that the lowest economic grade of ore could be mined."[11]

The late W. H. (Bill) Andrews, for many years one of South Africa's foremost white labor leaders and a champion of African rights, commented in 1943 on how the mining companies "conjured up a glorious vision of ore yielding only one pennyweight per ton being worked at a profit, which would prolong the life of the industry for a hundred years. Excellent! Only one step further and road-metal could be profitably milled. It reminds one of the story of the donkey who was trained to eat less and less until he was reduced to one straw a day, when the cantankerous brute upset the experiment by dying."

Grievances and Strikes

The mine operators' donkey didn't die, but it frequently kicked. There was, for example, the African mineworkers' strike of July, 1913, following on the heels of a riotous strike of the white workers. Africans in several of the mine compounds refused to go to work without increase of pay, entirely disregarding the orders and exhortations of the white compound managers. A Government inquiry report describes what happened:

Mounted police were called in, but this produced no effect at all. The natives were quite prepared for a stand-up fight with these police, and at one mine they actually stoned them. The resistance was only quelled by calling in a company of soldiers [with] fixed bayonets . . . who succeeded in arresting the leaders in each compound. . . . There is no doubt that, on this occasion, we were within an ace of a native outbreak on a serious scale. [Lucky that it didn't occur two or three days earlier, for] there would have been neither police or troops available; they were both fully occupied with the white rioters.[12]

The grievances? First and foremost was the demand for more pay. They complained that there was cheating on their daily work records, that there was no promotion, that no matter how often they were re-hired, they had to start at the bottom rate, that they were required to work long hours overtime and on Sundays without extra pay. They particularly protested against the color bar (Jim Crow) system. The black miner argues, said the inquiry report, "that if he can do the same work as white men, there is no reason why he should not receive the same remuneration. That in many instances he can do it and in some instances is actually doing it, admits of no doubt."[13]

There were other complaints about the sordid compound quarters and starvation rations, about brutality and assaults from overseers, about inadequate safeguards and too frequent accidents down in the mines and the paltry compensation granted when they occurred (management, for instance, paying £10 to dependents, if known, in a case of accidental death; £500 if the worker happened to be white).

The Government's investigators noted down all these grievances, but their real concern was with the "unmistakable signs" of the "breakdown" of such "safeguards" as the personal influence of the compound managers, African respect for European authority personified in the police, and "the inter-tribal jealousies which have rendered it possible, in the last resort, to protect Europeans by utilizing one tribe against another." It was noted that in all the compounds the workers regardless of tribal differences "acted absolutely together" in the strike.

To meet this situation the investigators proposed certain "precautions to be taken against a general outbreak among native mine laborers." They included organization of a dormant military organization among the whites at every mine, establishment of a permanent white guard at each mine, an intelligence or spy system in the compounds, closer supervision of compounds at night, searches for arms at regular intervals, and more complete separation of tribes both in the compounds and at work.[14]

Even thus chained down, the mineworkers could not be kept permanently passive. There was a big strike in 1920 and a still bigger one in 1946 when White South Africa, startled, asked, "How is it possible?" Ah, yes, Communist trouble-makers—that was the explanation. So various Communist leaders were rounded up in 1946 and extended trials were held, but the Government's case collapsed for lack of evidence.

Foreign guests who take a look at South Africa's gold mines usually come away with the memory of the Sunday exhibitions of tribal dances in the compound yards uppermost in their minds. Lest they get the wrong impression, such observers should recall the experience of the late Bishop David Henry Sims of the African Methodist Episcopal Church. As he was being conducted on such a tour down in the mines, his guide, a mine official, stopped and asked the African workers if they were satisfied with their wages and working conditions. They all answered "yes." When the official's back was turned, Bishop Sims, a Negro, asked them the same question and they all shouted "No!" That was an example of "protective psychology," said the Bishop later, adding that it explained why the white South African could not possibly fully understand the African.[15]

The system of recruiting unspoiled "tribal Natives" and housing them in the protective environment of the mining compounds was copied in other territories from South Africa. And also, of course, the basic Jim Crow, cheap labor pattern. In many instances, the diamond, gold and copper mines in South West Africa, Angola, Rhodesia, and the Belgian Congo were opened and put into operation with the assistance or direction of expert advisers or mining officials from South Africa. Moreover, the majority of the white workers in the mines of Northern and Southern Rhodesia initially came from South Africa.

The spread of the South African mining system to other areas went hand in hand with the development of the big mining syndicates based in South Africa—biggest of all: the Anglo American Corp. of South Africa headed by the late Sir Ernest Oppenheimer, who was heir to John Cecil Rhodes' corporation empire. The free-lance individual prospector of the early diamond and gold rush days gave way to company mining as big-scale, long-pull operations became necessary. The smaller companies were bought up or pushed out by the bigger ones. Those in the gold mining industry in turn became parts of a "group system," linked together in seven "houses," each under centralized control, through interlocking shares and directorships. Similar unified control was established in diamond and other mining.

"*Many of Us Die for 22s.6d.*"

We may take Rhodesia as an illustration of how the South African system of exploiting black mine labor operated in other parts of the continent. Gold mining under European auspices got under way in Southern Rhodesia soon after Rhodes' conquest. The Matabele and Mashona, added to the theft of their land and cattle and the violation of their women, found themselves compelled by force to labor in the mines and flogged when they tried to run away. They revolted. They could not win. But what else had they to lose? "The crushing of the rebellion by the imperial authorities was attended by great loss of native life and by many terrible incidents, amongst others the dynamiting of the caves in which the Mashona had taken refuge."[16] That was in 1896.

The big mines began operating in the Northern Rhodesia Copperbelt between 1929 and 1933. One morning in April, 1935, a notice was found posted in one of the African compounds. As translated from Chiwemba by a mine clerk (and reproduced here without editing) it read:

> Listen to this all you who live in the country, think well how they treat us and to ask for a land. Do we live in good treatment, no; therefore let us ask one another and remember this treatment. Because we wish on the day of 29th April, every person not to go to work. He who will go to work, and if we see him it will be a serious case. Know how they cause us to suffer, they cheat us for money, they arrest us for loafing, they persecute us and put us in jail for tax. What reason have we done? Secondly, do you not wish to hear these words, well listen, this year of 1935, if they will not increase

us more money stop paying tax. Do you think they can kill you, no. Let us encourage surely you will see that God will be with us. See how we suffer with the work and how we are continually reviled and beaten underground. Many brothers of us die for 22s.6d. [for 30 days work], is this money that we should lose our lives for. He who cannot read should tell his companion that on the 29th April not to go to work.[17]

That is the first recorded strike call by African copper miners in Northern Rhodesia. The strike swept three mines, two of them, Roan Antelope and Mufulira, being properties in which the American Metal Co., a Morgan interest, had made large investments in 1929. Unfortunately the workers did not strike simultaneously; even so, for eight days company officials, the police, and the military had a tense time of it. The police were responsible for opening fire on a crowd of Africans (unarmed except for stones) massed in front of the compound manager's office at Roan Antelope, killing six outright and wounding 22 others.

What of the workers' demand for more money (their poll tax rate had just been increased from 12s.6d. to 15s.)? The Government Commission made the customary question-begging reference to prevailing wage standards—the cut-rate Jim Crow standards for Africans. The mineworkers' wages, said the Commission, "compare favorably with the wages paid in other forms of employment in Northern Rhodesia and with the wages on the mines in adjoining territories."[18] Was the miners' wage, or the other wages used for comparison, sufficient to provide a decent living standard? The Commision did not bother to go into that.

Nor did it even mention the gap, wider even than in the South African gold mines, between white and black workers' wages. In 1938 the Copperbelt mines employed 2,700 whites and 23,000 Africans; there were 5,879 whites, 36,147 Africans in 1953; 7,794 whites and 52,757 Africans in 1955. The comparative wages are seen in Table 4.

TABLE 4. AVERAGE MONTHLY CASH WAGES (INCLUDING BONUSES) NORTHERN RHODESIA COPPER MINES[19]

Year	African	White
1938	$ 3.78	$131.60
1946	5.88	162.40
1950	9.24	231.00
1953	17.64	281.40
1955	18.72	381.50

(*Converted from pounds sterling at present exchange rates*)

A glance back to Table 3 will show that the black Copperbelt miner has climbed the wage ladder a little faster (from a lower starting point) than his brother in the South African gold mines. Organization did it. The early Copperbelt strikes of 1935 and 1940 (when troops killed 17 Africans and wounded 65) were demonstrations of desperation by unorganized workers; those of 1952 and 1955, to be reviewed later, were disciplined and effective trade unions actions, and some gains—even if not enough—were won. But nowhere else in Central and Southern Africa have black mine workers yet been allowed to make their collective strength felt.

To sum up, the entire history of European extraction of African gold, diamonds, copper and other minerals has been marked by the continuous struggle of the African mine "boy"—whose labor was and is indispensable—to be treated as a *man* and to be paid a *man's* wages. Here and there some concessions and compromises have been won. But in the areas of white settlement and white political control the prevailing mine labor policy remains one of employing every expedient—migrant labor, tribalism, the spy system, legal duress, police and troops—to prevent the development of black labor solidarity. High mining dividends require that the African mineworker be kept a "boy."

4. White Cities and Black Workers

SUCH URBAN CENTERS as Kano (Northern Nigeria) and Timbuktu (French Sudan) were well-established communities for many centuries before the European penetration of Africa. Most African cities of today, however, owe their expansion or origin to the development of mining and agricultural production for overseas export and to the foreign capital investments and, in some areas, the influx of Europeans which accompanied that economic activity. The concentration of investments in South African gold and diamonds, for instance, meant an earlier and more rapid rate of urbanization there. But down to World War II the growth of urban areas in Africa as a whole was slow or moderate. The war brought a general upturn which became more pronounced with postwar investments and enterprise. The movement cityward was no longer simply a drift. The African population of Dakar and other French West African cities doubled between 1945 and 1950; that of the major towns in Northern Rhodesia doubled in three years, 1948-1950.[1]

One has to be cautious with such figures, however, remembering that they still represent only a fraction, usually small, of the total dominantly rural population, and remembering also that a great many of the Africans in the cities are migrant workers with roots still in their countryside homes. But after making these qualifications the fact remains that the urban minority, by the very nature of its new way of living and working, is cast in a special role. It is the yeast of the whole loaf.

While the problems of social readjustment confronting the newly urbanized millions in all sections of Africa have certain common characteristics, there are added difficulties of an extremely obnoxious kind in that part of Africa where resident whites hold sway. The difficulties stem from the fact that these whites—those who hold power and others down the scale—regard the cities in which they live as being exclusively their own, and consider it necessary to do whatever they can to *keep* them exclusively their own. That is what is implied when Col. Stallard, a former Minister of Mines in the South African Government, says:

> The standard by which we should introduce Natives into our towns should be the standard of what is required and what is not required for industry, for the use of the white population. . . I regard [the Africans'] wives in town as a nuisance. They may be a convenience on the farms, but my view upon this is that we should have a system of migratory labor; that is to say, practically the same policy that is pursued on the mines at the present time.[2]

The first rule in the white cities might be framed: keep the Africans out unless their labor is needed. The second rule: they can work *for* us but not live *with* us. The net result of the application of these two rules over the years is seen everywhere in the special "Native" areas, slum districts, set apart from and on the periphery of the white cities.

Shanty Towns

There is a monotonous repetition of the same sordid details in the pictures of these places. Algiers has its Bidonville—"a settlement of the very poorest people, crowded into huts made of rotting wood and beaten-out petrol tins, devoid of the most elementary sanitary provisions." Casablanca, Morocco, has its *Carrières Centrales*, a poverty-stricken suburb of old tin huts. Dakar has its Medina district housing 150,000 Africans in make-shift dwellings lining alleys of loose sand, with here and there stand pipes for water and latrines.

The Belgian Congo's non-rural Africans, numbering 1,500,000 adults and 840,000 children in 1949, were quartered in eight "native cities" and 33 "extra-customary centers"—the Belgians have things systematized. One of the 'native cities,' today crowded with 350,000 Africans, adjoins Leopoldville where 20,000 whites live apart in a suburb described as "far too big for them."

"Settlements of closely packed huts are to be seen on the fringes of all the larger towns in East Africa," states a recent British Royal Commission survey of the area. It cites an official but unpublished report describing Africans employed in Nairobi, Kenya, in 1948 living "in dangerous shacks in the swamp, in buses parked on the roadside, and fourteen to the room in Pumwani, two to a bed and the rest on the floor."[3] Just prior to the so-called Mau Mau "emergency" in 1952, it was officially stated that there were 10,000 bedless and homeless Africans in Nairobi.

In the vicinity of Salisbury, capital of Southern Rhodesia, there lived an estimated 80,000 African men, 8,300 women, and 18,200 children in 1955. (The disproportion between men and women, almost incredible in this instance, rises in direct ratio to the dependence on migrant workers; the pernicious social consequences are obvious.) Many of these were homeless. Some, it was reported, "find shelter in old motor cars or structures made out of motor-car doors, old petrol drums and soap boxes. The floor is generally the bare earth."[4]

More often described to the world are South Africa's notorious dormitory "townships" like Alexandra, "locations" like Pimville, and municipal slums such as Moroka with their hundreds of shanties of sackcloth, cardboard, and discarded oil drums, the homes of the scores of thousands of Africans employed in the cities.

Bus Boycott

Alexandra Township with its 80,000 crowded tenants lies nine and a half miles outside Johannesburg. Every morning and every night there are long lines of African men and women waiting to board the buses that carry them to and from work in the city. A Commission of Inquiry in 1944 stated: "The national policy of segregation and the necessity for finding land needed to house Africans under this policy, away from the areas occupied by other races, have created in South Africa the unique phenomenon that the lowest paid workers have to live furthest from their work."[5]

In 1943 the bus companies increased the Alexandra-Johannesburg fare from 4d. to 5d. Instead of paying it, about 15,000 men and women in a procession stretching about three miles *walked* the nine and a half miles to Johannesburg—and back home again after a hard day's work. They did it for nine days; there were a few cars and trucks made available, some by friendly white persons, for older people and women with babies, but most just walked. On the ninth day the fare increase was rescinded.

All on account of a one penny increase in fare? Yes. It was the last straw piled on top of starvation wages, high rent, soaring food costs, taxes and Jim Crow. Even the Government's Inquiry Commission was forced to say: "Transport charges in relation to the worker's wages, or even to the total family income, are beyond the capacity of the African workers to pay. Indeed, it may be said that they cannot afford to pay anything. They certainly cannot afford to pay anything more in any direction, except by reducing still further their hunger diet."[6]

Nevertheless, a few months after the end of the nine days strike, a fare increase was again announced. It was suggested that the Africans should collect the extra fare from their employers. The proposal was rejected and the strike was resumed. "Many washwomen, carrying burdens, plodded along with bowed shoulders, feet unshod," a newspaper reported. The buses continued to run, accompanied by police escorts, but nobody rode. The boycott lasted seven weeks. At last the companies agreed to keep the fare at 4d. during weekdays if a coupon book were purchased; the fare would be higher only on weekends and for those with no coupon book.[7]

There was a repetition of the bus boycott early in 1957 by the people of Alexandra to keep the fare at 4d. It lasted three months this time. And there were other "We won't ride" demonstrations last year in Cape Town, South Africa, against Jim Crow seats on busses, and in Salisbury, Southern Rhodesia, against increased fares. It is natural that South Africans would watch with keen interest the progress of the year-long bus boycott of 1956 in Montgomery, Alabama.

"He Must Obey the Laws of the White Man"

In 1937 there occurred two violent clashes between black South Africans and the police. That some of the latter were killed shocked the white population. The whites were becoming convinced, said General Hertzog, then Prime Minister of the Dominion, "that there was a deep-rooted and far-reaching hostility, perhaps organized, among the Natives towards the white man." This was bad, he said. The white people's sense of "security and confidence" must be quickly restored. Drastic measures would be taken. "This use of force by the Native on the European must cease forthwith," Hertzog declared (no comment on the reverse use of force), "and no punishment or means by which this can be accomplished must be left untried. Here, where the Native lives in the domain of the White man, he must obey the laws of the White man . . . regardless of what the Native may think of the law—whether it is the pass laws, the liquor laws, or anything else."[8]

The domain of the white man: the cities of South Africa built by African labor, dependent upon African labor for their functioning, but closed to the African except in terms of the white rulers' laws. The Natives (Urban Areas) Act of 1923, for instance, with all its many amendments, which, among other things, empowers the Governor-General to "declare that . . . all natives within the limits of any urban area or any specified portion thereof . . . shall . . . reside in a location, native village or native hostel;" and to bar Africans, if so requested by local authorities, from entering any urban area "for the purpose of seeking or taking up employment or residing therein." Another section of this same Act itemizes numerous regulations as to documents (passes) the African must secure, keep, and show on request, together with other conditions pertaining to his entry or stay in "proclaimed areas,"—that is, urban areas designated as out-of-bounds for him.

("The white man," said Prime Minister Hertzog, "is quite determined to carry out faithfully that fatherly care which has been promised to the Native ever since the laying of the foundations of the white man's settlement in South Africa.")[9]

To illustrate the meaning of this legal labyrinth, let us take the case of an African in the Transvaal Province who wants to go to Johannesburg, one of the "proclaimed" urban areas. He first has to produce his identification pass to the district pass officer and obtain a traveling pass. On arrival in Johannesburg he has to report to the pass office within 24 hours. There he gives up his travel pass and gets a permit to look for work. This is good for just six days; it may sometimes be renewed, but not more than twice. If it isn't renewed or if he doesn't find a job within the allotted time, he must leave Johannesburg or face arrest. If he does find a job, he then has his service contract registered. He must report to have this registration renewed every month. If he wishes to travel anywhere, he must secure his employer's permission and a travel pass from the pass office.[10]

Though the South African Dominion may perhaps claim the prize for the sheer weight of its restrictive legislation relating to the African in the city, it has no monopoly on this article. A number of other territories including South West Africa, Southern Rhodesia (whose laws in many cases are almost duplicates of her southern neighbor's), Northern Rhodesia, Kenya, the Belgian Congo, and Portuguese colonies likewise impose registration and pass regulations on the African, restrict his presence and movement in urban areas, and provide him with segregated townships and the like. "These regulations," the Kikuyu Central Association declared in 1932, "make Kenya Africans strangers in their own land; they subject Africans to a control which is only accorded to criminals in other countries, and which give rise to constant hardship and resentment."

Despite the people's protests and demonstrations, despite the expressions of legal authorities and Government commissions as to the injustice of the pass system, it continues to grind on and on in South Africa, adding yearly to the African jail population. Ask a black worker in Johannesburg what a police state is, and he will tell you about the petty tyranny of the local pass offices; about the police who stop him on the street or invade his home to examine his registration papers (a carry-all "reference book" has been used since 1952); about the magistrate's courts where hundreds of pass offenders are daily tried, convicted and sentenced in assembly-line fashion. Here are a few figures corroborating the black worker's answer to your question.

TABLE 5. CONVICTIONS OF AFRICANS UNDER PASS AND ALLIED [a] LAWS IN SOUTH AFRICA[11]

1930	1940	1950	1955
42,000	99,000[b]	217,387	337,603

TOTAL CONVICTIONS OF AFRICANS IN SOUTH AFRICA

Year	African Population (millions)	Number of Convictions	Convictions % of Population
1936	6.6	459,911	7
1954	8.5	1,032,421	12.1

[a] Curfew regulations, registration of documents, location rules, etc.
[b] In Transvaal only.

Thus it is seen that the current jailing of Africans under the all-white Government of the Union of South Africa proceeds at the yearly rate of about one for every eight in the country, including women and children. As for the whites there were 174,336 convictions in 1954, 6.6 per cent of the white population, and this covers all minor offenses such as traffic violations. The rate of white convictions, it should be added, is also considerably lower than the rates for the Asian and Colored sections of the population.

Prison Labor for Hire

Eight or nine of every ten Africans convicted in the South African courts must go to jail in default of payment of fine—they can't afford to pay it no matter how small. What happens then? They become part of a cheap manual labor force of no mean size controlled and exploited by the Prisons Department. Recent reports indicate about 1,400 long-sentence prisoners being supplied daily to the gold mines, another 2,600 to the state-owned railway and harbor systems for quarrying and other such work. Besides the prisoners supplied to other private and governmental industry, a considerable number of those sentenced to less than five months are hired out to individual farmers.

The prisoner receives no pay; the Prisons Department gets 9d. (10¢) a day from farmers for each prisoner taken, and 2s. (28¢) a day from the mining companies and other industrial employers. The revenue received from these sources in 1952 amounted to $523,270, while the value of the convict labor used by the various Government agencies (Railways, etc.) and departments, including the Prisons Department itself, was $1,184,546.[12]

The practice of supplying convict labor to the farms of South Africa is over twenty years old. "Free" black labor scorns the miserable wages paid by the farmers; prison labor has no choice in the matter. In 1949 some Transvaal farmers got an inspiration. Instead of having to get convicts from the city, they would get together and build a jail right there near the farms. And so they did, and the Department of Justice agreed to fill it. The Minister of Justice, Mr. Swart, described this "private jail"—thirteen of them had sprung up by 1953—as "a monument to the enterprise of the farmers" and pictured convicts "living in the congenial atmosphere of the countryside."

Mr. Swart, of course, knew better. He knew the prisoners weren't going to the farms to recline in hammocks. Year after year South African newspapers have reported outrage after outrage, including death by flogging, committed upon prison laborers on the farms. One report in 1956 tells of their being chained at night by their ankles to a post in the center of a shed where they slept, and lashed every time they tried to straighten their backs from the task of sorting potatoes.[13] All for 10 cents a day—paid to the Prisons Department.

We shall pass over some other white settler territories where the system of collecting black prisoners and putting them to work might be compared with South Africa's. But on Kenya we must pause. For there the system, all its vicious ugliness plainly exposed, has been used to enslave scores of thousands of Africans. There is a long background.[14] Kenya had a Collective Punishment Ordinance as far back as 1909; it was amended and expanded in 1930. A system of detention camps, supplementing the prisons and cheaper to maintain, has been in operation in the colony for more than 30 years. In 1930 there were 32 such detention camps (besides 29 prisons) housing 8,431 prisoners; in 1938 it was officially noted that detainee labor was becoming "more efficient and productive"; in 1951 there were 47 camps containing 18,247 inmates. Prisoners from outlying jails were brought to Nairobi Prison to labor at the quarry and concrete works. Prison industries in Kenya provided a revenue of £14,851 in 1938, £74,118 ($207,530) in 1951. In addition, the "prisoners contributed much to the building of roads and other public works by their free labor."

That was the prelude. In October, 1952, came the Mau Mau "emergency," and within a few days Sir Evelyn Baring, the Governor, was telling the Kenya Legislative Council that as soon as "arrangements for the reception and segregation of the considerable numbers of prisoners" could be made, "the policy of the Prisons Department of dispersing convicts from the security prisons to temporary prison camps from which convict labor is employed to the economic advantage of the Colony . . . will be extended."[15] It was, indeed. That story comes in a later chapter.

In the "domain of the white man"—in spite of all his efforts to keep it restricted and exclusively his own—the African increased in numbers and began to discover how to make his numbers in the city count. He could not be taught how to stay on his knees. Instead, during the hungry depression 'thirties and inflationary wartime 'forties, he acquired through hard experience an understanding of what was needed for his people to win their rights as workers and human beings.

"The facts we have before us," said a leader at a South African organization's conference in 1937, "are a clear proof that there will never be any improvement in the conditions and wages of the Africans until we learn how to unite as a race. . . . We have to pass from a group of leaders expressing pious resolutions into an active body representing the interests of our oppressed and exploited people."[16]

Something like that was also being said by leaders in other parts of Africa, east, west, and north. Even if their trade unions had no legal standing and were set upon by the police when they dared strike, Africans organized. Even if their movements for land security, for decent urban housing, for freedom from pass law slavery, and for political rights were alternately ignored and outlawed, they organized. A powerful and irresistible demand for African liberation was building up.

Part Two: *African Aims and AmericanInterests*

5. World War II: The Conflict Grows

AFTER A DECADE of Cold War doubts and fears, it is rather difficult now to recall the spirit of hope and promise that was so widely felt in 1945 at the end of the war. It survived only a few months. Soon it was no longer fine and patriotic to talk of "one world"; it was subversive. For a brief period, in millions of minds there dwelled the conviction that the victory over fascism must necessarily usher in a new order of things. Africans, no less than other peoples, believed it.

In some sections of Africa, of course, they did not wait for the end of the war—in Morocco, for instance. There the Istiqlal Party presented the French administration with a petition for independence in January, 1944. Recovering from the shock of amazement, the authorities replied by jailing and exiling nationalist leaders and answering the protests which followed with 18 months of military suppression and mass arrests.

In Algeria, Moslems holding a victory parade in Setif on V-E Day, May 8, 1945, dared to carry the forbidden green-and-white national banner along with the flags of the allied powers. That was the apparent spark which set off widespread fighting between Moslems and French. American planes and tanks given to France under lend-lease were turned against Algerians in a campaign of bloody repression. Some reports tell of 40,000 slain.

By May, 1946, it was said that the French thought they had succeeded in stamping out the fire. They were "so confident of keeping the nationalist movements under control in Tunisia, Algeria and Morocco that they have now released all the major Nationalist leaders in the three territories. The critical period of post-war change and confusion has passed."[1] But in 1947 French troops were again busy in Tunisia battling and killing workers during a general strike, and in Algeria patrolling the Kabylie region "to discourage any attempt on the part of the turbulent Kabylie Berbers to take advantage of France's difficulties in Indo-China and Madagascar and give her operations on a third front."[2]

Although sheer hunger was an important motivation, political demands claimed the main attention in these struggles in the French North African colonies, and also in Egypt. Here the war's end saw King Fuad's police clubbing and jailing students and workers in Cairo and Alexandria for their too vociferous demands for the scrapping of the 1936 treaty of "perpetual" alliance with Britain and the immediate withdrawal of all foreign troops. Economic and political factors both figured prominently in the origins of the 1947 war in Madagascar and in the post-war ferment of organization in France's sub-Sahara colonies.

The French occupation of Madagascar (a protectorateship was declared in 1889), like that of Morocco, entailed the continuous military suppression of uprisings down to the mid-'thirties. The French settlers and concessionaire agents of the big Paris trusts got four million or more acres of land and made the dispossessed peasants work for them. It was to maintain this profitable system and smash the developing trade unions and rising political strength of the Malagasy (given some small scope by the 1946 Constitution of the French Union) that reactionary Vichy elements in Madagascar engineered a provocation in March, 1947, followed by the unleashing of a savage assault upon the people. Women and children were massacred, whole villages burned to the ground. A figure of 89,000 killed was officially admitted. Some of the thousands jailed have not even yet been released. But with all that, the workers were not crushed. A major strike, for example, occurred in December, 1950, at the Diego-Suarez arsenal and maritime base.

In West Africa the most pressing incentive to militant organization at this time in both the British and French colonies was the

WORLD WAR II: THE CONFLICT GROWS   63

people's reaction against the war economy pincers' squeeze of fixed prices on the farmers' cocoa, palm oil, or peanuts as against the constantly rising cost of consumer goods. A number of new farmer, labor and political organizations emerged on the scene. The most important of these in the French colonies was the RDA or African Democratic Rally (*Rassemblement Démocratique Africaine*).

Its first Congress in October, 1946, at Bamako, French West Africa, opened with a mass meeting of 15,000 supporters and was attended by 800 delegates representing peasants, workers and some sections of the African middle class. They came from all over French West Africa, Togoland, Cameroons, and Chad (the only territory of Equatorial Africa from which delegates were permitted to come). A solid working apparatus was established reaching from the smallest country villages to Paris. It stood for "a struggle for the political, economic, and social emancipation of French West Africa, within the framework of a French Union based upon the principle of equal rights and duties"; and for "the union of all Africans, irrespective of their political or religious beliefs, their origins and social conditions, in the struggle against colonial rule."[3] Its influence spread rapidly.

By the time of its second Inter-Territorial Congress at Abidjan in April, 1949, rightist forces in Paris and in French West Africa had launched a counter-attack against the RDA. It was called Communist because its representatives in the French Parliament, although maintaining an independent position both on particular issues and Marxism in general, happened to be aligned with the French Communists in votes on colonial and international policy. RDA leaders and members in the Ivory Coast were jailed on trumped-up charges of armed insurrection. This was answered by protest meetings and demonstrations and a general boycott of imported goods. Then came the police attacks and the killing of men and women at Grand Bassam and Dimbokro, Ivory Coast, at the end of 1949 and in January, 1950. Thousands were jailed. Finally came the official ban, February 1, 1950, on all meetings of the RDA "for having provoked disorder."

Later in the year a section of the leadership of the RDA headed by President Felix Houphouet-Boigny made its peace with the government and a strategic retreat from the organization's militant program. It continued to function—in collaboration with the French administration, not in opposition to it. Those who rejected this line, leaders such as Gabriel D'Arboussier, a founder and prime organizer, were purged; and those unreformed sections of the movement in Senegal and the Cameroons were ultimately expelled, though continuing to function. The trade union movement tended to replace the RDA in the leadership of mass struggle in French West Africa.

Like the RDA, the NCNC (National Council of Nigeria and Cameroons), founded in August 1944, was a united front movement, in this case representing a broad alliance of varied organizations. Dr. Nnamdi Azikiwe, now Prime Minister of the Eastern Region of Nigeria, served as the first general secretary of NCNC and shortly became its president, which he remains. The Council was primarily concerned with democratic constitutional reform, but it soon found its strength tested in a bread-and-butter struggle in 1945 involving 150,000 organized workers in transport, communications and other government services. The workers had long vainly petitioned for a minimum daily wage of 2s.6d. (50¢) and a 50 per cent increase in cost of living allowances which had remained stationary since 1942 while prices soared. At last they served notice that unless their "extremely modest demand" was met within a month, they would "proceed to seek their own remedy, with due regard to law and order on the one hand and starvation on the other hand."

Their strike lasted a month and a half, bringing the colony's traffic and business to a full stop. Arrests, "emergency" restrictions, and the banning of Azikiwe's newspapers for supporting the strike availed not. The crisis united the people and gave the NCNC a new drive. In 1947 its delegation, acting on behalf of 183 political, labor, farmer, tribal and other organizations, carried a mandate to the Colonial Secretary in London. It denounced the crown colony system as "despotic and obsolete" and demanded a time-table for the handing over of political responsibility to the people of Nigeria. The demand was brushed aside at the time, but could not be long ignored. The British Government has always disliked giving the appearance of being *forced* to grant anything.

Struggles around economic issues likewise spurred united political organization and action in the Gold Coast. There a country-wide boycott of stores operated by the UAC and other big merchant traders to force the lowering of prices culminated in rioting in Accra, Kumasi, and other towns in late March, 1948. The trouble started when a group of unarmed African war veterans, marching to lay a petition before the Governor, was fired upon by the police.

WORLD WAR II: THE CONFLICT GROWS 65

The news of this coincided with the discovery by thousands of angry shoppers that they had been cheated out of price reductions which had been promised for ending the boycott. Stores were looted and fired; 29 persons were killed and 237 injured in the restoration of "law and order."

The public feeling reflected in these events led Kwame Nkrumah and other younger Gold Coast leaders to the conviction that the people wanted something more than the moderate constitutional reforms which Dr. J. B. Danquah and other more conservative leaders of the United Gold Coast Convention, founded in August, 1947, were prepared to accept. Nkrumah and his followers split from the UGCC and established the Convention People's Party (CPP) in June, 1949. Their slogan was "Self-Government Now." And this, with all that it meant for the exploited worker and farmer, coupled with Nkrumah's program of "Positive Action" for achieving it, soon made the CPP the supreme organization in the land. The weapons of "Positive Action" were defined as "(1) Legitimate political agitation; (2) Newspaper and educational campaigns; and (3) as a last resort, the constitutional application of strikes, boycotts, and non-cooperation based on the principle of absolute non-violence."[4]

The stage of "last resort" was reached on January 8, 1950. A government workers' strike was already in progress, and a general strike was launched on January 7 by the Gold Coast Trade Union Congress. Political non-cooperation was merged with trade union non-cooperation. The Governor declared a "state of emergency" and put Nkrumah in jail, along with his political lieutenants and labor allies. He emerged from James Fort Prison in Accra on February 12, 1951, to become Leader of Government Business (the title of Prime Minister came a year later) after the CPP had swept to victory in the country's first general election.

Elsewhere in Africa few territories were unaffected by labor upsurges stemming from the inflationary pressures of the period. In 1944, the year that the Kenya African Union was organized, there was a general strike at the port of Mombasa, followed by another one of two weeks duration at the same place in 1947. In 1945 there were serious strikes at Douala in the French Cameroons (eight killed), in Uganda (six killed), on the Southern Rhodesia railways, and in the Belgian Congo where a railway line was cut, a power station was seized, and dockworkers at the port of Matadi engaged Belgian troops in barricade street fighting (seven killed).

In 1946 came a general strike in Dakar, and strikes by 1400 Union Steel Corp. workers and 60,000 gold mine employees in South Africa (nine killed). From November, 1947, to March, 1948, the railway system throughout French West Africa was crippled by a strike of 20,000 African workers demanding equal pay and equal job status with white employees.

Europe Rediscovers Africa

While Africa struggled for a taste of the Four Freedoms so widely heralded during the war, Europe at the end of the conflict faced the problem of bankruptcy. How to solve it? Once again, as in the last quarter of the nineteenth century, statesmen and financiers in London, Paris and Brussels turned toward Africa. "In view of disappointments registered in Asia," said *France Overseas,* an organ of French capital, "the European heart started to beat for the African continent."

Africans asked for time-tables for freedom; their rulers hurriedly prepared time-tables for "economic development" in Africa. France's Four Year Plan, 1949-52, for example, stated:

> Morocco will take an active part in the recovery of France by . . . supplying manganese, cobalt and lead ore, canned goods and agricultural produce, to enable the French Union to subsist on its own resources as much as possible. . . . France will find in Morocco a market for the products of its recovering industries, particularly as regards textiles and the products of the steel industry.[5]

Said Sir Stafford Cripps, Laborite Minister of Economic Affairs, addressing a conference of governors of Britain's African colonies in 1947:

> We must be prepared to change our outlook . . to colonial development, and force the pace so that within the next two or five years we can get a really marked increase of production in coal, minerals, timber and raw materials of all kinds, and foodstuffs and anything else that will save dollars or sell in the dollar market. . . . The whole future of the sterling group and its ability to survive depends, in my view, on the quick and extensive development of our African resources.[6]

Following the Governors' Conference, the black, brown and white members of all the Legislative Councils in Britain's African colonies were called to London in September, 1948 (the first occasion of any such assemblage, and there has not been another to date) to hear more of the same urgent pleading. They were told that exploitation in the colonies was obsolete; they were also told to be mindful of keeping the spirit of nationalism in Africa within bounds, not allowing it to become a "destructive force." On the main point of the agenda, the picture of Britain's financial crisis was clearly drawn: if the current dollar drain continued, there would be nothing left by 1950 to buy anything from the United States or other hard currency countries, and the pound sterling would drop to a third of its value.

Dr. J. B. Danquah was present (this was a year prior to the eclipse of the UGCC by the CPP) and has given an account[7] of what else was said on this point:

> We were told at the Conference that a simple solution had been found to meet the crisis, that solution is this: Africa, with her vast and massive resources in raw materials . . . could redress the balance of old Europe if she could sell increasing quantities of those massive resources to the United States. America needs Africa's goods. America would pay dollars for them. Such dollars would go to Britain and the sterling areas, and thereby stop the dollar drain. Would Africa come to help?
>
> There is yet another way in which Africa could help. . . . Would Africa restrain herself for the present, buy less and less from the United States, so that the dollars earned from Africa's raw materials sold to America should not again be taken to the United States except for really essential needs. . .

This, said Dr. Danquah, "is a great call, the greatest call of the century upon this old continent." One detail is omitted from his exposition. At one point in the Conference an African chief arose and politely asked about his people getting fair prices for their products. There were no mineworkers present to ask about wages.

The War and African Raw Materials

The "simple solution" of keeping Britain in dollars with Africa's raw materials was not quite so newly conceived and suddenly inspired as its proponents suggested. It amounted, in effect, to an extension and expansion of an exchange system which began operating in June, 1943, and went by the name of reciprocal aid or reverse lend-lease. Under this system wartime United States aid to Britain was repaid in part by raw materials and foodstuffs shipped from British colonies to the United States on United Kingdom account. (Britain's lend-lease bill was later cancelled.)

Except for rubber, mostly from Ceylon, the reverse lend-lease exports to the United States—copper, chrome, asbestos, graphite, sisal, palm oil and kernels, peanuts, cocoa and others—came mainly from Africa. To the end of the war they amounted to over $215 million in value, according to a United Kingdom report.[8] There were also other forms of wartime dollar-earning based on African resources. The Chairman of De Beers Consolidated Mines, Mr. H. F. Oppenheimer, reported at his company's meeting in 1946 that the De Beers Group's "sales of gem diamonds during the war secured about 300,000,000 American dollars for Great Britain and the Commonwealth."[9]

The wartime disruption of European-African shipping meant the re-channeling of African exports to the United States and into American war production. An even greater increase took place in the supply of American manufactures to Africa. In one year, August, 1940, to August, 1941, United States imports from Africa rose by 120 per cent while exports to Africa went up by 178 per cent as compared with the preceding year. With the arrival of American troops in North Africa in 1942, Washington dispatched an economic mission to promote trade relations in that area. Other missions visited the Congo, British and French West African territories, Ethiopia, Liberia, and South Africa.

These explorations were often concerned with general business prospects and not simply immediate military and wartime needs. The United States Foreign Economic Administration in 1944 announced that it was organizing economic "missions of businessmen" to visit various war areas, including North Africa, "to examine trade conditions and possibilities for practical private operations in such areas."[10]

Even before Pearl Harbor such a publication as *Fortune* magazine (November, 1941) had pictured Africa as "the jack pot of World War II." By the end of 1942 others saw "prospects that the war for the first time will bring the United States into close trading and other connections with the great continent of Africa."[11] And in 1943 the State Department was already looking ahead to the postwar period, as evidenced by one official's statement: "I feel certain that the American principle of equality of opportunity in trade will remain a paramount factor in Africa, applicable in the colonies of whatever nationality. . . . Africa needs our skills and services in order to achieve greater productivity, just as we need access to Africa's resources."[12]

Equality of opportunity—the open door for American access to Africa's raw materials—was an important part of the price paid by the European colonial powers for the postwar grants-in-aid they received from the United States. A London publication in 1947 put it this way: "On the one side are the indispensable economic requirements of the British peoples, and on the other side the tenaciously held theories of Americans who make no secret of their determination to 'bust wide open' the markets of the Empire."[18]

And in the middle—the Africans.

Cross Currents

In the days of bright promise at the war's end, did we not believe that Africa was to march forward with the rest of the world? That was what labor delegates from Nigeria, the Gold Coast, Sierra Leone and other colonies declared at the first World Trade Union Congress held in Paris in October, 1945. That was what Jomo Kenyatta, Kwame Nkrumah and others said at the Fifth Pan-African Congress held later the same month in Birmingham, England, and presided over by Dr. W. E. Burghardt Du Bois, founder of the Pan-African movement in 1919.

"We are unwilling to starve any longer, while doing the world's drudgery, in order to support, by our poverty and ignorance, a false aristocracy and a discredited imperialism," the Pan-African Congress Declaration read. "All colonies must be free from foreign imperialist control, whether political or economic."

Opposing this came the demand for Africa and Africans to produce more and more of the raw materials required by Europe and America, to recoup the imperialist losses sustained in Asia, and to remain subservient.

Thus arose the series of revolts, strikes and boycotts throughout Africa in the years immediately following the war and in subsequent years.

6. Loot—and More Loot

To SEE THE European-American postwar drive for Africa's resources in proper focus, one must first perceive something of the general dimensions of what the whole long history of foreign exploitation of these resources has amounted to.

Let us consider here only the *mineral* wealth of Africa. Bear in mind that Europeans have been taking this from the continent for nearly five centuries. It was in 1471 that the Portuguese first sailed around the western bulge of Africa to find and take away gold dust, naming the place where they got it the Gold Coast (the inhabitants have now chosen to call it Ghana). Remember, too, that such things as gold and diamonds do not replenish themselves. Once they're gone, they're gone. You can always look forward to another harvest of cocoa or corn or cotton, but when mining is done, there's nothing left at the end but a hole in the ground.

Twenty Billion Dollars Worth—Plus

European mining in South Africa is said to have had its beginning in 1852. Some time after the initial development of diamond and gold mining, toward the end of the century, they began to keep official records of all mineral sales. The total of such recorded sales in the Union of South Africa through the year 1955 comes to $13.7 billion.[1] Nearly four-fifths of that amount came from gold— some 18,874 tons of it. Over 40 tons of diamonds—if you can visualize them—came second in order of value.

The figures in table 6 represent what the minerals were worth at the time sold. What is their worth at current prices? Well, if one were to value at today's price of $35 an ounce all the South African gold marketed since 1911, it would come to over $17 billion. As a

TABLE 6. THE VALUE OF PRINCIPAL MINERALS PRODUCED
IN SOUTH AFRICA[2]

	Value Realized from Recorded Sales through 1955 ($ millions)	Percentage Increase in Production from 1937/39 to 1952/54
Gold	10,568.3	1
Diamonds	1,304.7	124
Coal	823.5	75
Copper	299.9	174
Asbestos	138.6	321
Uranium*	136.4	
Manganese	71.1	6
Chrome	52.6	216
Iron Ore	32.2	280

* Production started in 1953. Amount includes other "prescribed materials."

result of both high prices and increased production, South African minerals marketed during only the four years, 1952-55, amounted to $2.7 billion. That is about one-fifth of the total value of recorded mineral sales in the whole history of mining in the country. And add another $803 million for the minerals taken out in 1956.

In Northern Rhodesia, from the time exports began through 1955, mineral production—mainly copper—has had a total sales value of $2.1 billion.[3] About one-half of this was realized during the four years 1952-55. Southern Rhodesia's main minerals in order of importance are gold, asbestos, coal, chrome, and tungsten. These and other minerals produced through 1955 have had an aggregate value of $983 million.[4] The output of mines in both Rhodesias came to $528 million in 1956, Northern Rhodesia accounting for 85 per cent.

In the Belgian Congo the European mining of gold began in 1904, copper in 1911, diamonds and tin in 1913. Cobalt and manganese are other major exports. Mineral production averaged under $7 million a year in 1936-38; for the five years 1950-54 it averaged over $50 million for a total of $258 million. Add to this the undisclosed but probably substantial value of uranium and other fissionable materials exported.

The northeastern corner of Angola is diamond country. Smaller amounts of manganese and copper are also produced in this colony. The Diamond Co. of Angola has been called "Portugal's most notable private enterprise." In terms of its revenues, perhaps, yes. Since 1917, through depressions and wars, it has year after year unfailingly continued to produce thousands of diamonds. Through 1953 the total came to 17,653,000 carats.[5]

Which is all very nice. But the Diamond Co. of Angola can also probably claim the distinction of having about the lowest paid mine workers to be found anywhere in Africa. In 1953 over 7,000 of its 17,000 African employees were forced workers supplied "by intervention of the authorities," and they received 67 escudos ($2.33) a month.[6] The net profits of the Company for 1953 were $9,377,375 and combined profits for 1954 and 1955 came to the total of invested capital plus another 40 per cent.

This, then, is the general picture of the mineral wealth taken from South Africa, the Rhodesias, the Belgian Congo and Angola. To this must be added, in this region of the continent, diamonds and other minerals from Tanganyika, asbestos from Swaziland, and more diamonds, lead, zinc, and so forth from South West Africa. All told, one might give a conservative estimate of at least $20 billion as the value of the minerals taken by the white man just from that part of Africa which lies below the equator.

Without extending this survey to the whole continent, we may note a few facts with reference to the British West African colonies lest the impression be conveyed that the European extraction of gold and diamonds and base minerals has been confined to the areas of white settlement in Africa.

In 1945 the Director of Geological Survey in the Gold Coast estimated the value of the minerals extracted by the British from that colony since 1880 at $480 million, gold representing three-fourths of that amount. But long before 1880, in the early eighteenth century, British, Dutch and Danes settled on the Coast were sending home gold to the value of about $700,000 annually. The Ashanti Goldfield Corp., weathiest of the present-day mining companies in Ghana, was established in 1897 with a nominal capital of £250,000 ($700,000), and now has an issued capital of about $3.5 million. Up to 1954 it had produced some seven million ounces of fine gold, today worth $245 million.[7]

Diamonds and manganese are the other chief mineral exports coming from Ghana. In Nigeria it is mainly tin; from 1910 to 1954 a half million tons of tin ore, valued at $336 million, was exported.[8] And in Sierra Leone it is diamonds and iron ore, the latter chopped from two hills of iron rising from the Marampa plain. From 1933 to 1952 over 15 million tons of ore was taken;[9] 1,328,000 tons of it was exported in 1956.

Africans and Mining Rights

There is one significant difference in the character of the mining industry in the West African territories and in white-settler countries like Rhodesia, South Africa or the Belgian Congo. In the latter the big corporations have preempted the field with government's blessing and protection; African mining is virtually non-existent. If the African digs any minerals it must be for the corporations. Illustrating their zeal in this regard Belgian Congo authorities in 1950 arrested in one swoop 300 Africans suspected of illegal mining and illegal business in gold, sentencing 79 of them.

On the other hand, in the British West African colonies and Uganda, and also in French West Africa and, recently, Tanganyika, Africans have in varying degrees engaged in prospecting and mining on their own account—outside the concession areas held by the white companies, of course. The African, lacking capital, naturally cannot compete on equal terms with the big mining concerns. His equipment is usually no more than that of the typical individual mining prospector. Even so, in the case of the Gold Coast, the hundreds of African diggers working on their own have collectively produced more diamonds each year since 1950 than the British companies with their large-scale modern, mechanized mining operations. The Africans have complaints, however, against the diamond marketing system in Accra controlled by foreign buyers.

We have already seen what little affection West Africans had for UAC (United Africa Co.), which inherited from the Royal Niger Company the 99-year right to collect half the royalties on all minerals. At the end of the war, about the time when it became unfashionable for the British to characterize their West African colonies as "unprepared for self-government in the foreseeable future," the UAC and other companies with long-established and long still-to-run monopoly privileges began to have second thoughts. The demands were becoming louder, the current was flowing fast. Better perhaps to withdraw gracefully—at a price, than to be forced out, who knows when, with nothing.

The UAC in any event entered into lengthy negotiations with London colonial officials as to the basis for relinquishing its minerals royalties and mining rights in Nigeria. In 1950 the price was finally settled—a million pounds ($2.8 million). Only then, when the Nigerian Legislative Council was called upon to ratify the deal, did the people learn of it. Despite a clamor of protest, the deal was approved.

Another case was that of the Sierra Leone Selection Trust, a subsidiary of Consolidated African Selection Trust, which in turn is part of the De Beers-Anglo American investment complex presided over by Sir Ernest Oppenheimer. SLST in 1934 secured exclusive rights for 99 years to prospect and mine diamonds throughout the whole of Sierra Leone, some 28,000 square miles. In 1953 Africans began finding diamonds in abundance outside the area being actually worked by SLST. Notwithstanding the Trust's exclusive rights, the people saw no reason to let the diamonds lie around waiting for somebody else to come and claim them. Illegal mining and diamond marketing soon became too much for the authorities to cope with.

The Trust, to get the Government's increased protection of its rights, agreed to give it a somewhat larger share of its revenue ($3.7 million gross profits in 1953, while African employees averaged $3.75 for a 51-hour week). When this failed to bring a stop to the illegal mining, SLST decided on partial withdrawal—at a price. In 1955 it was agreed to limit the area of the Trust's operations and rights to 450 square miles, and to cut the duration of these rights from the 77 years still remaining to a maximum of 30 years—in exchange for compensation in the amount of $4,396,000 to be paid SLST by the Sierra Leone Government ($19.6 million was asked at one time). Again it was the Colonial Secretary in London who had the final word on the price to be paid. The opposition minority in the colony's Legislative Council fought against paying the "compensation," Dr. Bankole Bright calling the terms "diabolical and iniquitous," and Mr. I. T. A. Wallace Johnson speaking for four hours against the payment. But it was paid. Thus illegal African mining in most of Sierra Leone became legal.

In 1956 another concessionaire in the same colony underwent some wing-clipping. The Sierra Leone Development Co., which in 1931 acquired exclusive mineral rights in the Marampa area and then in the Tonkolili District, agreed that in the latter place it would curtail its rights from 99 to 33 years, relinquish its monopoly over minerals other than iron ore, and increase its rental and tax payments to the Sierra Leone Government.

In Rhodesia the BSA (British South Africa Co.), after getting the equivalent of over $17 million in 1923 for the loss of its royal charter, received another $8.5 million in 1933 from the Southern

Rhodesia Government for giving up its rights to mineral royalties in that territory. As for Northern Rhodesia, not until 1949 did BSA agree to share 20 per cent of its mineral royalties with the local government, and to terminate its rights without compensation in 1986. It refused to yield more than that. The De Beers Corp. in 1955 also agreed to give up its diamond mining rights in Northern Rhodesia in 1986. But in the present relationship of whites and blacks in Rhodesia these concessions add nothing to the possibility or opportunity for independent mining by Africans, who continue to challenge the validity of the 1890 "treaties" with the African chiefs by which BSA originally claimed its mineral rights.

Profits and Poverty

Twenty billion dollars worth of minerals, more or less, from sub-equatorial Africa and additional massive quantities from other areas—and yet they say Africa is poor. If by that is meant the mass of the population, it is certainly true. But why should the people be poverty-stricken when the continent's sub-soil yields such wealth? The answer is obvious: the mineral riches and the profits therefrom are taken by non-Africans.

It is a serious charge to make—that the wealth of Africa is drained away, [writes Dr. Rita Hinden, a Fabian Socialist, in *The Challenge of African Poverty*]. Minerals are one of Africa's precious assets, yet the mines are almost always operated by European capitalist companies, which pay dividends to their overseas shareholders, heavy remuneration to their directors, as likely as not the lion's share of their taxes to the British Exchequer, royalties to venerable but functionless companies, and enormous wages to local European employees. What remains for the African workers and for the African exchequers are the crumbs from the rich man's table.

And a Nigerian comments: "The fabulous sums drawn away from our mines alone, had they been at the disposal of a government of Nigerians, might have transformed the face of our country in a decade. We would have had those things which we are now vainly seeking for: schools, factories, hospitals."[10]

From 1870 to the end of 1934 the diamond mining companies in South Africa paid net dividends of more than £80 million on a capital investment of £20 million. "This wealth," says Lord Hailey, "has probably been greater than that which has been obtained from any other commodity in the same time anywhere in the world, when the size of the industry is taken into account." Gold mining companies in the same country—those that failed as well as those that prospered—paid between 1886 and 1932 dividends of £255 million on invested capital of £200 million.[11] By 1945, after sixty years of gold mining on the Rand, the shareholders' dividends had climbed to £479 million (then equivalent to $2,547 million).[12]

With regard to the Belgian Congo former Governor Pierre Ryckmans, lately a leading opponent of the anti-colonialists in the United Nations, is on record as stating that during the 13-year period, 1927-1939, Belgian stockholders had received 5,366 million francs in dividends and mining companies 4,208 million in net profits on paid-up capital of 1,700 million francs.[13]

No, you could hardly say that investors in the mining companies have found Africa poor. And we have not yet come to the postwar record of profits.

But minerals once taken cannot be taken again, as we have already observed. Decades of looting must eventually wear out even the richest of mineral deposits. South African diamonds, of course, are not as plentiful as they used to be, and until the new mines in the Orange Free State were opened, the country's gold production had been declining since 1941. Even with the new mines, according to the calculations of the South African Government Mining Engineer in 1947, all but a small fraction of the remaining gold reserves will be exhausted by 1990. The Diamond Co. of Angola has had diminishing returns since its peak output of 1946. The Shamva gold mine in Southern Rhodesia shut down recently after 44 years. As for West Africa, the Managing Director of the United Africa Co. stated in 1949 that tin production in Nigeria and gold in the Gold Coast had "passed their zenith." One gold mining company in the latter country, its prosperous years over, shut down permanently in January, 1956, when its 3,000 striking workers refused to return without a wage increase. The mine was simply flooded and the men dismissed. One more hole in the ground.

The Postwar Drive for Strategic Minerals

Those in Europe and the United States who turned eager eyes toward Africa after World War II did not bother to mention how much of her mineral wealth had already been mined and exported. Instead, everyone talked about the continent's "vast untapped resources." To bring Africa's raw material resources, tapped or untapped, to the service of governments and industries in the United States and Western Europe in maximum amounts and minimum time was the job assigned a veritable expeditionary force of administrators, scientists, technicians, and assorted experts and businessmen which descended upon the continent.

The general plan of attack was indicated in the European Recovery Program or Marshall Plan, and the staff headquarters for directing and coordinating the campaign was the Economic Cooperation Administration (ECA) in Washington, together with its overseas auxiliary, the Organization for European Economic Cooperation (OEEC). From them emanated the detailed tactical plans—how much to spend, where, and for what, toward getting the resources from colonial Africa (1) to satisfy United States requirements and (2) to save and earn dollars for Britain, France, Belgium and Portugal.

Putting colonial production into high gear meant not only opening up new sources of raw materials and pumping the old ones harder, but also providing new and better means for getting the stuff out of the continent—roads, railroads, and harbor facilities. For all this, in addition to ECA and OEEC, there were created by each of the colonial powers, if they did not already exist, various agencies and funds for channeling state and private investments into the colonies where needed. The contribution of private capital was small. There is little or no profit to be made from providing the basic production needs in colonial countries, and as someone has said, there is nothing as shy as a million dollars unless it happens to be tax-payers' money.

So the financing job was done in the final analysis by Joe Smith in the United States, who paid for the direct ECA colonial grants and loans (actually payments for colonial raw materials) or for the Marshall Plan aid to Europe which directly or indirectly made possible at least part of the contributions of the colonial powers toward expanding their colonies' production. It was done, secondly, by Jean or Thomas in France, Belgium and England, who paid for the remaining part of the colonial powers' contribution. And it was done, thirdly, by Jomo or Mohammed in the African colonies, whose governments were called upon to match the contributions of the metropolitan countries.

When the Marshall Plan was first launched, it was thought that by its scheduled termination at the end of 1950 Europe, supported by its colonies, would be able to go it alone. But, of course, OEEC lived on and the functions of ECA were taken over by MSA (Mutual Security Agency) which in turn gave way to FOA (Foreign Operations Administration) and (since July 1, 1955) ICA (International Cooperation Administration). We need not concern ourselves here with the organizational and ideological permutations of this evolution. The point is that the American-European program of economic expansion in Africa continued on after the end of the Marshall Plan, and still continues.

From 1946 through 1953 approximately $3.8 billion was spent for specific economic projects and programs in the whole of Africa, excluding Egypt and the Union of South Africa. By far the largest part of this came from France and her colonies—$2 billion spent in North Africa and $700 million in her other African colonies. $287 million of regular Marshall Plan grants to France were earmarked for expenditure in her colonies. Direct United States grants and loans to all African countries, including the Union of South Africa, during the same period totalled about $600 million.[14] This is a comparatively small amount as such items go, but what benefits accrued from it and to whom will be seen as we proceed. Additional substantial sums went from the United States Government to some parts of Africa, notably the Union of South Africa and Rhodesia, during 1954 and 1955.

A major item in both ECA and OEEC priorities was geological surveying, aimed at discovering new mineral deposits. Teams of experts were dispatched from America and Europe to all sections of Africa. The British staff of overseas geological experts, for example, expanded from 58 in 1947 to 186 by 1952, while the French staff, consisting of 25 experts in 1947, was enlarged to 155. All kinds of minerals needed by modern industry and particularly the armaments industry have been sought, but above all the search has been hottest for uranium and radioactive substitutes such as thorium and monazite. Important deposits of these minerals have been reported discovered within the past year or two in widely scattered places including Mrima Hill in Kenya north of Mombasa, at N'Boko-Songo in French Equatorial Africa, and in Madagascar. The list of Mozambique's mineral production in 1952 included 49,409 metric tons of "radioactive minerals." In the same year 1952 the Mutual Security Agency announced that "at least 26 highly-specialized American technicians and the most modern American scientific equipment" were being sent to Portugal's Mozambique and Angola for "the largest combined aerial and ground search for new mineral deposits ever undertaken with United States support."[15]

But private capital is not content to leave this prospecting job entirely to government. An American engineer who found the Nchanga copper mine in Northern Rhodesia in 1924 again took up the search for more copper there in 1956 on behalf of a United States company. American capital is also backing a search for uranium in Southern Rhodesia. The London Tin Corp. with holdings in Nigeria set up a subsidiary company in 1953 for mineral exploration in Nyasaland. In Tanganyika the competition in uranium-prospecting has become such that the Government has arranged to protect the interests of a prospector using an airborne scintillometer-detector by barring other persons from the area so that observers on the ground will not "jump" his claim.

Northern Rhodesia is a concentration point of the big mining companies. Two powerful combinations have launched ambitious prospecting programs there since 1954. One combination consists of Rio Tinto, Tanganyika Concessions, and Zambesi Exploring. The other embraces the British South Africa Co. and Anglo-American Corp. of South Africa. A subsidiary company of the latter (all of whose directors except one are South African) is in Kenya.

Other high priorities on the list of American-European government investments in Africa have been electric power and transportation. Mines have no value, of course, without power facilities to work them, railroads to carry away the ore, and ports where ships can dock and take it on board.

An ECA report to Congress in 1951 told how the Governments of France, Belgium and Britain were all concentrating on transport facilities and public works in their colonies. The French were improving the port of Conakry, "which is the outlet for a rich mineral region in West Africa," and the Pointe Noire-Brazzaville railroad "to facilitate access to the area in French Equatorial Africa where strategic materials are being developed." Belgium's 1951 investments of $160 million in the Congo would go mainly "for the improvement and development of transportation and power to facilitate the processing and transit of such critical commodities as palm oil, rubber, bauxite, quinine, pyrethrum and diamonds." And Britain's 1951 investment program of nearly $200 million would likewise concentrate on "construction and improvement of trunk

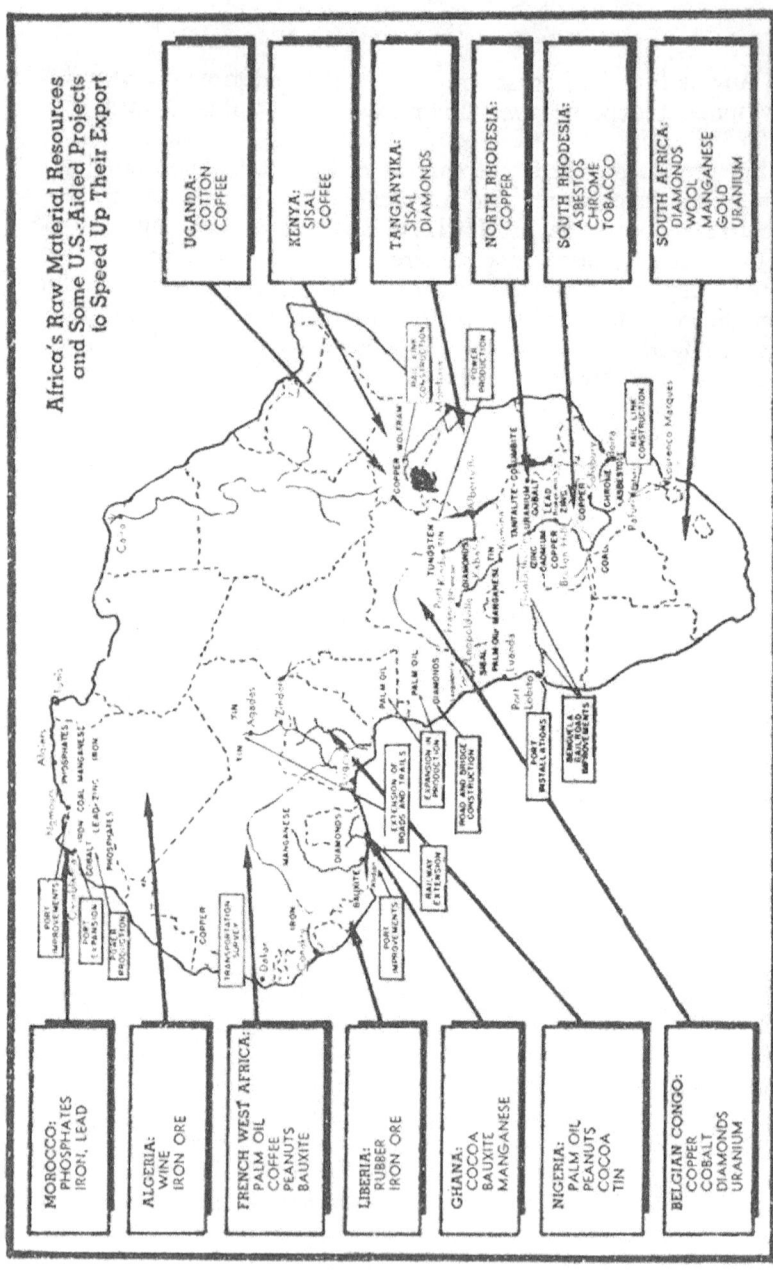

Main present exports of principal countries are shown in panels left and right.

and feeder roads and of rail links (to) expedite the production and export of such scarce materials as copper, manganese, lead, zinc, tin and diamonds from the United Kingdom territories in Africa."[16]

"The interests of the African peoples are given first consideration," said the State Department official, speaking of the Marshall Plan and Africa. And meantime in the Gold Coast complaints were raised because there was no bridge across a river and the people had to wait unsheltered through the night for the ferry, while the "government goes on its way to construct double manganese railway lines from Takoradi to Tarkwa for nothing but to facilitate taking away huge quantities of our manganese and other minerals to enrich other nations."[17]

It may be said that the British and French Governments were making geological surveys and investing in railroads and other public works in order to promote the production and export of colonial raw materials long before World War II and before the Marshall Plan and ECA came on the scene. That is true, of course. Such is the nature of economic colonialism. Europeans did not need Americans to teach them that. The new elements in the postwar drive for Africa's resources were the vastly enlarged scale and accelerated tempo of the operations, and the role of the United States Government whose control of the wherewithal, so it implied, gave it the right to set the pace and dictate production targets and expect the individual and collective compliance of those on the receiving end of the dollar bounty, the rulers of Africa's colonies. "The United States," British Laborite Ernest Bevin once said, "are a great country of free enterprise in America, but wonderful planners outside."

In a dispatch from Dakar, French West Africa, an American newspaperman, Edwin A. Lahey, in 1953 wrote:

> Imperialism would be a nasty word to describe our own expanding interest in Africa, but the list of American projects to develop the vast mineral resources of this continent suggests that the 19th century imperialism of England, France, Belgium and Portugal is child's play by comparison. . . .
>
> If Africa were just a matter of minerals, the continent would be strictly something for the metal trades publications to write about. But the whole business is distressingly complicated by the presence of a good many million natives, whose labor is needed for the digging, and who are clamoring with varying degrees of militancy and viciousness to be elected to membership in the human race.[18]

Call it viciousness or what you will, from the Africa's point of view people come before things—even uranium.

7. Dollars and Empire

AT THE BEGINNING of this century when British imperial power was at its peak, J. A. Hobson noted how England's ruling families, then concerned with the profitable outcome of Cecil Rhodes' enterprises in South Africa and Rhodesia, "have had an ever increasing incentive to employ the public policy, the public purse and the public force to extend the field of their private investments, and to safeguard and improve their existing investments." In speaking today of the policy and investments of the United States Government in Africa, we should remember the extent to which that government reflects the aims and interests of the ruling families, the top business circles, of New York and other American cities.

Back in the 1912 election campaign Woodrow Wilson characterized the government in Washington as "a foster child of the special interests." Franklin D. Roosevelt and others, including an occasional Republican, have assailed the American money lords' dominating control over government. Mr. Adlai Stevenson spoke of business having too big a voice in the Eisenhower administration, but at the same time he reminded us that "Every frontier in American progress has been, and will always be, opened up by the joint enterprise of business and government." Presumably in his view Africa, where Mr. Stevenson recently traveled extensively on undisclosed business matters, is one of those frontiers.

The war-time administration of Roosevelt, notwithstanding his forays against privileged wealth during the 'thirties, also called upon the services of a considerable number of industrial and financial leaders. The late Edward R. Stettinius, Jr., a director of U.S. Steel, General Motors, General Electric, Metropolitan Life and other corporations, was Lend-Lease Administrator and then Under-Secretary of State during 1943 when the agreement for construction of a port and port works at Monrovia, Liberia, was negotiated and signed. Soon after leaving the post of Secretary of State in 1945, Mr. Stettinius organized the Liberia Co.

Another Secretary of State, James F. Byrnes of South Carolina, has for some years been a member of the Board of Directors of Newmont Mining Corp., which holds wide interests in Africa. Another director of Newmont, H. De Witt Smith, served as Executive Vice-President of the Government's Metals Reserve Company. Still another Newmont director, Fred Searls, Jr., now Chairman of the Board and also a director of the American Metal Co., with which Newmont is associated in several African enterprises, held a number of government positions. In 1951, when serving as consultant on mineral policies to Charles E. Wilson, then Director of the Office of Defense Mobilization, Searls came under attack in the Senate when it was disclosed that he was opposing government assistance to other mining enterprises at the same time that Newmont-backed companies in the United States and Africa were benefiting from such subsidies. He resigned from his government post, but the subsidies remained.

Government Cooperates with Private Enterprise

The three main institutional channels of American investment in Africa have been ECA and its successors; the Export-Import Bank (Eximbank), a federal United States lending agency with global scope; and the International Bank for Reconstruction and Development, or more simply, World Bank. While the latter is nominally a United Nations agency and is composed like that body of representatives of member governments, its headquarters is not in New York or Geneva but in Washington, D. C. Headed by Eugene R. Black, former Vice President of Chase National Bank, the World Bank is in fact regarded as "an arm of the United States Government."[1] American banks sometimes participate in financing its loans.

ECA and the Eximbank have made many direct loans to private mining enterprises in Africa, but the main function of all three agencies in relation to that continent has been to provide the previously discussed basic supporting facilities of production— roads and railroads, electric power and ports. "The improvements in basic equipment brought about by the public authorities," said OEEC, "should . . . lighten the task of private enterprise by providing the conditions essential for its success."[2] The leader of a World Bank mission to Southern Rhodesia in 1951 put it this way: "We do not like to compete with private enterprise, but try to pave the way for further expansion by them."

Besides aiding foreign enterprise in Africa by relieving it of some heavy overhead costs and charging them up to the taxpayer, the great trinity of financing institutions has also benefited some sectors of stay-at-home American industry. Through them came orders, again paid for out of the public treasury, for millions of dollars worth of specialized electrical apparatus; construction, conveying, and mining equipment; tractors and other heavy agricultural machines; motor vehicles, engines, and parts—all to be used on various African projects.

ECA releases describing these operations read like something out of Hollywood. "The Marshall Plan has stepped into French West Africa to bring potential wealth out of the desert and into the world's trade markets. The ECA said today that most of the $31,000,000 worth of American goods and machinery allocated to the territory [is] for the improvement of roads, ports and airfields, the mining of gold and ore deposits, and the cultivation of rice and peanuts." Another release boasts: "Rare tropical woods from the French Cameroons in Africa soon will be turning up in the world's living rooms" as a result of "$1,600,000 worth of American machinery" sent by the ECA and Eximbank to a sawmill and logging camp "in the jungles of the French Cameroons."[3]

As regards the Point Four Program, which was launched with such great fanfare seven years ago, it has been of relatively minor significance in Africa both in scope and in the size of the appropriations doled out. Liberia, Ethiopia, Libya and Egypt have been the only African recipients of Point Four aid. It parallels the technical assistance given under ECA, etc.; there are the same expert survey of transport facilities and resources, preparing the way for mining, lumber operations, and so forth.

Grants for education, sanitation, eradication of disease, and agricultural production for local consumption (instead of export) come usually at the bottom of the list. And it is not being cynical to ask whether such help when given is for the benefit of the general population or in the interest of some economic venture which requires the elimination of local health hazards and a supply of reasonably qualified and able-bodied workers. For one can find it plainly stated in a British Colonial Office report: "Natives in

European employment cannot be permitted to live in dirty and insanitary quarters, if only from the point of view of the welfare of their masters."[4]

On August 27, 1950, ECA announced (release No. 1681) the assignment of two American scientists under its technical assistance program to help British authorities fight disease-carrying insects in West Africa. Highly laudable, it would seem. But it was explained: "Tapping of Africa's rich resources, long impeded by the prevalence of disease, soon may be accelerated. . . . With the control of certain types of insects, the British plan to embark on large-scale agricultural and industrial projects in the Gold Coast." One could perhaps call this "aid with a rope attached." Under the circumstances the people of that territory might prefer to bear with the insects a little longer.

Doubtless some benefits do accrue to Africans from educational, health and other Point Four or technical assistance projects promoted by the United States Government. But the evidence suggests that the social objectives of such projects are incidental and subordinate to other economic objectives which accord with European or American rather than African needs. This judgment can be amended when we see Washington announce an educational program for some part of Africa having the same urgent time-table schedule and generous outlay of money and equipment as have characterized the many strategic materials programs in that continent.

Stockpile Bonanza

The people of Europe were told that the Marshall Plan would bring them economic security. We in America were informed that it would promote our "national interests" and those of the "Free World." The practical-minded members of the United States Congress were advised that the enabling legislation proposed was "designed to assist the United States wherever feasible to obtain materials for stock piling purposes . . . from a participating country or its colonies or dependencies . . . under an aggressive plan of exploration, development, and expansion of productive facilities, or by other actions. . . ."[5]

The stockpiling program, started in 1946 when the war was barely over, aimed at securing huge quantities of some 67 strategic materials within five years; $3.2 billion was to be spent for them.

Both the expenditure and time limit were subsequently extended. An ECA list of 21 of the desired stockpile materials, ranging from antimony to zinc, indicated some part of Africa as the source from which they were all to be procured. They were needed, it was urged, to produce the planes, tanks, guns and bombs for the defense of the United States and its western allies who came to be organized in NATO. Some Americans, braving castigation and ostracism, argued at the time that the made-in-America weapons might in fact be used not to stop the feared Soviet aggression but to keep Asian and African peoples in subjection. Events proved them right.

Meantime the stockpiling program has richly rewarded some mining interests. Consider, for example, the mineral columbite. This is a very rare heat-resistant steel alloy which lately became highly prized for its efficiency as a jet-engine metal. Virtually all of it comes from one place, Nigeria. Before 1953 the mineral had been regarded as a practically worthless by-product of tin mining. Then came the stockpile orders from Washington, with offers of a bonus price of about $6,300 a ton during 1953 and slightly less from 1954 through 1956. The producing companies in Nigeria stepped up their production and did handsomely; production costs amounted to between $1,400 and $2,240 a ton and even half the U.S. offer would have given a nice profit. The United States Government made available close to a million dollars for one company to enlarge its production capacity, the amount to be repaid, plus five per cent interest, in columbite at the fancy prices indicated.

The United States got $10.4 million worth of Nigeria columbite in 1953, $14.4 million in 1954. In the latter year the United States took 2,176 long tons, the United Kingdom got 245, and other countries 103. But by May, 1955, the ride was over. No new stockpile orders were forthcoming, the target having been achieved. By August the price had dropped down to about $3,000, with few buyers around. Stockpile suppliers of other minerals enjoyed a longer ride.

The Main Objective—Investment and Control

It was not long after the launching of the Marshall Plan that the Congressional Joint Committee concerned with this program called attention to the fact that one section of the enabling Act was not being adhered to. It referred to a clause which stated that

Americans be given "suitable protection for the right of access" to raw material sources, emphasizing that it was Congress' intent not only that the European countries should spur the production of strategic materials, but also that "the United States should share in this production." "It is precisely that Congress wished to obtain access to new sources for both stock pile and American industry" that it wrote that section in the law, said the Joint Committee. "It is certain," the ECA Director of the Strategic Materials Division stated, "that the participating countries view with some anxiety the stipulation that United States industry be given equal recognition with their nationals in the development of their resources." They were resorting to "obstructionist tactics," he said.[6]

The point is that awareness was developing in European circles that the Americans were not merely interested in *buying* more raw materials in the African colonies. They wanted to invest in the mines and other colonial enterprises, own them, control them. The prospecting for new mineral deposits, the railroad expansion, and the new harbor facilities financed by the United States were designed to pave the way primarily for *American* private investment.

There were cries of alarm from some quarters in London, Paris and Brussels. A speaker on Britain's overseas radio broadcast service in 1949 warned: "If America is allowed to invest too much capital, the mineral wealth of Africa will become American before it is dug from the soil. The chance that Africa will have to sell her minerals for dollars to America will be gone. . . . Do not let us think for one moment that Africa, watered by a stream of American gold, will flower as an English rose. The national flower of America is Golden Rod!"[7]

From Africans came different expressions of concern. State Department officials admitted that African resentment and hostility were widespread, but they naturally attributed these reactions to "misunderstanding." The general tenor of this criticism, exemplified in the words of a Nigerian, is that the Marshall Plan policy of utilizing Africa's resources to serve the needs of Europe and the United States "is creating the impression of 'American Imperialism' in Africa. The implications of this policy are hopelessly inimical to the freedom of Africa from European colonial imperialism."[8]

The Point Four Program was intended to win back the disillusioned, but its glowing humanitarian sentiments soon sputtered out when tested in action. Although American private investment in Africa advanced, it was far off the pace which government investment had set for it in the first flush of the Marshall Plan—except in a few areas where the welcome mat remained in front of the open door.

Under the Republican administration the aims of Government became more openly and clearly identified with those of Big Business as expressed, for instance, by the United States Chamber of Commerce. When Mr. Preston Hotchkis, the United States representative, addressed the United Nations Economic and Social Council, April 7, 1954, on the subject of Economic Development of Underdeveloped Countries, he took as his text President Eisenhower's capsule summation of his foreign economic policy, to wit:

> Aid—which we wish to curtail;
> Investment—which we wish to encourage;
> Convertibility—which we wish to facilitate; and
> Trade—which we wish to expand.

To further implement this policy in Africa the Foreign Operations Administration in 1954 dispatched Mr. R. T. Wise, a consultant of its Office of Trade, Investment and Monetary Affairs, on an extended tour which covered a number of African territories including Morocco, Liberia, the Belgian Congo, Rhodesia, and Portuguese Angola and Mozambique. In the latter country, explaining to the local press and businessmen FOA's plan for setting up "partnership" concerns to handle Africa's business, Mr. Wise said quite bluntly,

> Its motif is profit. It is profit for either partner. The participation of FOA is an assurance that financial adventurers shall not be permitted in such plans. The selection criterion in these projects is to reconcile the interests of the American capitalists with those of the Portuguese partners, with preference to such enterprises as adequately meet the requirements and progress of the Province [colony].[9]

There have been no small number of other grand tours of Africa, with the same objective of opening up new investment channels, by the top executives of American banks and corporations, not to mention the numerous junkets of visiting Congressmen. The general picture is one of friendly hand-in-hand cooperation between Wall Street and Washington in promoting American business enterprise in "the continent of the future," as the *New York Times* calls it.

Attractive Investment Climates

To the axiom about the shyness of a million dollars, unless it happens to be taxpayers' money, should be added another qualification—unless it is following after another million dollars. United States postwar investments in Africa, both governmental (omitting military bases) and private, have been directed to the same concentration areas where foreign capital was attracted during the first three decades of this century (the earlier American investments—on a much smaller scale, of course, than Europe's—included those of Thomas F. Fortune and Daniel Guggenheim, who in 1907 helped finance one of Leopolds' main concessions in the Congo, *Forminière;* and those of Morgan and Rockefeller in South Africa, Firestone in Liberia, and the already-mentioned holdings in Northern Rhodesia's Copperbelt). The proportionate distribution of World Bank and Export-Import loans to African territories parallels almost exactly the pattern of prewar capital investments. Those areas that got the most twenty years ago are still getting the most, as seen in Table 7.

TABLE 7. EXIMBANK AND WORLD BANK LOANS IN AFRICA COMPARED WITH EARLIER FOREIGN INVESTMENTS[10]

	Foreign Investment per Head of Total Population, 1936[a]	Eximbank 1946-1955 ($ millions)	World Bank to June 30, 1956 ($ millions)
Union of South Africa	$279	149.7	180.2[b]
N. and S. Rhodesia	192	22.4	122.0
Belgian Congo	65	15.5	70.0
Angola, Mozambique	49	17.3	none
British East Africa	40	none	24.0
British West Africa	24	none	none
French Territories	16	none	18.1[c]

[a] At 1936 exchange rates. [b] Includes following loans financed by New York private banks: $10 million in October, 1949; $10 million, January, 1951; $25 million, November, 1955. [c] Includes $609,000 loan financed by J. P. Morgan & Co., June, 1954.

ECA-FOA, etc. grants and loans (for which the Union of South Africa is ineligible) raise United States Government investments in Rhodesia higher, and similarly with the Belgian Congo and French territories, these being the chief recipients of such grants and loans. Including them, the Union of South Africa still ranks far ahead at the top in over-all non-private United States investments, followed by Rhodesia, the Belgian Congo, the French territories (mainly Morocco and Algeria), British East Africa (mainly Kenya), and the Portuguese colonies, in that order. British West Africa is at the bottom of the list.

Other Eximbank loans to Africa through 1955 have been $25.3 million to Liberia, $7.3 million to Egypt, and $27 million to Ethiopia. The only other World Bank loan in Africa also went to Ethiopia in the amount of $8.5 million.

Even though we are dealing here with American *government* investment, it seems that the same criteria determine where it goes as in the case of private investment. Obviously, South Africa, Rhodesia, and the Belgian Congo draw the greatest number of dollars because (a) they have strategic materials that the United States wants, (b) they have already established a reputation for paying good dividends on investments, and (c) they represent a healthy investment climate of "political stability" in that they are and may be expected to remain (at least so it is thought) under the political control of those in whom the investor has the fullest confidence.

The third criterion also explains why even Kenya and Mozambique rate higher in the investor's book than Nigeria or the Sudan. One infers that by this standard white political control is desirable. But it is clearly not necessarily essential. Color aside, what the dispensers of federal funds look for is a government with certain tenure of office, unchallenged control over labor and the general population, unquestioned loyalty to the West, and a hospitable attitude toward foreign investors. The regimes of President Tubman of Liberia and of Emperor Haile Selassie of Ethiopia qualify under these standards. It remains true, however, that the white-ruled sections of Africa have been getting the most dollars from the United States treasury.

A Kenya official, after a month's visit to the United States in 1953 at the invitation of the American Departments of State and Commerce, had only the most optimistic report to give. "Through the kindness of Mr. David Rockefeller," he said, "I was able to meet many of the leading investment bankers of New York, and, I believe, engage their interest in Kenya as a country of rapidly growing opportunities." He stated that the bankers whom he met had not been very concerned about Mau Mau (the revolt in Kenya was then in full motion) and regarded it as "much less serious than the impediments to capital investment in other parts of the world."[11]

Confirming this attitude a 1953 economic report on Kenya prepared by the United States Department of Commerce expressed the belief that the Kenya Government would succeed in converting the Kikuyu and other African inhabitants from rebellion to cooperation. It stated further, "The energy and confidence of those in Kenya who have kept, and are determined to keep, the economy in running order should have a stimulating effect on potential immigration and investment."[12]

It apparently did not matter to the authors of the report that keeping Kenya's economy in running order involved, among other things:

—the exaction of forced communal labor from Africans, without pay for 90 days out of the year, under penalty of six months imprisonment or a $14 to $70 fine;[13]

—putting scores of thousands of Africans, mainly women, at communal labor clearing trees and bush, laying new roads, making ditches, fences, and furrows, and building houses in the new Kikuyu, Embu, and Meru villages where between 750,000 and 1,000,000 men, women and children driven out of their former abodes were to be compelled to reside permanently;[14]

—using Mau Mau convict labor to build a new airfield on the coast near Lamu, and another, described as "the world's first hand-made international airport," covering seven square miles with four runways, at Embakasi, eight miles from Nairobi (there had been difficulties in financing the project; the sweeping Mau Mau arrests provided a solution of the problem in line with the previously mentioned declaration of Kenya's Governor of his intention to enlarge the use of convict labor "to the economic advantage of the colony")—several thousand prisoners laboring under armed guard at a million-ton excavation job, filling in craters, laying a half million tons of stone with nothing but shovels, stone-hammers, and their bare hands.[15]

There may not be another Embakasi Airport, but in South Africa, the chief beneficiary of United States Government loans, and in other territories, too, as we have already seen, it is convict labor and other forced labor of various types that help keep the economy in running order, just as in Kenya. And millions of dollars, let it be noted, have been contributed directly to these countries' railroads and other public works which regularly depend on such coerced labor. Note also that the absence of trade union rights for black workers is a common characteristic of most of the African territories in which American capital is mainly interested,—South Africa, the Congo, Liberia, Ethiopia, and the Portuguese colonies. Only in Kenya and Northern Rhodesia, among the favored territories south of the Sahara, are there functioning African trade unions, and their status even in these places is precarious, labor leaders being among the first to be rounded up and jailed whenever the authorities see fit to declare an "emergency."

In British and French West Africa and the Sudan the workers' rights are better protected as a result of their organization. Is this one reason why investment capital has been less interested in these territories? The United States in 1948 wanted more manganese from the Gold Coast. ECA officials went to see Mr. Thompson, the president of the African Manganese Co., which operates there, and asked him about speeding up production.

Mr. Thompson was very cooperative with his facts [the ECA men reported] but insisted that it is infeasible to expand production on account of the labor supply, the difficulties in dealing with labor since the recent strike. . . . Mr. Thompson stressed the labor problem, and pointed out that it is a black man's country . . . the natives are more advanced and independent than most Africans. . . . He described the country's labor policy as very progressive. He viewed importation of either white or outside colored labor as infeasible and bound to provoke trouble.[16]

Since the local management could not be budged, the ECA men discreetly suggested that it might be in order to take the matter up with the American owners—African Manganese is a London-registered company but most of its shares are held by Union Carbide and Carbon Corp. of New York. This was presumably done and production was speeded up. The incident, nevertheless, points a moral. Labor in a black man' country has certain rights which the investor is bound to respect; on the other hand, in African countries where the people are under the domination of a more or less permanently installed oligarchy, white or otherwise, the investor has privileges which labor is forced to submit to.

As we have said, the key problem is in the areas of large non-African minorities where ideas and practices of "white domination" flourish. These same areas are the ones favored by United States capital. "Do your American businessmen always leave their ideas of equal pay for equal work at home?" asks the President of the African National Congress in South Africa, Albert John Luthuli. "I've visited and admired a great deal of America, but are none of your democratic practices for export?"[17]

8. Bases and Oil

THE MILITARY, of course, has also played its part—probably the most important part—in determining the shape and content of United States-African relations.

In the United Nations it was the Pentagon rather than the State Department that decided what was to be done with Libya, Eritrea and Somaliland, which Italy held before the war, just as it decided the special kind of trusteeship that the United States should exercise over the Pacific Islands previously held by Japan. "Considerations of military strategy," the *New York Times* (Nov. 26, 1948) reported, "have determined the attitude that the United States Delegation has adopted on the question of the Italian colonies." In the Pacific Islands the United States has its major testing area for atomic weapons; in Libya it has a major air force base; in Ethiopia, to which Eritrea is federated, it has acquired long-term military base rights; and in Eritrea it still maintains an armed forces radio relay station established during the last war.

Strategic considerations—North African bases and South African uranium—many commentators believe, have likewise decided the stand of the United States on other United Nations questions: its support of France's blunt rejection of any advice or assistance from the world body at times of crisis in Morocco and Algeria, and its support of South Africa's parallel and equally adamant attitude with regard to its *apartheid* code and practice.

Military bases require railroads and other supporting utilities just as do mines. "It is essential that the bases [in North Africa] be serviced through adequate port, internal transportation and electric power facilities."[1] But military operations entail more than mining. Africa, as viewed from the Pentagon, "may be considered

93

in one sense as an aggregate of separate base areas and in another, in its entirety, as a vast defense complex."[2] Thus, not only local facilities but a network of interbase communications is required.

This was the main subject of the military conferences of the colonial powers in Africa (including South Africa and Rhodesia, and with the United States represented by observers) held in Nairobi, August, 1951, and at Dakar, March, 1954. Liberia, invited to Dakar, was the only independent or nearly-independent non-white-governed state to take part in the conferences. Such private discussions of high policy at exclusive gatherings of representatives of the white ruling powers in sub-Sahara Africa, with the United States accepted as a *de facto* member of the club, contrast markedly with the same powers' indignant resentment and rejection of efforts on the part of the United Nations to make inquiries or recommendations regarding matters in African territories under their rule.

Hardly anyone will argue that transport for meeting either stockpile or logistic requirements has anything to do with satisfying African needs. As Hans J. Morgenthau of the Center for the Study of American Foreign Policy, University of Chicago, has said, the United States "has subordinated the long-range objectives of technical assistance"—we have already indicated our views on those objectives—"to short-term military advantages. Ports, airfields, and railroads are built primarily in view of immediate military contingencies rather than for the long-term improvement of the living conditions of the native population."[3]

In some sections of Africa as in other parts of the world, military bases and oil concessions appear to have an affinity for one another. A government which will accommodate one will often welcome the other. And a military base may be regarded in some circles as a sort of insurance against expropriation of oil properties.

Oil remains one of the big economic question marks in Africa. The search for it in some areas dates back decades. Thus far only Egypt has achieved even a small regular production, enough to provide for about two-thirds of its own consumption needs. Algeria and Morocco have to date yielded only a little fraction of Egypt's output. Elsewhere there has been a good deal of exploration and drilling, but while occasional oil traces and strikes are reported here and there, no substantial finds of the liquid gold have yet been disclosed.

Yet with so little to show for their efforts, the oil companies continue their search and extend their concession holdings. The hope of happening on oil riches like those just across the Red Sea is slow to die. And it should not be forgotten that the companies can write off their fruitless expenditures in Africa as capital losses against taxes on profits in other areas. Finally, there is the objective of establishing control over potential oil areas in order to shut out competitors, even where there is no prospect of immediate gain. It's another form of calculated risk, one might say, when Standard Oil or Gulf takes a flyer in Africa.

Claimants in Ethiopia

The Sinclair Oil Company's concession in Ethiopia, obtained in 1945, a year after the visit of a United States economic mission, was the first robin in the springtime of American postwar private investment in Africa. The 50-year agreement gave Sinclair exclusive prospecting rights in the whole of the country for five years, in a half of it for the next five years, and in one quarter thereafter. Prospecting results to date have not been good.

Ten years before Sinclair got its concession, Standard-Socony, operating in utmost secrecy and frantic haste through a British promoter and a dummy corporation chartered in Delaware, negotiated a 75-year concession in Ethiopia. Mussolini was then threatening an invasion and Emperor Haile Selassie, finding no succor in the League of Nations, hoped to gain the protection of the United States. When the news broke in the London press, Britain demanded cancellation of the agreement. The Emperor refused. But the United States State Department then intervened, bringing pressure on the oil company and the deal was dropped. "Since that time," said the *Christian Science Monitor* (Sept. 7, 1945), commenting on the Sinclair agreement and the failure of the earlier deal, "America has had a change of heart about foreign entanglements, and now it seems almost a logical outgrowth of global war that there will be global investment as well . . . oil is a vital stake in the game of world politics."

Though nationals of other countries are prominent in Ethiopian commercial and governmental affairs, the United Nations having supplied a considerable number of its technical assistance experts, Americans predominate. They hold such positions as chief engineer of the imperial gold mines and director of the State Bank. There were some 80 Point Four and FOA personnel in the country in

1954. Americans have replaced the British military mission which formerly trained the Ethiopian army and advised the Emperor on military matters, and a "mutual defense" agreement with the United States was signed in May 1953. There have been unconfirmed reports that Washington received 99-year rights to establish military bases in the country.[4]

The government-owned Ethiopian Airlines is operated by America's TWA, and nearly all of the money lent by the World and Export-Import Banks has been for the improvement of transportation and communications. The latest and largest loan, $24 million in 1955 from the Eximbank, was reported to be "for the development of commercial airfields and aviation facilities throughout the country." All this has obvious significance in relation to the country's strategic potential, in which Washington is interested, as well as to the further expansion of Ethiopian exports of coffee, lumber, meat, grain, and hides. There may be still bigger stakes than such commodities, and even oil; during his state visit to the United States in 1954 the Emperor was reported "laying the groundwork" for a loan of $100 million to be used mainly for the development of rich uranium deposits said to exist in Ethiopia.

The "Great White Hope" in North Africa

The North African countries from Morocco east to Egypt have attracted the greatest amount of exploration attention from American oil companies. And in this strategic area, in Morocco and Libya, are found the air and naval bases manned and maintained by the United States military command. In addition to these, there are the major "strategic platforms"—Casablanca, Algiers, Oran, Tunis, Bizerte and others—which were and presumably still remain available for United States use in terms of NATO provisions and the "gentlemen's agreement" between Washington and Paris.

Wheelus Airfield, the United States base near Tripoli toward the western end of Libya's coast, is called by *Time* magazine the "key airfield in the Strategic Air Command's ring around Moscow." The 12th Air Force was reported conducting guided missile tests from this point in March, 1956. Near the other end of Libya's coastline, right next door to Egypt, is Britain's important but little-mentioned air and naval base, Tobruk.

Oil interests converged on Libya soon after the agreement on the Wheelus air base was signed in 1954 after three years of protracted negotiations. By early 1956 no less than six American and two British companies (Anglo-Saxon Petroleum and British Petroleum) had received oil prospecting concessions stretching across the country. Standard Oil (N.J.) held rights over 18.8 million acres. Conorado Petroleum, a combination of Continental Oil, Ohio Oil, and Amerada Petroleum, acquired concessions totalling over a hundred million acres. Texas Gulf Producing Co. (51%) and W. R. Grace & Co. (49%) shared a 50-year concession covering 25 million acres under the name of the Libyan American Oil Co. Another stakeholder was Bunker Hunt, son of H. L. Hunt, the millionaire businessman and "Facts Forum" propagandist of Dallas, Texas (the family has also recently secured a big oil concession in Pakistan).

Some of these companies such as Ohio Oil formerly operated only in the United States; they have decided to go after more lucrative overseas business. Ohio Oil's interests in Libya and other African countries are said to cover a total area of 173 million acres.

Unfortunately for newly independent Libya, most of the country's land is desert, and unless oil is found there is no other known subsoil resource except water. So with the commitments it has made, the country stands between the Scylla of the oil interests and the Charybdis of British and American military occupation, for which the Government receives annual subsidies from London and Washington.

"The great white hope of Algeria and Tunisia is oil," it was reported in 1953, when continued French political control of these territories was still taken for granted, "and millions of dollars in direct and indirect American money and in French francs are being expended in a frantic search for it."[5] There had then been four years of prospecting efforts in Tunisia by the *Société Nord Africaine des Pétroles*, which is 65 per cent Gulf Oil and 35 per cent Tunisian Government. Standard Oil (N.J.) is reported as controlling the *Compagnie Algerienne des Pétroles Standard*, and sharing with Socony-Vacuum, through another company, principal control over Morocco's oil deposits. Currently the vast Sahara region, crisiscrossed by a checkerboard of oil concessions, has become the new "white hope" of France. And that is a major reason why it fights to hold Algeria.

Egypt's oilfields are located in the Sinai Peninsula and Western Desert areas bordering the Red Sea. They have for many years past been worked by Socony-Vacuum, Anglo-Egyptian Oilfields

(Royal Dutch-Shell), and Standard Oil (N.J.). The latter suspended operations in 1949 after twelve years in the country because of disagreement with the Government's oil price policy. In 1954 Conorado Petroleum acquired a 30 year concession, renewable for the same period, and the Cities Service Co., Continental Oil, and Richfield Oil Corp. together shared another concession. Still another American company, Southern California Petroleum, is participating with Belgian and Swiss interests in developing Egyptian oil production.

General Nasser's thunder-clap proclamation of July 26, 1956, cancelling the Suez Canal Company's concession and nationalizing the operation of that strategic waterway naturally cast a sudden, heavy cloud over the sundry oil concessions in Egypt and the surrounding area. The cloud of course became darker and heavier with the Anglo-French invasion of Egypt in November. Particularly bleak was the immediate outlook for Anglo-Egyptian Oilfields, the largest British commercial interest remaining in Egypt with assets of $98 million including a refinery at Suez. The stand of the United States Government in the United Nations against the invasion action probably served to strengthen the position of the American oil companies at least momentarily, but their long-range prospects are contingent on the course of further developments in this area of the world.

Oil Concessions and War Bases

The entire east coastal area from the Somaliland horn down to and including Mozambique is currently undergoing oil exploration. In British Somaliland we find Standard-Vacuum Oil and Conorado. In Somaliland under Italian trusteeship it is Conorado and Sinclair, each holding 50 per cent of a 56 million acre concession. Continental Oil (part of Conorado) as of March, 1956, had interests adding up to 44 million acres in Libya, Egypt and Somaliland compared with holdings of 17.9 million acres in the United States and Canada.

Further south, in Kenya, Tanganyika and Zanzibar, subsidiaries of Shell and British Petroleum are doing most of the surveying and drilling. American geologists in 1950-52 made a survey for the ECA in Kenya and concluded that oil prospects were reasonably good. Whether that be true or not, it is planned to build a huge oil refinery near the port of Mombasa, Kenya. This has been under discussion since 1952 when the probable cost was estimated at nearly $200 million. The project was then described as "a vital factor in the Commonwealth defense system, safeguarding petroleum production in the event of wartime severance of supplies from Middle East oilfields. Naval forces guarding the Indian Ocean could refuel at Mombasa as well as at Trincomalee, Ceylon, and reports from Nairobi speak of Mombasa's possibilities as an actual major naval base."[6]

With the Ceylonese bidding the British quit their bases there, the Suez gone, and Cyprus hardly comfortable, Mombasa and its projected oil refinery assume considerable strategic significance. In this light the Kenya Government's ruthless suppression of the Kenya African Union and dissident African leadership in the colony takes on additional meaning. So also do the optimistic talk about Kenya's coming boom, the visit of four American destroyers to Mombasa in 1954, and the grants from MSA (1954) and World Bank (1955) toward the building of deep water berths and other improvements at Mombasa.

In Mozambique Gulf Oil in 1948 acquired a 47,000 square mile concession. The Government, as is the custom with Portuguese concession grants, received a one-third interest in the subsidiary prospecting company. In Portuguese Angola, where an oil strike has been made near Luanda, Standard Oil (N.J.) in 1950 renewed a search which Sinclair Oil had undertaken in 1923.

West Africa has also been the scene of considerable oil prospecting. Shell and British Petroleum have been looking around in Nigeria since 1937. A few years ago police had to be sent to Owerri to deal with people who objected to the oil company "poking its nose into their soil," and a Nigerian newspaper asked, "Are we to understand that the Government has signed away Nigeria to the Shell Company?"[7] Late in 1955 Socony Vacuum obtained a license for a subsidiary company to take up the search in Northern Nigeria. The French associate of British Petroleum received an exploration license in 1956 covering a large area of Senegal, French West Africa.

In the Gold Coast Gulf Oil was granted exploration rights in February, 1956. The Government is to receive fifty per cent of net profits, 12.5 per cent going to chiefs from whose land oil is taken. Special dispensation was made to exempt the Company from liability under an existing concession ordinance providing for the cancellation at any time of a foreign concession deemed prejudicial to the public interest. The explanation given by Dr. Nkrumah's Minister of Trade and Labor, Mr. Ako Adjei, was that the Company must "obviously be protected against any sudden or arbitrary cancellation of its concession before it commits itself to the very substantial capital investment involved."

There was considerable discussion aroused a few years ago when a seven-man United States air mission visited Nigeria for the stated purpose of familiarizing themselves with airport facilities in the area. "Others feel," said the *West African Pilot* (Feb. 28, 1952), "that the more correct reason is to look for suitable sites for air bases. Since 1946, America has abandoned the Monroe Doctrine as it affects other nations, and has been busy ringing the world with a string of air bases and army outposts." The mission visited Kano and Maiduguri, both of which were American-British air bases during World War II, and Lagos. Since then the Kano airport runway has been greatly enlarged to meet international standards.

United States military personnel have made the rounds of air and port facilities in other parts of Africa, including the 125,000-acre military air base near Kamina in the Belgian Congo with its accommodations for three airborne divisions. There have been reports that the United States had a hand in building the base, but Belgian authorities deny it. They do not deny, however, that the base will be available to United States forces if required. The 300-mile rail link from Kamina to Kabalo, completed in 1956, represents part of a trans-continental communications system extending from Lobito on the west coast to Dar-es-Salaam on the east coast.

Along with Kamina, Kano, and the Mediterranean bases, there are other African "strategic platforms" extending to Diégo-Suarez and Tananarive in Madagascar. Along with Casablanca, Mombasa, and Lourenco Marquez are other ports which have lately been improved and equipped with deep-water berths, such as Dakar and Abidjan in French West Africa; Monrovia, Liberia; Takoradi in Ghana; and Djibouti, French Somaliland, Ethiopia's outlet to the sea, where dock workers clashed with the French in August, 1956. While made necessary by Africa's expanding foreign trade, these modernized harbors at the same time form part of the continental aggregate of potential base areas in the military calculations of Washington, London, and Paris.

The United States naval air bases in Morocco and Libya have alone cost somewhere in the neighborhood of a billion dollars to construct and maintain, and each year several millions more have to be paid out for them. For what? Leaving aside the question of whether establishment of the bases can be justified, can it be denied that military installations and strategy considered expedient and essential in 1950 have been rendered irrelevant and obsolete by political changes in North Africa and by today's missiles of destruction? In Africa as elsewhere national pride stimulates popular demands upon the big powers to kindly pack up their strategic baggage and get out. United States bases in Africa are a very expensive anarchronism.

Governments and not the people of Africa have given their assent to base rights and oil concessions. The people have not been asked. Even with a Libyan Parliament so elected as to guarantee approval of British and American war bases in the country, the proposal for the lease of Wheelus Airfield to the United States was put before that assembly by the Prime Minister "in guarded, almost apologetic, terms [and] was opposed by sensitive patriots in the press and streets."[8] The President of the Libyan Senate, Omar Mansour Kihia, who opposed the base agreement, was dismissed from his post and from membership in the Senate on the same day the vote was taken.

In the 1955 French budget was a special appropriation of six billion francs ($16.8 million) for improvement of military establishments in the colonies, including the equipment of Dakar, Diégo-Suarez and Djibouti as strategic bases. When this was voted in the Assembly of the French Union, the only members in opposition (27 to 107) were Communist representatives and representatives from the colonies, members of the *Indépendents d'Outre-Mer*.

The people will yet have their say in Africa. If we accept that premise there will be no cause for shock and alarm when they repudiate agreements made for them, agreements which are contrary to the public interest and which violate the principle of national sovereignty.

9. Liberia's Open Door

THE LIBERIAN REPUBLIC, established in 1847, was not recognized by the United States until 1862—by President Abraham Lincoln. It continued to be more or less ignored officially and otherwise by Americans for the next half century. Then came the participation of J. P. Morgan banking interests in an international loan to Liberia in 1912, and the establishment of the Firestone Rubber Plantation in the country in 1926. The latter provoked some public discussion in the United States, but interest soon waned again, livened only by the concern of the Garvey Movement and the League of Nations with Liberian affairs. Not until American troops landed in Liberia during World War II can it be said that American attention turned full-face toward the West African Republic. During the last fifteen years the earlier long neglect has been cancelled out by a belated American embrace.

The freed Negroes from the United States who were settled by the American Colonization Society on West Africa's coast in 1821, though of African ancestry, did not think of themselves as returning home to live with their people. They sought liberty, but did not conceive of sharing it with the native inhabitants of the land where they settled. They set themselves up as the rulers, the privileged, like other colonial settlers, and remained apart from the Africans whom they ruled, acquiring for themselves the name of Americo-Liberians. Naturally the unhyphenated Liberians rebelled, just as Africans did against other like-minded settlers.

But where the Europeans in Africa had the backing of European capital and governmental authority, the Americo-Liberians had nothing of the sort from the United States. They had only the inadequate and short-lived financial support of American missionary organizations and the occasional protective presence of an American warship. That difference—and not the complexion of the ruling group—is the fundamental source of the much talked about "backwardness" of Liberia as compared with other African countries. The preservation of the Republic for 110 years, considering what little help and what formidable handicaps there were, must be rated as no small achievement.

From the circumstance of being orphaned settlers, coupled with their failure to weld a united nation which could build up the country, arose the Americo-Liberians' financial difficulties resulting in the country's being continuously mortgaged to foreign lenders at high interest rates. It started in 1871. Until 1912 the loans came exclusively from Europe. Since the advent of Firestone in Liberia they have come exclusively from the United States. The Firestone 99-year million-acre concession was "bought" with a loan of $5 million (only half of which was used) at 7 per cent interest advanced by the Finance Corporation of America, a Firestone subsidiary. The terms of neither the concession agreement nor the loan were to the liking of the Liberian Government, but they were reluctantly accepted—under pressure from the American State Department, some charged.

Sharp criticism of the transaction was voiced in the United States. For example, at a meeting of the Academy of Political Science in New York, July 1926, it was maintained that "if Mr. Firestone's project of turning Liberia into one great American rubber plantation succeeds, it will make Liberia very much more definitely an appendage of the United States. It will mean the extension of United States' imperialism, whether we call it that or not, whether we allow the Liberian flag to wave or not."[1]

The heavy costs of the Firestone loan multiplied Liberia's financial difficulties. The Government was hard pressed to meet its obligations. Extraordinary measures which infringed on the country's sovereignty were imposed to force its adherence to the loan terms. An American historian has pointed out the "striking fact" that while the State Department "tacitly supported" these measures and even withheld recognition of President Barclay until he promised in 1935 to keep up interest payments, it did not protest when Latin American governments defaulted on American loans but instead extended new credits to them through the Export-Import Bank.[2]

With the war the State Department moved into a more open

and direct relation to Liberia's economic affairs. The Liberian flag continued to wave, but the American dollar as of 1943 became the official currency of the country. In 1934 only about 15 per cent of Liberia's foreign trade was with the United States; since 1941 this country has taken 90 per cent or more of her exports and provided about two-thirds of her imports. Liberia's national bank is a subsidiary of the First National City Bank of New York.

The Fruits of American-Liberian War-Time Relations

"The resources of the country are virgin, just now at the threshold of development. . . . Opening of the country is now possible for the first time because (due to World War II activities) the basic facilities exist for transportation: a. fine harbor, b. international airport, c. trans-country road." The quotation is from the 1948 prospectus memorandum of Mr. Stettinius' Liberia Co. The airport referred to is Roberts Field, built at a cost of $5 million by the United States. After the war United States Army maintenance continued for a time and then operation of the Field passed to Pan American World Airways, with maintenance costs divided between it and the Liberian Government. Mr. Stettinius' relation to the construction of the $22 million deep-water harbor at Monrovia has already been mentioned.

Firestone had agreed in 1926 to build the harbor, the cost to be repaid by the Liberian Government. But the project was abandoned when it was found that the cost would be far beyond the $300,000 limit Firestone stood committed to spend. Oared or motor craft continued to transport cargo and passengers to and from vessels standing off shore. Then with the war came Washington's realization of Liberia's strategic importance and investment possibilities, and the United States Navy got the assignment of directing the construction of the Monrovia port.

But the vision of Liberia's potentialities had been seen much earlier. Even before Mr. Firestone set foot there, one of America's advocates of racial *apartheid* had proposed taking over Liberia, if not a larger section of West Africa. "Peopled by our negroes," he wrote, in just that way, it "will mean the opening of the riches of Equatorial Africa to our trade. . . . From Liberia, our influence, if not our control, will permeate far inland." Among other advantages, he pointed out, "Liberia offers the possibility of a splendid naval base, which may not only dominate the western coast of

Africa but be within a comparatively short distance of South America."³

Article 7 of the Port Construction Agreement signed at Monrovia December 31, 1943, gave the United States "the right to establish, use, maintain . . . and control . . . such naval, air and military facilities and installations at the site of the port, and in the general vicinity thereof, as may be desired . . . for the protection of the strategic interests of the United States of America in the South Atlantic." The sweeping language and the absence of any time limit whatsoever led one Liberian newspaper to remark that the Agreement amounted "to the ceding of a portion of Liberian territory to a foreign power, without any expressed act of cession or any treaty on our part to that end."⁴

Leaving aside the matter of United States base rights (a United States-Liberian military assistance pact was signed in 1951), there remains the question of when the Liberian Government will come into ownership of the port and be able to control even its ordinary commercial operations. According to the Agreement this can come about only when all costs of the port, port works and access roads have been fully repaid by the Liberian Government from revenues of the port, and after all administrative and operating costs of the port have been met from the same source. From 1948, when the port was opened to shipping, up to 1954 only $150,000 had been repaid the United States.

Meanwhile, until such time as repayment of the $22 million is made in full, which now seems a remote eventuality at best, control and operation of Monrovia's harbor are vested in an American firm called the Monrovia Port Management Co. As organized by the United States State Department it consisted of representatives of seven United States business concerns operating in Liberia: two oil companies and two shipping lines plus Firestone Plantations, Liberia Co., and Liberia Mining Co.

The new port, said Liberia's Secretary of the Treasury in 1950, was "an invitation to capital investment" as well as to shipping. But though the harbor was certainly of prime importance, foreign investors also required some other facilities. So the last of the Firestone loan was paid off in 1950 (by means of advances from Firestone Plantations against its income taxes for the next three years) and the Liberian Government thereby became able to secure Eximbank loans in 1951 for modernizing its water supply and sewerage systems ($1,350,000) and for highway construction and improvement ($5 million). In his 1955 report to the Legislature President Tubman said that top priority would continue to be given to new roads "for thereby trade and commerce will be expanded."

One reason for the emphasis on road building was the revelation of a United States forestry expert in 1954. Liberia, he reported, possessed some nine million acres of high forest whose timber yield was worth at least $120 million, but the first requirement was transport facilities to get at the timber, there being only one road into the interior.[5] Early in 1955 another Eximbank loan was granted to Liberia, $15 million (at 4.75 per cent—20 years) for highway construction, with the Bank's explanation that "These roads will open for development the rich agricultural area in the western province . . . and will give access to valuable timber resources."

Making It Easy for the Concessionaires

The report of the forestry expert is one example of another kind of service rendered by the U.S. Government, in cooperation with Liberian authorities, on behalf of American business. Various specialists and missions were sent from Washington, prior to the negotiation of concessions, to find out and report where and what the resources were. And then there was the Point Four brigade, numbering 84 technicians in 1953. Liberia was the first country to sign a general Point Four agreement embracing its entire economy. Pursuant therewith a photogrammetric survey was made resulting in the location of a number of industrial minerals. The aerial survey covered 87 per cent of the country—a higher proportion, it is said, than the photo coverage of the United States.

The director of the economic mission sent by the Foreign Economic Administration in 1944 has stated that Washington's instructions were "to work toward Liberia's development with the help of the United States and for the mutual benefit of both countries." And this was interpreted to mean in part that "large corporate concessions should go to American rather than European firms."[6] A detailed four-year soils survey prepared the way for Stettinius' Liberia Co. and its program for developing cocoa and other agricultural and mineral exports. A geological survey confirmed the value of the Bomi Hills iron ore and led to Landell K. Christie's Liberia Mining Co. concession. The previously mentioned forestry survey, which began in 1951, was of very real assistance to Mr. R. G. Le Tourneau, the American millionaire manufacturer of bulldozers and dispensers of bibles, who in 1952 secured 80-year rights to lease a half million acres of Liberia's timber land for his profit-making and soul-saving pursuits.

The Bomi Hills deal was the first major concession granted by the Liberian Government following the Firestone concession 20 years earlier. It was also the first and most important of the several grants made since World War II. The Liberia Co. had a far more ambitious and all-embracing program planned, but this was drastically reduced after the death of Mr. Stettinius in 1949. Liberia Mining Co.'s 80-year concession covers an area of 25,000 acres of which Bomi Hills is the hub. Christie agreed to pay the Government $100 a month until actual mining started and then five cents an acre per year for land selected, and five cents royalty plus five cents port charges on each ton of iron ore shipped. President Tubman later decided that the Government ought to get more.

This concession agreement, like the port construction agreement, is said to have been acted upon by the Government in apparent secrecy and without prior publication as required by Liberian law. There was considerable public opposition to the manner, terms and duration of the concession grant. These objections were embodied in a petition to the Legislature signed by 57 citizens. Three magistrates who were among the petitioners were forced to resign, and other signers were reported prosecuted. Our State Department's pressure in the matter, according to the *Afro-American* (Feb. 9, 1946), reached the point of American war vessels anchoring threateningly in Monrovia harbor, but this was categorically denied in Washington.

The Liberia Mining Co. needed a railroad to transport the ore 45 miles to Monrovia. Washington again came to Christie's assistance with a $4 million Eximbank loan. Another $4 million came from the Republic Steel Corp., which in 1949 bought controlling interest, about 60 per cent, in Christie's company and contracted to buy 400,000 tons of ore yearly, reserving the right to take 66 per cent of total output. Thus financed, the Liberia Mining Co. has done pretty well by itself. In 1952, the first full year of production, it netted about $3.5 million—about 35 per cent profit on the total investment.[7] Republic Steel also has had nothing to complain of: it got Liberian iron ore of superior quality at $4.75 a ton (plus shipping costs) when the world market price was $12.50—besides the dividends on its investment.

Since succeeding Edwin Barclay as the Republic's eighteenth President in January, 1944, William V. S. Tubman has repeatedly asserted his belief that the Open Door policy would mean the economic salvation of his country. He has succeeded in impressing his views upon most of those who make up the government and governing class, and also, it appears, upon the chiefs in the hinterland, whose cooperation and support he has taken pains to win. Those who disagree either remain silent or risk the loss of property, liberty, or life.

Deference to the foreign investor is expressed with unabashed frankness, for example, in *The Listener* (May 11, 1951) a Monrovia newspaper owned and published by the Secretary of the Treasury, Mr. Dennis: "The highest aim of Liberia has been to win friends in the international market. In the process she has been very tolerant to their nationals; she has given them every opportunity to amass wealth, which the competitive economy of their states would not have, in the longest life, afforded them." More specifically, quoting from an official Liberian source,

> In 1948 and again in 1951 the amendment and liberalization of the corporate legislative code encouraged the establishment of "Liberian corporations" by non-resident foreigners. Low taxes, relatively light charges for social welfare, the absence of complicated government regulations, the granting of long-term lease concessions, the absence of foreign exchange controls, and low tariffs have encouraged the beginning of capital formation and the attraction of foreign capital.[8]

Generous helpings of Liberia's postwar concession pie have gone to United States capital. Besides the awards already mentioned, there was an 80-year grant of 600,000 acres in 1954 to B. F. Goodrich for a rubber plantation, and a 70-year allotment of 320,000 acres in 1953 to the American-Canadian financed Liberian American Minerals Co., headed by Johnston Avery, a former deputy director of the U S. Technical Assistance Program. Other beneficiaries included two Spanish companies, a Liechtenstein-Swiss trust, and two German enterprises interested in timber, minerals, and plantation crops. Although something over 3,200,000 acres of the country had been turned over to foreign concessionaires by the end of 1954,[9] the door remained still wide open to others.

Adding Up the Results

The concession boom has undoubtedly brought prosperity to the families of Liberia's ruling aristocracy. Gone are the lean years of the 'thirties when government salaries sometimes could not be met. The President reported in 1950 that salaries and allowances of government officials and employees had been increased by 75, 100 and 150 per cent. Mr. Tubman himself now enjoys an annual salary of $25,000, a presidential yacht purchased from Holland in 1952 and refitted at a total cost of about a million dollars, and a country estate in what is described as a sort of Alpine setting.

A former Acting Chief of the State Department's Liberian Desk has written that "an examination of the Point Four program [for Liberia] as it was originally set up will show that the bulk of highway developments will benefit the ruling classes principally and Mr. Tubman's rubber plantation in the Eastern Province notably."[10]

Besides President Tubman and members of his family there are reported to be some 750 independent rubber producers among Liberia's elite. The owners of the private plantations totalling 18,000 acres regard them, it is said, as "a form of insurance against political and other vicissitudes." Firestone without question also considers them as its own insurance against the same, for it supplies the independent producers, who include virtually all Liberia's present and past presidents and cabinet members, with plants, gives them advice on production, collects their rubber milk, and pays them the world rubber price less the cost, without profit, of processing.

The independents, with one or two exceptions, have no processing facilities of their own; without Firestone they could not market their produce. They need the big American concessionaire for their personal gain; the concessionaire needs their good will to protect and maintain its control of Liberian rubber production. Processing is the key to that control. Regardless of the number of independent producers, without their own processing plant Liberia will continue to remain America's dependent rubber colony. No such industrial undertaking is yet in sight.

If Liberia's first families are prospering, the same cannot be said of the workers. There have been no wage increases for them like the salary boost for those on the government payroll. The tappers and laborers who comprise the great majority of the 30,000 workers on the Firestone Plantations, the country's chief employer, were still of late getting only 28 cents a day. And most of that is spent at the Company's own stores. There have been large-scale desertions.

In fulfilling its agreement to help the rubber concession "secure and maintain an adequate labor supply," the Government established a Labor Bureau, which sent out requisitions to Native and District Commissioners in the bush country, who in turn indicated the quota of workers to be supplied by the chiefs. The concessionaire paid the chiefs and the Labor Bureau each a cent a day for every worker hired. Thus Firestone made it "financially worthwhile for the Government and the chiefs to keep the plantations supplied."[11] However, when a League of Nations Commission in 1930 investigated forced labor conditions in Liberia, it said that it could find no evidence that the Firestone Plantations Company "consciously employs any but voluntary labor." Whatever compulsion there was, the Commission said, was at the instance of the Liberian Government, "over which the [Firestone] Company had little control." Firestone still continues to send its recruiting agents to arrange with the chiefs the quota of workers each is to supply and what payment they will receive for this service.

The Company claims credit for having trained staff assistants, mechanics, truck drivers and construction workers who have set themselves up in business. But after 30 years of operation in Liberia it yet says nothing about the placement of either Liberians or colored Americans on the managerial or administrative staff of Firestone Plantations—"assistants" excepted.

Though unorganized, the employees of Firestone and other enterprises in Liberia have from time to time forcibly brought their grievances to the attention of management and Government. In December, 1945, there was a strike of workers on the port construction job. The wage differential between Liberian and foreign workers was a main grievance. In 1946 engineers, deckhands and warehouse laborers on the Firestone Plantations' river transport division struck, demanding $1.50, $1 and 50c a day respectively instead of the 50c, 30c, and 15c paid. In February, 1950, workers on the Firestone and Bomi Hills concessions struck simultaneously. The Government proclaimed a state of emergency and rushed machine-gun squads to the affected areas.

A Liberian Commissioner of Labor, Mr. Tilman Dunbar, in his official report for the year 1952-53, noted that the general level of wages was far below the cost of living. He urged the Government's help toward developing trade unions: "Collective agreement through trade unions is the only means through which equitable terms of remuneration and conditions of work may be obtained." President Tubman, questioned on this point, maintains that it is the responsibility of the workers, not the Government, to organize trade unions. But does his administration fulfill its responsibility of insuring that Firestone and other employers *permit* their workers to organize?

American Boasts and Liberian Facts

Mr. Preston Hotchkiss in his statement to the United Nations, referred to earlier, regarding what the United States thinks about aid to "underdeveloped countries," spoke of Firestone's investment in Liberia as "a classic example of foreign capital investment which has contributed to the economic strength, political stability, and social progress of an underdeveloped country." It would seem to be more in keeping with diplomatic tact and ordinary modesty to quote what Liberians themselves say on the subject instead of assuming the right to speak for them. Is it perhaps that appropriate quotations were difficult to find?

What Mr. Hotchkiss means by "economic strength" we don't know. We have already seen how Liberia rid itself of one foreign debt only to contract another much larger one in order to provide a port, roads and other facilities to pave the way for the concessionaires. A United Nations tabulation of the 1949 national incomes of seventy countries indicated Liberia's to be the very lowest of all, and the country's per capita income of $38 was also far down on the list and exactly level with that of Ethiopia, which had no Firestone concession to contribute to its economic strength for over two decades.

And "social progress" ("political stability" will wait for a moment)—how is that measured? By educational provisions and standards? The Director of Liberia's Bureau of Census and Statistics has reported that in 1950 there were 24,526 children in all schools, mission and private, fewer than one out of every 20 of school age. In 1954 the figure was 43,000. The January 1955 report of President Tubman to the Legislature included reference to the failure to complete the erection of school buildings in several places, the inadequacy of buildings in other places, and the "need for the erection of buildings for elementary education throughout the country."

Or do you measure "social progress" by the health and physical well-being of the population? A United States Department of Commerce report speaks of the "poor health status of the majority of the people," which does not permit the highest standard of work.[12] The same 1955 report of President Tubman tells of the "appalling need for the employment of additional doctors," there being only one to every 50 or 75,000 inhabitants (depending on the estimate of the total population, there having been no census). Let it be conceded that Firestone made a sizeable medical contribution to Liberia, particularly in the area of the rubber plantations. Still it was necessary to send a United States Health Mission to clean out the malaria, plan public sanitation facilities, and perform other functions when it came time for big-scale investment in the country. And still the medical needs remain "appalling."

The poor health conditions, moreover, can be traced in large measure to the Africans' loss of their land and the dislocation of their traditional cultivation of rice, the country's staple food crop, which resulted from the concession grants, starting with Firestone's. An American State Department official in 1946 denied that any more than 5,000 persons had to be removed from the Bomi Hills concession area—others put the number much higher—and as for their land claims in the area, that was the responsibility of the Liberian Government, he said. To prevent the practice of rice farmers moving into timber concession areas and clearing the ground for planting after the larger trees had been logged, a law was passed in 1953 making this illegal. Meanwhile, the people go hungry. As the foreign concessions multiply, food costs rise with no corresponding increase in wages. The supply of rice is far below the demand, and thousands of tons have to be imported annually to prevent famine or near famine.

The final test of what Firestone has done for Liberia is how much it has directly contributed to the country's revenue. You will recall the seven per cent interest rate charged the Government on the Firestone loan. Contrast that with what the Company agreed to pay for its concession rights: *one* per cent of the value (at New York price) of rubber it exported and six cents an acre per year for the land actually used (by 1956 90,000 acres had been planted making this the world's largest continuous plantation). Up to the end of 1951 Firestone's total payments to Liberia amounted to $8 million.[13] In the same period the Company exported rubber valued at more than $160 million. Is that what one would call a contribution to Liberia's economic strength?

In the parent company's annual report for the year ending October 31, 1930, Mr. Firestone assured shareholders that expenses for the Liberian concession were being kept "to a minimum" and that "no matter at what price rubber will be sold in the future, we can produce it in Liberia as cheap as or cheaper than it can be produced in any other rubber-growing country."

The earnings of the Company's Liberian concession are not a matter of public record. However, in 1951 when the Korean War pushed rubber up to 83 cents a pound, the Company reported that its Liberian plantation had "accounted for a larger portion" of its total profits of $48.4 million. The Liberian Government's share of those earnings was $1.3 million out of $45.7 million worth of rubber exported from the country.

Corporations and individuals became subject to a Liberian income tax for the first time in 1951, and in 1953 the Government raised Firestone's income tax rate from 14 to 25 per cent. But it refunded, at President Tubman's recommendation, $792,797 paid by the Company under protest when tax experts in the United States, to whom the matter was referred, ruled in Firestone's favor. In 1954 Liberia received $2.5 million in tax on nearly $20 million worth of rubber exported. Even with the augmented income from additional taxes and new concessions the Government's revenue from *all* sources in 1955, though considerably higher than a decade earlier, was still less than half the value of the country's rubber exports and only 27 per cent of Firestone's net over-all profits.

As for the second most profitable concession venture at the present time, the Liberia Mining Co., Mr. Tubman took another look at the agreement with Christie when iron ore exports began

TABLE 8. RUBBER EXPORTS, FIRESTONE PROFITS, AND GOVERNMENT REVENUE IN LIBERIA[14]

Year	Value of rubber exports from Liberia ($ million)	Rubber as percentage of total exports	Net income, Firestone Tire and Rubber Co. ($ million)	Liberia Gov't. revenue from all sources ($ million)
1937	1	52.6	9.3	1
1945	11	96.6	16.4	1.9
1950	26.8	96.8	33.3	3.9
1955	31.5	73.6	55.4	15

to flow during the second half of 1951. The sharp fall in the price of rubber in 1952 added to his concern. In June of that year officials of Liberia Mining and Republic Steel were invited to the Executive Mansion. There Mr. Tubman told them that the royalty of five cents a ton, which "was so low as to be insignificant," had been agreed to with the expectation "that indirect benefits would flow to the country and its people. However, these anticipated benefits have been negligible."

In the first place, he said, there was little employment of labor because of the highly mechanized production, and this "in conjunction with a low wage scale of less than fifty cents per diem results in a situation which does not inure to the welfare of the country and its people." Secondly, Government itself had paid the costs, for which it was indebted to the United States, of access roads and a bridge which the concessionaire had been expected to construct and pay for. And it had likewise paid the full expense of American geologists to verify the value of the ore deposit.

"Moreover," Tubman said, ". . . as other interested mining companies would expect to receive similar terms, Government wishes to establish a condition of general application." The concession stood to make a profit of $7 million to $18 million a year on a common stock issue of $4.5 million, he pointed out. The Government's share of less than one-half of one per cent of the returns was "inequitable, immoral, and unjustly apportioned in favor of the Company."[15]

In two months a new agreement was reached. The concession remained tax free. The Company was allowed a grace period until April 1, 1957, to pay off its Eximbank loan, during which time the Government would receive between $1.5 million and $2 million a year royalties. After that date, or upon liquidation of the loan if earlier, it would get 25 per cent of net profits for the first five years, 35 per cent for the next ten years, and 50 per cent thereafter. No price preferentials for any company would be permitted. The Government was given three directorships on the Company's 13-man Board (Republic Steel has seven).

The Open Door has remained open, but the cover charge has gone up.

Political "Stability" or Democracy?

How are Liberia's additional revenue receipts to be spent? Will there be more schools and teachers, hospitals and doctors? Will there be the sorely needed improvements in agriculture to provide an ample and balanced diet for the population? Will there be the establishment of Liberian-owned industries and not simply cheap-labor rubber plantations?

The Government in 1951 levied a health tax of $1 on everyone, male and female, aged 18 to 60—to be collected "in the Hinterland areas of the country from each hut, through the Paramount Chief in the usual manner . . . [who] shall be compensated in the amount of 5 per cent of the sum so collected." A "development tax" of $1 was also levied on everyone aged 16 to 60. These were in addition to the customary hut tax of $2. In the same year these special taxes were enacted the President's annual salary was increased by $10,000.

Paramount chiefs in Liberia are not salaried but are allowed a commission of 10 per cent on all annual taxes collected, some receiving as much as $8,000 a year in this way. There are other emoluments that go with the chief's office. "Under the present administration, many paramount and clan chiefs own and operate large coffee, cocoa, oil palm or rubber farms. . . . A number of them own cars and beautiful homes in the capital city."[16]

Yes, some Liberians are growing rich, rich from the people's taxes, while the average Liberian is barely existing, and yet the taxes keep piling up, [a Liberian newspaper commented in 1953]. It is an ordinary thing for some of these "fortunates" to build 10, 15, 20, 30, or 50 thousand dollar houses. . . . We do not mind paying taxes if there will be no favored ones, no hoarding by the selfish or squandering by the foolish, no discrimination, no leakages in our national coffers, whereby some may gain illicit wealth.[17]

The income tax revenue in 1951 paid for the newly built and furnished executive mansion and for the 1952 inauguration, the new Centennial Pavilion where it was held, decorations, fireworks, new police uniforms, and so forth.[18] The 1956 inauguration was another gala affair. A young Liberian watching the fireworks display exclaimed, "That show would have built a school in my village, and the money used on the floats in the parade would have supplied schools for my whole chiefdom."[19]

It finally comes down to the question of for whose benefit the country is governed—and who governs. The opinion has often been voiced that the long-entrenched power of the True Whig Party, comprising Liberia's ruling aristocracy, and the circumstances of President Tubman's continuance in office for three successive terms (the first of eight years, the others four years) do not bespeak the kind of "political stability" that is wholesome. In the last two elections when rivals for the presidency dared come forward as candidates, the surface calm was shattered by open, ruthless despotism of a sort often seen in this hemisphere.[20]

Mr. Tubman deplores the use of the term Americo-Liberian; he insists that the country and its people are one. And under his administration Liberia has seen the extension of the voting right to all adult inhabitants of the country, even if the conduct of elections still remains questionable (with an estimated population of 2,500,000, 246,000 votes were reported cast in the 1955 election with only 1,198 for the opposition). There has also come some representation for the tribal groups and Hinterland Provinces in the House of Representatives, though not yet in the Senate, and the appointment of individuals from among the Grebo, Vai and other indigenous peoples to various high government offices for the first time in the country's history.

But one is left wondering whether these reforms represent a genuine advance toward political democracy in Liberia. The reforms taking place in neighboring British and French colonies made it virtually impossible for the True Whig Party to remain the exclusive source of all political authority in Liberia. And even in countries like Kenya or Rhodesia the white rulers have talked much about "partnership" and yielded some appointments and governmental representation to Africans. There still continues in Liberia as in the white settler colonies the wide gulf between rulers and the ruled, bridged only by district commissioners and chiefs. Unless and until such archaic, authoritarian control is replaced by popular self-government locally and nationally, there is not likely to be any New Deal for the Liberians.

The West African Republic will come into her own as a truly free and independent nation when the people—*all* of them—run their country in the interest of *all* of the inhabitants.

10. Uranium and Other South African Attractions

"I WOULDN'T INVEST a dime in your country in its present circumstances," said an American businessman in Johannesburg recently, after touring South Africa to judge investment prospects. The straight-talking visitor, Mr. Walter Kreiger, president of the Chicago Tool and Die Institute, said he objected to the country's racial and monopolistic policies.[1]

When set beside the usual run of comments on South Africa by American business executives, that statement stands out like a single tree on a wide expanse of sand. "General Motors has great confidence in the future progress and development of South Africa," says that corporation's regional manager in Africa, for example. He is echoed by the managing director of Ford's South African plant, who speaks of "the faith we have in South Africa." Mr. H. de Witt Smith of the Newmont Mining Corp. says, "We regard the Union [of South Africa] and Canada as the best investment spheres outside the United States." That is a sampling.[2]

"In South Africa legitimate American mining companies and white persons are given every encouragement to bring their capital to the Union and to engage in productive mining operations." So reads a statement sent from the American Consulate in Johannesburg to Washington and released there by the Department of Commerce in 1955. No one along the line apparently saw anything wrong in the use of the qualifying adjective "white," or any need to apologize for it. When that can happen, can one doubt the readiness of those in power in Washington to do business with those in power in South Africa on the latter's own "for whites only" terms? Whether it is done with unvoiced misgivings or bland indifference to the code of racist oppression doesn't much matter. It is done.

Africans throughout the continent, most Asians, liberals in other parts of the world, colored people in the United States, and even much of the general press in this country have long assailed the Smuts-Malan-Strijdom principle and practice of white supremacy as an evil menace. But to Washington South Africa remains "a dependable friend," quoting Senator Hickenlooper following his visit there in 1953. This official characterization has been most heavily underscored since the agreement was reached in 1950 concerning South African production of uranium for the United States. At the highest level President Eisenhower has expressed it in his warm felicitations to the South African Ambassador: "The good relations which so happily exist between our two countries are a source of the greatest satisfaction and encouragement to me, and I assure you that we share with you the desire that the traditional ties of friendship and understanding between us shall be strengthened and maintained to our mutual benefit."[3]

American Business in South Africa

Before looking at the mutual benefits of the South African uranium transaction, let us see something of the nature and scope of American private enterprise in the Dominion. As indicated earlier, United States business interests are not newcomers to South Africa. The big American oil companies have been selling their products there since 1897, and Caltex, Atlantic Refining, and Standard Vacuum (the latter opened a new $22-million refinery at Durban two years ago) have for some time dominated the oil business in the Union.

A representative of the Guaranty Trust Co. and an associate of J. P. Morgan were among the board of directors of the Anglo-American Corp. of South Africa, established in 1917. Ford set up business in South Africa in 1923. General Motors came on the scene about the same time. Other American automobile and tire companies followed. In 1943 United States direct private investments in the Union amounted to $50 million, 39 per cent of all such investments in the continent. By 1949 United States companies had doubled their direct investments in South Africa, and by the end of 1955 they had jumped to more than five times the 1943 figure.

The new postwar private capital came from the already established oil, auto, and tire companies, which added to their plants and operations (reinvestment of profits); from a host of fresh arrivals concerned with the manufacture and sale of everything from tractors and industrial machinery to cosmetics and breakfast cereals[4]; and from the entrance of new American interests into South African mining.

General Motors in 1955 completed improvements costing $1.4 million on its assembly plant, the largest in Port Elizabeth, an auto and rubber industrial center, and planned spending $5.6 million more on expansion. Ford has also enlarged its plant. Firestone has done likewise for the fifth time since coming to South Africa 20 years ago. The shortage of white workers has brought about the hiring of more Africans and Colored in these plants during the last five years, despite the official prohibition against their employment in skilled jobs. Firestone, for instance, uses almost exclusively African labor except in supervisory posts. There are, of course, the usual separate dining and sanitary facilities according to color, and the usual wage differentials going from the white scale down to the Colored and further down to the African.

In some fields one finds American capital elbowing South African capital out of the way. For example, Masonite Corp. of American in 1949 bought a minority interest in Masonite (Africa) Ltd. In 1956 it gained control by buying up several large blocks of ordinary shares held by South African companies, thus increasing its holding from one-third to 80 per cent. Twentieth Century-Fox Film Corp. in 1955 acquired 90 per cent control of African Consolidated Theatres, owned by South African, Rhodesian, and East African interests. It paid $14 for shares formerly valued at $9.80. The $28 million deal gave the American company control over the South African entertainment industry, 140 (Jim Crow) theatres, plus others in Kenya and Rhodesia.

The Newmont Mining Corp. and American Metal Co. in 1945 jointly acquired 57 per cent controlling interest in the O'okiep Copper Co. in South Africa. In 1947 they took over a lead-zinc-copper mine, Tsumeb, which the Germans had taken from the Herero in South West Africa (Newmont 56.3 per cent, American Metal 19.7 per cent). In 1955, beginning with a small minority interest which was expected to grow bigger, they took up the Winkelhaak Mines in the new gold mining area of the eastern Transvaal Province. Winkelhaak is scheduled to begin producing gold and uranium in 1958. British and South African companies are participants in all three ventures.

At O'okiep and Tsumeb the American companies have had the benefit of African labor at the prevailing low wage rates and "the sympathetic cooperation of the South African Government." A financial weekly points out that "Owing to the higher copper content of its ores and the relatively low wages paid native workers, production costs at O'okiep are among the lowest in the world."[5] This mine, incidentally, received a contract in 1952 to sell all its tungsten concentrates until April, 1958, to the United States Government.

Tsumeb employs 3,100 Africans who come to work at the mines on fifteen-month contracts without their families, and live in the usual mining compound quarters, twelve to a room. Their pay for a day's work ranges from 25 cents to $1.54 (for a few). Tsumeb's white skilled workers get $6 a day plus $75 a month cost-of-living bonus and may rent a five-room house from the company for $6 a month.[6]

Shareholders in these mine properties have good reason to say complimentary things about South Africa. Tsumeb, which cost $4 million in purchase cost and $3 million to start production, had net earnings of over $8 million in the first three years operation. O'okiep paid sky-high dividends of $6.44 per $1.40 share in 1951-52 and 1953-54 and $6.72 in 1952-53. In the four years 1952-55 the net profits (after tax) of O'okiep and Tsumeb together came to $74.7 million, and $26.4 million of this went to Newmont in dividend payments and $14.5 million to American Metal.

Among the less publicized minerals in this area in which American investors are currently interested are platinum and iron ore. Stock exchange circles report United States purchases of substantial parcels in Rustenburg Platinum Mines in South Africa, the world's largest producer. Bethlehem Steel in 1954 completed a two-year mineral survey in the Kaokoveld, South West Africa, and is said to have found immense iron ore deposits. But to get the iron out of the country requires building over a hundred miles of railroad and a port. The U.S. Steel Corp. has contracts to buy yearly between 30,000 and 50,000 tons of manganese ore mined in South West Africa by the South African Minerals Corp.

Interviewed by a Johannesburg newspaper in 1949, the American Minerals Attaché—a new quantity in diplomatic personnel—announced, "Here in South Africa you have an enormous variety of minerals nearly all of which the United States wants to buy more eagerly than it wants gold." He listed twelve of them available in South Africa, tactfully omitting uranium, and suggested that opportunity was knocking at the door.

One South African company, Consolidated Murchison Goldfields, in 1951 benefited to the tune of 800 per cent dividends on ordinary shares having a par value of $572,400 as a result of supplying urgent Washington demands for antimony, an alloy used to stiffen other metals. Two of the wanted minerals, manganese and chromite, were produced in such quantity that the railway system could not handle the traffic. The unshipped ore piled up at the mines. Another strategic mineral, industrial diamonds, presented no such difficulty.

The Diamond Monopoly

The American businessman with whom this chapter opened objected to South Africa's monopolistic as well as racial practices. It is a good bet that he had the De Beers-Anglo American diamond monopoly in mind. Without industrial diamonds the tool and diemaking industry can function about as well as a gun without bullets. During World War II the monopoly pinch hurt American industrialists; there was an unsuccessful attempt to buy diamonds directly from *Forminière* in the Belgian Congo, which is part of the De Beers empire. In 1945 the Department of Justice brought an anti-trust suit against De Beers, eight associated companies in Africa, and seven important American stockholders or officers in the companies.

Sir Ernest Oppenheimer retorted that the United States courts lacked jurisdiction. Furthermore, he said, control in the diamond trade was a matter of national policy of the South African Government, and the Government was itself "actively associated" with the policy of control, being a producer of diamonds and a member of the Diamond Producers' Association, the trade's regulating body.[7] Sir Ernest was saying to the United States authorities, in effect, "Well, do you want to sue the Government of the Union of South Africa?" The answer, of course, was "No."

There was another effort to break through the monopoly.

The ECA in 1950 financed the efforts of a French company to open up new diamond sources in French Equatorial Africa. Not much came of that either. Two threats still hang over the monopoly: one is the "man-made" diamonds that General Electric scientists have been working on; the other is the recent statement of the Soviet Minister of Geology and Mineral Conservation that his country planned to use its diamond resources in foreign exchange and thus break the South African monopoly.

But meanwhile the De Beers syndicate remains in full control of the marketing of 90 to 95 per cent of all the non-socialist world's diamonds, which really means Africa's diamonds. The United States, buying three-quarters or more of the supply, has spurred a rising production of gem and industrial stones, particularly the latter for the strategic stockpile. While the sale of gem stones through the De Beers syndicate increased from $72.1 million in 1946 to $140.8 million in 1955, that of industrial diamonds mounted from $9.8 million to $67.2 million in the same period. In those ten years 1946-55 the syndicate's total diamond sales amounted to $1,407.6 million, of which $393.4 million was in industrial stones.

In 1955, with a new high in diamond sales, the De Beers Group enjoyed a profit of $58.8 million after paying $23.2 million in taxes to the South African Government. The profits of one company, De Beers Consolidated Mines in South Africa, have alone ranged between $25.8 and $28.8 million a year since 1951. The 12,000 African miners in that enterprise get wages of under $280 a year per man. It has been figured that their total wages for eleven years to 1956 amounted to only about 8 per cent of the value of the diamonds they produced in that period.[8] And yet it is said that Africans must learn that "the worker is worth only what he can earn"!

The Uranium Deal

It was from the Belgian Congo, to be dealt with in a later chapter, that the United States during World War II began getting its main supply of the essential ingredient of atomic bombs. The 1950 United States-Britain-South Africa agreement on the terms of uranium production in the latter country opened up a valuable new source of the mighty mineral for the United States. At the same time it served to bolster up South Africa's then shaky economy—and, incidentally, the prestige of Premier Malan and his Nationalist Government.

The last-mentioned consequence of the agreement has had little attention. In the late 'forties the South African Government was experiencing serious difficulties with its balance of payments and dollar shortage. Imports from the United States in 1947 were ten times the value of South African exports (excluding gold) to this country. In 1948 the imports increased still more, while the exports dropped. In both years United States imports outranked the British. From April 1948 to September 1949, when devaluation of the sterling pound occurred, the total gold and exchange resources of the South African Reserve Bank declined from $1,086 million to $210 million, and cash reserves of the country's commercial banks dropped from $776 million to $199 million during the same period.[9]

Devaluation of the pound sterling was a windfall, of course. But neither this, nor the purchase of $10 million from the International Monetary Fund, nor the imposition of import controls (November 1948), cutting down the dollar and gold out-flow, provided any sufficient or lasting remedy. The *Wall Street Journal* (Dec. 8, 1948) foresaw the need of a billion and a half dollars in United States loans to South Africa over the next five years.

In 1949 Mr. Havenga, South Africa's Minister of Finance, came to the United States and talked with officials in Washington and bankers in New York. He wanted two things, American agreement to an increase in the world price of gold and a loan of at least $70 million. He went home with neither—only a $10 million loan from four commercial banks. Back home Mr. Havenga made it known that he had failed because South Africa, so he said, was "not a distressed borrower" and "could not accept the strings attached" to a Government loan—namely, the deposit of gold as security and "inspection and supervision of South African internal affairs."[10]

Now, the United States Government's interest in South African uranium had been aroused as early as 1944 by a secret report of an American geologist who visited the Rand. By the time Malan came to power in 1948, research work had confirmed the earlier findings. One of Malan's first acts in office was the promulgation of a law in September 1948 (amended 1950) reserving to the State the ownership of "prescribed materials" and the right to prospect and mine for them and enabling the State to grant authority for such mining and prospecting.

It was in November, 1949, about the time of the Finance Minister's return from his unsuccessful mission to Washington,, that United States and British representatives were invited to South Africa for "exploratory" talks about the country's uranium production. Is the coincidence of these events merely accidental, or was the Malan Government pressed to the wall? And if the uranium deal had not been consummated a year later, where and how could the capital injection have been found to halt the disintegration of the country's financial position and prevent the political embarrassment for Malan and company which certainly would have ensued?

The agreement provided that the United States should advance two-thirds and Britain one-third of the cost of installing the uranium plants and other required facilities. A ten-year production schedule was set. Three-fourths of production was consigned to the United States, according to the *Wall Street Journal* (May 25, 1953). The South African Government, through its Atomic Energy Board (which includes mining industry representatives), grants authority to approved companies to mine and produce uranium. The AEB allocates the capital needs for production and governs all relations between buyers and producers.

The selling price formula is such that in addition to ensuring "a reasonable margin of profit," the mines are enabled to redeem loans over a period of ten years and thus become full owners of the uranium installations. It was further agreed that uranium recovery should be regarded as incidental to gold mining and not interfere with it.[11] At first only four mines were considered for uranium production, but toward the end of 1951 the United States and Britain urged doubling or tripling the output schedule. By September, 1956, 26 mines had been authorized to participate in the program and more were expected. Only 18, however, had reached production stage.

From 1951 to the middle of 1955 the United States Export-Import Bank advanced $130.1 million to mines participating in the South African uranium program, amounts to individual companies ranging up to $13 million. It advanced another $19.6 million for the development of electric power facilities for the uranium separation plants. Although the World Bank was not a party to the agreement, it cooperated with Washington's plans, advancing loans from 1951 through 1955 totalling $60 million for power installations, turbo-generators and other electrical equipment required for the mines, and $75.2 million for the improvement of

South African transportation to handle the uranium and other strategic exports. United States commercial banks added another $35 million for the latter.

An official of the United States Atomic Energy Commission has said that "it is safe to predict that South Africa will be the leading producer of uranium for many decades."[12] The *Wall Street Journal* (May 25, 1953) cited South African experts as saying that 40 per cent of American uranium supplies would be coming from that country by 1956. The cost of the South African uranium program to the United States Government, the paper added, "will probably run something like $500 million in the next eight years. This big cash injection will let dollar-starved South Africa boost greatly its buying of U.S. goods in the near future. American taxpayers . . . will be tapped to supply these dollars, of course."

And who benefits? Well, the South African mining companies, of course, to begin with—and without any capital outlay or financial risk on their part. Since uranium is for them a by-product of gold production, the additional uranium profits count for the same thing as a substantial increase in the selling price of gold, so long demanded. Moreover, some of the dying mines whose gold yield no longer gives much margin over working costs—even when kept to the lowest minimum at the expense of black workers' wages—have gained a new lease on life. For them uranium production is now the main business, and gold simply a side-line. One gold mine which had stopped all production in 1953 is starting up again on uranium, thanks to about $4 million from the Eximbank. The first four years of South African uranium production reveal an exceptionally high and rising gross profit rate of well over 50 per cent compared with less than 25 per cent on gold production.

TABLE 9. SOUTH AFRICAN URANIUM AND GOLD: PRODUCTION AND GROSS PROFITS, 1953-56[13]
($ *millions*)

	Uranium			Gold (All Mines)	
	No. of Mines producing	Value of Exports	Gross Profits	Value of Production	Gross Profits
1953	5	10.9	5.0	411.6	96.5
1954	8	41.4	22.7	462.0	108.0
1955	16	84.0	49.3	511.8	124.0
1956	18	107.8	69.2	555.8	135.8

Thus far only one American company, the giant Kennecott Copper Corp., holds direct, controlling interest in any of the South African gold-uranium mines. Previously concerned only with operations in North and South America, Kennecott in 1948 began exploring the South African market. In 1949 there was an initial investment of $6.1 million in a mining property owned by a South African company and awaiting development in the newly opened Orange Free State mining area. The next year the American corporation put $7 million in another property under the same ownership adjoining the first. With further capital outlays in the two holdings, Virginia (O.F.S.) and Merriespruit (O.F.S.) Gold Mining Companies, Kennecott by the end of 1954 had a total investment of something over $21 million in each of them, giving it about 46 per cent equity in the first and 49 per cent in the second.

Both properties were early entrants in the uranium production program, Virginia receiving a loan of more than $10 million from the Eximbank for plant installations. This award was one of the three largest made by the Eximbank to mining companies in South Africa, generous assistance, indeed, to the venture of a corporation that in 1954 passed the one billion dollar mark in the aggregate of dividends distributed to stockholders during forty years existence. The two Kennecott holdings are now in full production; Virginia yielded its first gold ore in September, 1954, and Merriespruit started in February, 1956.

Kennecott's South African operations are conducted in association with the Anglo-Transvaal Consolidated Investment Co., which was the channel of a $20-million investment by New York and London banking groups in 1946. The chairman of Anglo-Transvaal at the Company's meeting in 1954 made mention of the fact that, in addition to the Kennecott interests, "private investors in the United States have built up a large holding of certain South African mining shares." Uranium prospects represented an attraction. And there would be many more such investments, he said, if South African shares were listed on the New York Stock Exchange.

Besides the mining companies and their shareholders, there are the suppliers of mining and electrical equipment. American firms have for some time past supplied machinery for the Rand mines; the new mines and new installations mean more orders. Power equipment for the uranium processing is obtained from such companies as General Electric. The Goodyear subsidiary in South

Africa announced in 1953 (net profits of $915,000 in that year) that it was enlarging its factory in order to produce materials to be used for uranium recovery.

The African's Share

The atomic boom, then, has added to the income of private enterprise and investment in South Africa. It has provided an inflow of much-needed dollars and credit. It has rescued the Nationalist Government from possible economic and political disaster. But it has in no way altered the basic pattern of the country's mode of life and work which prompted at least one American businessman to say that he wouldn't invest a dime there. The country remains split into two parts, economically, socially, and politically—the white governing minority and the subject African-Colored-Asian majority. The gulf between them has widened and the friction has sharpened since 1950—in striking contrast with the extremely amicable relations between the United States and South Africa on the official level and the growing attachment to the South African market exhibited by American capital.

Economic exploitation is at the root of the separation between black and white. We have already seen how this operates in South Africa's gold mining industry, and the widening distance between the wages of its white and African employees (Table 3) reflects the national illness. While the total wages of the relatively small white working force advanced from a little under 19 per cent in 1931 to 29 per cent in 1953 in relation to the value of gold production, the wages of the African working force in relation to the same fell from 16 to 12.5 per cent in the same period.

Overall dividends are not as high as in by-gone years before the better ore in the long-worked mines was exhausted. Yet the amount distributed to shareholders each year has with few exceptions remained more, and frequently considerably more, than the total African wage bill. There has been in recent years the opening of new higher-yielding mines, it is true. But the explanation of how shareholders year after year are assured good dividends even from the older mines is most likely to be found in the fact that the companies, while cutting down on the black wage bill in proportion to income, constantly pushed up the output schedule and got 55 per cent more ore dug and processed per African underground worker in 1953 (310 tons) than in 1931 (200 tons).[14] These underground workers, the backbone of the mining industry, comprise about two-thirds of the total African labor force in the gold mines.

In so far as South African uranium production is concerned, the considerably higher profits yielded as compared with gold production stem in large measure from the fact that little labor cost is involved. In most instances the same ore extracted for gold also yields uranium. The processing is a highly mechanized operation. As of 1955 the uranium project involved the special services of only 4,000 African employees (and 2,000 whites).[15]

Diamonds, then gold, and now uranium. The masters of South Africa's wealth from Rhodes to Oppenheimer have indeed been lucky. Will their luck hold? Can De Beers and Anglo American and the rest go on forever? And will Newmont and Kennecott and others from overseas who have come to join the sport continue to find the climate favorable?

Now and again there comes a turning point. A people's struggles, though repeatedly defeated and beaten back, engender an understanding and strength that are ultimately invincible. About the middle of 1955 there was being circulated throughout the cities, townships and countryside of South Africa a new expression of faith, of hope, of determination. It was listened to, thought over, debated and subscribed to by tens of thousands of Africans, Indians, Colored people—yes, and democratic-spirited white people, too.

It was a people's testament, called the Freedom Charter. It had been adopted by 2,844 elected delegates to the Congress of the People, June 26, 1955, sponsored by the African National Congress and other organizations, and held by many to have been the most representative gathering in South African history. One part of the Charter said, "The people shall share in the country's wealth! The national wealth of our country, the heritage of all South Africans, shall be restored to the people. The mineral wealth beneath the soil, the banks and monopoly industry shall be transferred to the ownership of the people as a whole." To the rulers of South Africa that was, of course, communism and treason. But those who endorsed the Freedom Charter considered it simply justice. And justice is what they intend to have.

11. Boom in Rhodesia

A WHITE HAIRED patriarch put the matter very simply: "The British have got Great Britain. The Indians have got India. God did not make a mistake in giving Nyasaland to us. We cannot turn the world upside down." The speaker, Chief Maganga, was one of a delegation of several Nyasa rulers who came to London early in 1953 with a final desperate appeal to the government and people of England to reject the scheme for linking their country and Northern Rhodesia with Southern Rhodesia in a new federal state dominated by the latter.

For three years African leaders and organizations in Nyasaland and Northern Rhodesia had appealed, petitioned, and demonstrated against the proposed Central African Federation. They asked for self-government and bitterly opposed annexation to Southern Rhodesia where African rights were even more rigidly circumscribed than in their own countries. A Nyasa chief was deported for supporting a ban on tax payments as an expression of resistance. Several anti-federation leaders in Northern Rhodesia were jailed, and 11 persons were killed in Nyasaland riots. Neither intimidation, nor fair talk of "partnership," nor "guarantees" of continued British "protection" of African rights could curb the opposition. So it was just ignored. The whites in the three territories proceeded to approve what the Africans (numbering more than 30 to each white inhabitant, and nearly 500 to one in Nyasaland) had disapproved, and the United Kingdom Government gave its assent.

Federation: Prerequisite for Large-Scale Investment

The formal establishment of the Federation of Rhodesia and Nyasaland in September, 1953—at least as viewed by resident political leaders such as Mr. Roy Welensky—was simply a transitional step toward the creation of a new British dominion in Africa, more skillful than the Union of South Africa in the handling of racial matters, but with white political power just as firmly and permanently intrenched as in the neighboring *apartheid*-ridden country. Such a union of the territories had been urged by white leaders in Southern Rhodesia for three decades.

There were those who prophesied that once federation was an accomplished fact, African opposition would fade away; there were benefits Africans, too, would gain, and they would soon come to realize that their betters knew what was best for them. That has not happened. We find Lord Malvern (formerly Sir Godfrey Huggins), for 19 consecutive years Prime Minister of Southern Rhodesia, chief architect of Federation and then its Prime Minister until his recent retirement, expressing official concern in 1956 over African movements in Northern Rhodesia which he described as political and even subversive. "Emergency" arrests and repression followed later in the year.

No, things have not quieted down. If anything, Africans are more dead set against Federation than in 1953. The six African members (not elected by Africans) in the 35-member Federal Assembly have proved, as was expected, to be little more than window-dressing; they cannot as yet eat dinner along with their white associates at the Salisbury Club across from the Parliament Building. Africans have witnessed the Federal Assembly's rejection of motions to end racial discrimination on the state-operated Rhodesia Railways, to eliminate Jim Crow in the post offices, to provide equal opportunities for all races in the civil service, to employ Africans as shunters and conductors in the railway service, or even to make a study of the principle of a multiracial community.

It is hardly surprising, then, to find the African National Congress of Northern Rhodesia in December, 1955, voicing the African people's desire that the Federation be "dissolved as soon as possible," or the Nyasaland African Congress earlier in the same year declaring that it "categorically reaffirms its determined opposition to the Federation of Rhodesia and Nyasaland and desires that the Nyasaland Protectorate be extracted from the Federal Scheme." The answer they get is that Federation is there to stay, and this reply is coupled with increased police surveillance and restriction of Congress activity.

The roadblock thrown in the way of the African freedom train

BOOM IN RHODESIA 131

simultaneously cleared the main track for the Bankers' Special. Federation provided the guarantees of long-term security and low-cost, high profit operations which were demanded of Rhodesia in return for foreign capital investment on the same grand scale as in the Union of South Africa. This was what the talk about the advantages of Federation for the "economic development" of British Central Africa boiled down to. And it was for this mainly that London pushed the scheme through. When Lord Malvern was reminded of the principle of partnership enshrined in the preamble of the Federation's Constitution, during the debate on the removal of separate post office windows for patrons of different color, the Prime Minister retorted, "Let us for the sake of Federation which was for economic advancement, not for the preamble which was forced upon us, have patience."

During the crucial year 1952, when the question whether to join the three territories was being hotly debated, there was ample expression on the matter from notable investment sources. With a $28-million loan to Southern Rhodesia early in 1952 for electric power expansion, the World Bank attached its advice that "full coordination of development in Central Africa could be most securely achieved through establishing a single political union."[1]

Sir Ronald L. Prain was more explicit. This gentleman is chairman of the Rhodesian Selection Trust group of mines and a director of International Nickel of Canada and other enterprises. In his annual report dated October 7, 1952, on the operation of Mufulira Copper Mines, one of the Northern Rhodesia properties largely financed by United States capital, Mr. Prain said:

> We are naturally closely concerned with the question of the possible federation of the Rhodesias and Nyasaland. The talks on this matter have now gone so far that it would be dangerous if finality should not be reached. A successful completion of federation would re-create conditions where investors could be confident about further investments in the Rhodesias. Without such investment it is not only difficult to see how some existing enterprises can be carried on, but also a great opportunity will have been missed of opening up these potentially rich territories for the benefit of the Commonwealth and free nations as a whole.[2]

In 1953 President Eisenhower sent a special envoy, Mr. William H. Ball, the glass jar manufacturer, to the Rhodes Centenary Exhibition. He told his Rhodesian audience that private investment interests in the United States and elsewhere had followed developments in Central Africa "with more than casual interest," and they hoped that Federation would "make possible the economic stability that offers an incentive to private capital."³

A little later the *New York Times* (Oct. 25, 1953), in the first sentence of a story on Rhodesian political developments, said quite candidly, "British Central Africa was federated into a new state to attract American capital for the development of its rich natural roseurces." From all this it should be apparent that certain circles in the United States must be held at least partly accountable for the decision to force a white-controlled federation system on the six or seven million Africans of Rhodesia and Nyasaland—and accountable, also, for the consequences of that decision.

Africans were not ignorant of what was behind the political move. A Nyasa leader, Mr. Y. M. Leonard Chirwa, wrote:

> Federation, we are told, will lead to "a very large capital investment from overseas." But what is it that will lead overseas capitalists to invest their money in Africa? We can answer that question simply: big profits and cheap labor. But big profits mean laying waste the natural resources of Africa which are our heritage, eroding the soil with "get-rich-quick" farming methods, exploiting our labor and robbing our wealth for the enrichment of overseas speculators in London or New York whose only interest in Africa is to squeeze it dry. . . . I do not want these things nor does any African patriot want them.⁴

In 1955 the United States Department of Commerce got Mr. G. H. T. Kimble, Director of the 20th Century Fund's Survey of Tropical Africa, to make a study of investment opportunities in the Federation and prepare a handbook on the subject for the benefit of American businessmen.⁵ And in 1956 the International Cooperation Administration appointed a former official of the National Trust Corp. of Chicago to act as "investment adviser" to the Federation Government on behalf of United States interests. If the Bankers' Special doesn't arrive on schedule, it won't be Washington's fault.

American Corporations in Rhodesia

Copper, which represents over 90 per cent of Northern Rhodesia's exports and about 60 per cent of the combined exports of Northern Rhodesia, Southern Rhodesia and Nyasaland, is the mainstay of the Federation's economy. Though Southern Rhodesia's production is more diversified than Northern Rhodesia's, it fails to cover imports with its own exports and must depend on copper to make up the deficit. Nyasaland—with only 6,700 whites and about 3,000,000 Africans—is the poor relation. Its only sizeable exports are tea and tobacco and its main contribution to the Federation's economy is the scores of thousands of Africans who annually leave their homes to find work in Rhodesian mining and agriculture (many going still further to South Africa).

Many of the same big American corporations supplying consumer and industrial markets in South Africa also operate in Southern Rhodesia, from which their business in Central and East Africa radiates. In addition, United States interests control most of Southern Rhodesia's chrome ore production and play a prominent part in asbestos and other primary industries. Subsidiaries of Union Carbide and Carbon, Metallurg Inc. of New York, and the Vanadium Corp. of America dominate the mining and processing of chrome ore—their African labor averaging about $9 a month in wages. The latter corporation, active in Southern Rhodesia since 1926, also gets manganese from its expanding mine properties. The American Chemical Corp. is one of the newcomers to Rhodesia; it is interested in developing a big fertilizer industry there.

Johns-Manville through its Canadian subsidiary holds controlling interest in Rhodesian Asbestos. Ltd. This is the operating company for Associated Asbestos Mines, which early in 1952 received a $288,400 loan for production expansion from the Mutual Security Agency (repayable in asbestos deliveries to the United States stockpile). A new Johns-Manville asbestos mill of 20,000 tons capacity was opened in 1954 at Mashaba.

Southern Rhodesia is one of the principal world sources of a little known mineral called lithium, used for making extra light aluminum alloys for aircraft and also, according to Rhodesian mining officials, in the manufacture of hydrogen bombs. Like uranium, lithium has become a highly attractive investment item. Bikita Minerals, controlled by Selection Trust, owns the world's largest known deposit of lithium, 45 miles from Fort Victoria. The American Metal Co. and the American Potash and Chemical Corporation hold a part interest in Bikita.

Turning to Northern Rhodesia, we find American, British and South African capital all concentrated in one thing—copper. Large-scale production by the four major operating companies—Roan Antelope, Mufulira, Nchanga, and Rhokana Corp. (Nkana mine)—began just 25 years ago. The first two companies are American-British owned, with control by American Metal exercised through

Rhodesian Selection Trust. The other two are South African-British holdings of Sir Ernest Oppenheimer's Anglo American Corp., represented locally by Rhodesian Anglo American. The chairman of RST puts the "historical value" of the capital invested in the copper mines at $430 million.[6]

As of December 31, 1955, the total investments of the American Metal Co., headed by Mr. Harold K. Hochschild until his recent retirement, were reported to have a computed value of about $207 million. Of this about two-thirds was in Northern Rhodesia copper and all but 13.5 per cent of the remainder was in the previously mentioned mining properties in South and South West Africa and Southern Rhodesia. The company's dividend income mushroomed from $748,000 in 1945 (when $24,703,000—*book value*—was invested in Africa and $2,070,000 elsewhere) to $15,347,000 in 1955 (from $28,854,000 invested in Africa, $4,507,000 elsewhere). In 1956 American Metal's profits soared higher, $20.6 million out of total dividends of $22.6 million being derived from its investments in Africa.

Besides the holdings of American Metal in Rhodesian Selection Trust (50.61 per cent) and Roan Antelope (32.65 per cent), additional shares in these companies have been bought on the New York Stock Exchange. The total investment holding of Americans in RST as of 1956 was estimated (in January) to be 61 per cent by the Company's chairman, though the British Colonial Secretary, Mr. Lennox Boyd, put it (in June) at 65 per cent. The total American stake in Roan Antelope was put at 41 per cent.

More Copper—with Washington's Help

Copper ore output in Northern Rhodesia was 204,000 tons in 1946; it was about double that in 1953, and it currently stands at about 500,000 tons a year. With higher copper prices prevailing and competition between government and industrial buyers for all avalable supplies, the companies have had every inducement to expand production and open new mines. Furthermore, they have had the help of ECA, Export-Import Bank, and World Bank loans in making this possible. Chibuluma, a copper and cobalt mine, one of three new properties in which Rhodesian Selection Trust (and consequently American capital) holds close to two-third's control, was put into operation with $14 million in loans (against metal deliveries) advanced by ECA, the company putting up only one-fifth of that amount out of its own capital.

Lured by the bustle in the Copperbelt some new companies are venturing in. During 1956 the American Smelting and Refining Co. took an option on a 1000 square mile concession where copper exploration is under way, and another concession was acquired by Anglo Transvaal Consolidated Investment, previously referred to as the holding company through which Kennecott Copper's South African investments are handled.

The increased mining activity developed as and when the companies saw plans being made and money becoming available for a corresponding improvement in transport and electric power supply. The existing railroads simply could not cope with the heavy freight awaiting export. Moreover, outdated and inadequate facilities were creating bottle-necks at the ports upon which landlocked Rhodesia depended, Angola's Lobito Bay on the west coast and Mozambique's Beira on the east coast (see map, p. 78).

ECA and MSA advanced $24 million toward improving Rhodesia's railway system. The World Bank added another $14 million toward the construction of a new rail line providing Southern Rhodesia with another outlet through the port of Lourenco Marques further south on Mozambique's coast, thus relieving pressure on Beira. Mozambique's part of this rail line was helped with a $17 million Eximbank loan—another interesting example of how the Eximbank and World Bank work together. Additional ECA funds went toward enlarging the capacity of the ports, such grants and those to the railways as well being repayable in deliveries of chrome, copper, tungsten, cobalt and other stockpile materials to the United States. But with all this, the complaint continues that the mineral exports are still not moving fast enough.

The provision of adequate electric power represented a bigger engineering and financing job. The Northern Rhodesia mines depended on coal from the Wankie coal-fields in Southern Rhodesia, and this entailed a heavy rail burden and cost. To supplement this fuel supply the Copperbelt companies took to cutting down forests and for a period imported coal all the way from the United States.

Two hydro-electric schemes were undertaken to overcome the power shortage handicap. One scheme, which went into operation in 1956, was arranged in cooperation with some of the big corporations in the Belgian Congo and brings power from installations on the Lualaba River in the Congo. This was financed with $22.4 million credit advanced by the Eximbank.

The other considerably bigger scheme is the much talked about Kariba Dam project on the Zambesi River on the border between Northern and Southern Rhodesia, the first stage of which is scheduled to be completed by 1960. The World Bank, having already made a loan of $28 million for improvement of Rhodesia's electric power facilities, granted another $80 million in one lump sum (at 5 per cent interest with 25 years for repayment) for the Kariba scheme. The World Bank requires that such big loans be matched by locally supplied capital. So this was generously provided—in the form of five year loans earning 4.5 per cent interest—by the mining companies and banking interests in Rhodesia.

Even with the surcharge on electric power which they have agreed to pay for six years, the companies' cost will be considerably reduced, since Kariba power is expected to come to only 22 per cent of the present cost. A further consideration is the fact that the Rhodesia Congo Border Power Corp., which serves Northern Rhodesia and links up with both the Congo and Kariba hydroelectric schemes, is the joint property of the four Copperbelt mining companies.

The Kariba project, estimated to cost $225 million for the first stage of construction, will enable Rhodesia to become "the industrial heart of the African continent," says the United States Consul General in the Federation. Some white Rhodesians see their country becoming the Ruhr Valley of Africa. All this makes for a very happy investment prospect. If Africans do not share this enthusiasm for Kariba, it is because they perceive that the rapid carrying-forward of the scheme is not unrelated to the whites' insistence upon political federation. This project, moreover, requires the flooding of land along both banks of the Zambesi where for generations past some 50,000 Africans (official estimates) have lived and farmed and made their homes. Now they have to move to other undeveloped land and start all over.

Copper Profits

The United States Department of Commerce considers that the economic future of Rhodesia "is an encouraging one." But it adds a note of caution: "However, Rhodesia is not well placed with regard to world markets, and its future will depend, despite its great

BOOM IN RHODESIA   137

mineral wealth, upon its ability to keep production costs at a low level.[7] Besides electric power, soon to be provided more abundantly and cheaply for the copper mines, there is another even more important factor of production cost—human labor power. "Here in the Copperbelt the ore is so rich and the labor so cheap that producers can reduce prices 50 per cent below the U.S. break-even point and still make money," a *Wall Street Journal* correspondent has reported (August 5, 1953). Is this what the Department of Commerce is talking about?

It cost about three times more to mine Northern Rhodesia copper in 1955 than in 1946, but the companies got paid about six times more for it on the London market. Thus production cost declined from 64 per cent of the London selling price in March, 1946, to 35 per cent in 1955. Table 10 shows the effect of this, coupled with increased production, on the mines' net profits.

TABLE 10. NET PROFITS, COPPERBELT MINES,
July 1, 1949 - June 30, 1956[8]
($ millions)

	Mufulira & Roan Antelope	Rhokana & Nchanga	Total Net Profits	Value of Production	Total Net Profits as % of Production
1949-50	6.7	11.2	17.9	104.5	17.1%
1952-53	23.6	47.5	71.1	227.4	31.3
1955-56	49.4	90.2	139.6	349.2	40.0
Total for 1949-1956:	168.4	324.3	492.7	1,551.6	31.7

Shareholders have obviously done well on Copperbelt investments. They couldn't ask for anything much better than Rhokana. Its dividend rate (return on ordinary shares based upon the par value of paid up capital) has gone steadily upward from 120 per cent in 1950 and stood at 262.5 per cent in 1955. Its dividend yield averaged 93 per cent annually from 1946 through 1950, and 51.9 per cent from the initial year 1935 to 1951.[9] "The copper companies," the London *Economist* noted (November 26, 1955), "are in vigorous manhood. . . . From mining assets stockholders expect —and will undoubtedly receive unless the bottom falls out of the market—rising dividends."

This optimistic forecast, it seems, is based upon the premise that the game will continue to be played according to the same old rules. We have seen (Table 10) how a larger and larger slice of the mining income was taken out as profits. But turning to wages we find that the total Copperbelt mine wage bill, the highly paid white workers included, amounted to 21 per cent of the value of the mines' output in 1949, varied between 17 and 18 per cent from 1950 to 1953, and was 20 per cent in 1954.[10]

To get a clearer idea of what the wage bill really represents, one has to isolate the amount paid the African workers and see its relation to the total income and expenditure. An examination of the copper industry's accounts for 1953 reveals (Table 11) that wages, bonuses and rations for the African workers, the mines' indispensable labor force, cost the companies about one-nineteenth of the value of the copper produced and between a quarter and one-fifth of what was paid out in dividends to do-nothing stockholders!

TABLE 11. INCOME AND EXPENDITURE, NORTHERN RHODESIA COPPER INDUSTRY, 1953[11]
(approximate)

Income: from copper exported		$251,000,000
Expenditure:		
PROFITS, ROYALTIES, ADMINISTRATION:		
Dividends	$57,300,000	
Royalties, British South Africa Co.	29,000,000	
Taxes, Northern Rhodesia Govt.	41,500,000	
Company reserve accounts	16,100,000	
Contractors' fees	11,100,000	
Rhodesia Railways freight charges, etc.	6,800,000	
Other local expenses	47,700,000	
		209,500,000
SALARIES, WAGES, BONUSES:		
To 5,874 white employees	27,900,000	
To 36,147 African employees	10,200,000	
Food rations for Africans	3,400,000	
		41,500,000
		$251,000,000

"We Have Had Enough of Slave Wages"

The problem confronting the Northern Rhodesia copper barons, causing them more headaches during recent years than transport or power supply difficulties, is that the African workers refuse to play any longer according to the old rules of the game.

The expansion of mining activity and an increasing shortage of all categories of labor tended toward the adoption of a stabilized African labor force in place of the old migrant worker system. This happened not only in Northern Rhodesia but in other developing areas such as the new minefields of the Orange Free State in South Africa, and the busy Katanga mines in the Belgian Congo. When Africans settle down in such places with their families and remain on the job for years instead of months, management has to answer certain questions. What to do about the wages of these workers after they have acquired long experience on their jobs? What to do about getting the maximum value from their experience by placing the workers in higher skilled jobs normally performed by white employees?

In South Africa and the Congo management has answered these questions as it saw fit. The distinguishing feature of the Northern Rhodesia Copperbelt situation is that there African labor, having become strongly organized, has come forward with some answers of its own. The Rhodesian copper mines in which American capital holds a big controlling interest have thus become a focal point of African labor's struggle to break through the chains of cheap labor serfdom in the continent's mining industry.

Out of the experiences of their earlier struggles the African mine workers on the Copperbelt by 1948 had built up a strong organization, the Northern Rhodesia African Mineworkers' Union (NRAMU). It was recognized by the companies in 1949 when the Government legalized trade unions, without reference to race or color, and their right to strike and picket. In 1951 the Union won its first victory, the payment of a wage bonus to Africans when the price of copper rose above a certain level. The white mineworkers (their union was organized in 1936 and in its early period was an adjunct of the white South African Mineworkers Union) had been getting such a bonus—a much bigger one, of course—since 1947.

In October, 1952, immediately following a demand by the white union for a 25 per cent pay increase which the companies agreed to settle by arbitration, the African Union called its workers out on strike. It asked for an increase in basic wages which would have about doubled the existing pay of 2s.6d. (35¢) or 3s. (42¢) a day. The Union rejected a first offer of 3 cents increase and a second of 7 cents. After seeing the strike continue for three weeks in a disciplined and effective shut-down, management agreed to negotiate. Pay increases were won ranging from 80 per cent for the lowest paid workers to 15 per cent for the highest.

In 1954 the companies granted African workers further rights previously reserved to whites in the form of annual holidays with pay and a pension for those over 50 with more than 20 years service. But pressure continued from the NRAMU for a *general* and *substantial* wage increase. "We have had enough of slave wages," said the Union's leadership; "we are now determined to change radically the whole wage structure for African miners and to raise it to a civilized level."[12] Toward the end of 1954 the NRAMU entered a demand for a down-the-line wage increase of 10*s*.8*d*. ($1.50) a day, to bring the lowest wages of $11.20 a month up to about $50 and the highest, about $53, close to $100. The companies flatly rejected the demand, calling it "irresponsible," though it would have cost them only about one-sixth or less of their current profits—ability to pay was not an issue.

After careful preparations for a long struggle, including the storing of food supplies for weeks in advance so that they couldn't be starved out, the Union launched its strike January 4, 1955. It was almost totally solid. The London *Economist* (January 8) commented on the emergence of "a new phenomenon in African trade unionism, and a very ominous one—a sustained and well-organized effort to create a powerful, militant and politically conscious mass union." The strike lasted 58 days, one of the longest and greatest in African history. The companies ordered the dismissal of all workers still out on January 25th, but later changed their minds, took the workers back without penalizing them and agreed to arbitrate. The increases awarded, ranging from $3.57 to $8.05 a month for all African workers, marked another advance for the Union but represented only a small fraction of what had been asked for.

The Chairman of Rhodesian Selection Trust, Sir Ronald Prain, will tell you that African labor costs on the Copperbelt have risen by some 316 per cent in the last 25 years. But if you're just adding pennies to pennies such percentage figures do not mean very much. On the other hand, the increases in the white miners' pay, which was high to begin with, add up to a horse of quite a different color.

The white mine worker occupies a special caste status everywhere in Africa, but nowhere in the continent—nor in Europe or even America—does a mine employee's income equal that of the white copper miner of Northern Rhodesia. In 1954 his average yearly pay, including basic pay, overtime and bonuses, was the equivalent of $5,102, while the African worker's yearly average wage, including the same, amounted to $217. In 1955 the white miner's early average was over $6,160.[13] And in 1956 the correspondent of one New York paper marveled at the "fantastic wages" of these white workers, some of whom got $1,400 a month.[14]

Obviously the inflated white wages, like the copper profits, are made possible by low black wages, and Africans know this. Yet while pressing their own demands for increases, they have never requested or hinted at a pay cut for white workers. Such a proposal has, however, been made. A study of the copper industry's wage structure was undertaken by Dr. Rheinhallt Jones, late president of the South African Institute of Race Relations and adviser on African labor to the Anglo American Corp. He maintained that the premium pay to white workers was no longer justified in view of the marked change in the environment since the early days when special inducements had to be offered them, and he concluded that equal pay for equal work by black and white workers should be achieved at a level of about 70 per cent of current white wages.[15] The study was filed away unpublished and forgotten.

From 1940 following the African miners' strike in that year down to 1954 there were no fewer than six other studies, all official, of the status of African labor in the Copperbelt mining industry. Two arbitration tribunals and four special commissions, the last in 1954, made their investigations and filed their reports. When there was trouble another commission would be appointed; otherwise Government preferred to leave the matter up to management. The Dalgleish Commission in 1948 offered some concrete proposals regarding African job promotions and wage scales. But it was not until after the 1955 strike that the companies took the first steps toward opening a few new job categories to Africans.

Actually, in the Rhodesian Selection Trust group of mines headed by Prain, Africans had for some time driven trucks, underground locomotives, and overhead cranes and performed other jobs formerly done only by whites. But they were not getting anything like the pay the whites got. This arrangement suited the RST management, but not the Africans—they demanded a complete review of African job classifications and wage structure, and a general leveling up of both.

Not being inclined to employ expensive white labor in jobs

which he could get Africans to perform at cheaper rates, Prain pressed for the white mineworkers' acceptance of a compromise formula which would in principle eliminate or eventually lead to the elimination of discrimination between white and black workers in job placements while maintaining the double wage standard with some slight modifications in the Africans' favor. According to the senior general manager of the RST mines in his testimony before the 1954 Board of Inquiry, Africans doing the same quality of work as whites would be paid more but in relation to "the African wage structure." The separate African and European (white) wage structures would remain, he said, "because of the dual society." Thus the political and social subordination of the African, here regarded as something permanent, is the justification offered for employing skilled African workers at unskilled labor rates.

In the other group of copper mines presided over by Sir Ernest Oppenheimer the Jim Crow job pattern has been more rigidly maintained as in the Union of South Africa, where the same South African-British interests have heavy mining investments. And Oppenheimer emphasized and reemphasized that his companies would make absolutely no concessions toward African advancement in the industry without the prior agreement of the white mineworkers' union, a reservation which Prain rejected.

The leaders of the white mineworkers have stuck to the position that any job promotion for Africans must be accompanied by "equal pay for equal work." This sounds very fine and is most certainly the goal of African striving. But in the immediate situation such an unqualified demand represents simply a barrier to *any* African advancement since, as the white union leaders know full well, the companies would certainly not give Africans equal pay at the *outset* of the promotion scheme, regardless of what they might later intend or be forced to do about it.

Moreover, the white union leadership demonstrated how little sincerity there was behind their "equal pay" advocacy by acquiescing in their membership not only continuing to work but even scabbing on African jobs during the 1952 and 1955 strikes when the NRAMU was fighting for wage increases. Let it be added that while the white union thus aided the companies and betrayed the interests of the African mineworkers, there was some rank-and-file protest among the white Copperbelt miners, and from Welsh, Scottish, and British mineworkers and other trade unions in England came several thousands of dollars to the NRAMU in support of the 1955 strike.

In September, 1955, after many long months of back-and-forth negotiation between the company heads and the white union leadership, an agreement was finally reached on "African advancement." The agreement embodied the Prain formula, with Oppenheimer on his part reserving the right of veto for the white mineworkers' union. Seventy-five former "European" jobs, 24 of them already performed by "non-Europeans" on the RST mines, were declared open to Africans with certain educational and other qualifications. As of March, 1956, 136 Africans were reported promoted to advanced jobs, and another 129 being trained.

Even if limited, these accomplishments represented a step forward, a breach in the wall barring African advancement which might be widened by continuing militant struggle by the NRAMU. But danger signs quickly appeared. At one of the mines 1,300 white workers struck in support of 12 of their colleagues who refused to work beside three Africans newly promoted to the same work as pipe-fitters. The African workers were promptly withdrawn. It was said that the withdrawal was temporary pending conciliation of the matter with the white union—"the avoidance of friction in the implementation of the advancement program is of paramount importance." We are familiar with that same phraseology from go-slow southerners in the United States.

Another more serious danger sign is the evident intention of the companies to use the advancement scheme as the means for creating a small hierarchy of more privileged and better paid African employes divorced from the NRAMU, thereby undermining the organization representing the mass of African mineworkers. The vehicle of this labor-splitting tactic is the African Staff Association, organized with management's blessing and help in 1953 and officially recognized by the companies in December, 1955, as the bargaining agent for its members. The Association has a no strike policy and its workers scabbed during the 1955 strike.

This body is composed of African workers in the supervisory and white collar grades who are paid on a monthly instead of daily wage basis. Now, it so happened that 62 of the 75 new jobs opened to Africans were classified as "staff jobs" even though they had been in the daily paid category when performed by whites. Management has declared its intention of dealing only with the African Staff Association in regard to the wages of the upgraded workers. The objective of the companies in turning their backs on the NRAMU appears to be to counter-balance the advancement of the few Africans by keeping the wages of the rest, the great majority, frozen at their present low level.

The NRAMU was, of course, alert to all these maneuvers and vigorously fought them. The Union recognized that its very existence was at stake. It stuck to the position expressed by its president, Mr. Lawrence Katilungu, in 1954: "The line taken by the African Mineworkers' Union is that they must not merely consider the few who would impinge on European employment, but that there must be universal economic advancement for Africans, regardless of grade or position."[16] A month after the agreement on African promotion was announced the Union entered a claim for a general wage increase of 6s.8d. (73¢) a day. "For us the battle of African advancement has only just begun," said the Union's secretary, Mr. M. D. Nkoloma.

But management is determined to block the Union's demand for *mass* advancement. Not content with undercutting and by-passing the NRAMU, the companies (as we shall see in a later chapter) resorted to more direct methods of smashing the Union. Thus the struggle on the labor front grows more acute, paralleling the sharpening struggle against white political domination. Those aboard the Federation's Banker's Special must sooner or later realize that the battle for African rights in Rhosedia has just begun.

12. Some Other American Interests

FOUR OUT OF every five dollars invested in Africa by United States private capital in 1955 went to either Liberia, the Union of South Africa, Egypt (where American oil companies had a $49 million stake), or Rhodesia. A considerable portion of what we may call the fifth dollar investment in Africa outside those four countries, amounting to $155 million in 1955, is represented by American petroleum marketing and distribution networks, such as Caltex, Standard Vacuum, Esso, and Texaco, which cover most of the continent. Texaco operations, for instance, extend from Morocco through all of French West and Equatorial Africa and the British West Coast colonies down to and including the Belgian Congo and Portuguese Angola. To oil selling we add the investments in oil prospecting enterprises reviewed earlier.

There is another network peddling another liquid over most of Africa—Coca Cola. There were 45 Coca Cola manufacturing plants spread over the continent in 1953; we have not kept count of the others opened since then. Pepsi-Cola and Canada Dry are also there.

North African Lead and West African Bauxite

The interests of a company like the Newmont Mining Corp. are scattered over most of the continent. In addition to its holdings in southern Africa, Newmont since World War II has bought into a French mining enterprise, the Zellidja lead-zinc complex on the Moroccan-Algerian border; acquired a 35 per cent interest in two

French companies holding mining concessions in French Equatorial Africa; and (in 1956) obtained a large mining concession in Southern Ethiopia in partnership with two other companies. Several million dollars were advanced by ECA to promote Newmont's ventures in North and Equatorial Africa, to be repaid as usual with stockpile deliveries. (For a mammoth copper mining undertaking in southern Peru the company, jointly with three other American corporations, got some really big money, $100 million credit from the Eximbank.)

Newmont's entry into North African mining is partly explained by the fact that one of Zellidja's board members is Mrs. Margaret Biddle, daughter of the founder of Newmont. Though its direct share interest in Zellidja is small—the St. Joseph Lead Co. also holds a small interest—Newmont derives a "substantial revenue . . . as fair compensation for technical and general assistance" it provides.[1] In addition Newmont and St. Joseph together hold nearly a half interest in the two companies which work the Zellidja lead-zinc complex, *Société Nord Africaine du Plomb* (lead) and *Société Algérienne du Zinc*.

Besides Republic Steel in Liberia and Bethlehem Steel looking toward South West Africa, the U.S. Steel Corp. is also interested in African sources of supply. It signed an agreement in 1953 to join with French government and private interests in exploiting manganese deposits in the region of Franceville, Gabon, lower French Equatorial Africa. Protests in France against the "handing over" of these mineral resources to Americans led to the reduction of U.S. Steel's share in the enterprise from 65 per cent as originally planned to 49 per cent, with six places on a 12-man board of directors. Production was scheduled to begin in 1957.

There were Nigerian protests, too, when the government of Eastern Nigeria granted a 30-year lease to the American Smelting and Refining Co. to develop lead-zinc mines in that region in association with a British mining syndicate. The venture, however, did not come up to expectations and the company terminated its option agreement amidst African "rejoicing that God has come to their aid when their own son, Okoi Arikpo, Minister of Land, Survey, and Local Development, could not put in a word of opposition when Ogoja people were being dispossessed of their land in favor of Americans."[2]

Another American mining company came on the Nigerian scene in 1955. With the price on columbite tumbling at the end of the stockpile joy-ride, Kennecott Copper decided it was a good time to buy a 52 per cent interest in Tin & Associated Minerals Ltd., British owner of a columbite mine and concentrating plant at Odegi, on the northern plateau of Nigeria. The mine, operated by primitive methods with the manual labor of some 3,000 African workers paid a few cents a day, does not represent a very important transaction money-wise for giant Kennecott. But it is a further indication of the Corporation's expanding African operations.

The British and French West African colonies—like some of their present or former tropical colonies in this hemisphere—have been the center of attention of another group of companies seeking and developing new sources of bauxite. From four tons of this ore is derived a ton of precious aluminum. Most of the bauxite ore exported from Africa now comes from mines owned and operated by an Aluminium Ltd. subsidiary on the island of Kassa off the coast of Guinea, French West Africa. The annual output of about a half million tons is less than a quarter of what the same company gets from British Guiana. Aluminium Ltd. is that part of the giant aluminum cartel that has charge of the global operations and interests of the Aluminum Co. of America (Alcoa) and its main subsidiary, the Aluminium Co. of Canada (Alcan).

Aluminium Ltd. in 1953 started enlarging its holdings in West African Aluminium (a subsidiary of Anglo-Transvaal Consolidated Investment), a company with concession rights and interests in bauxite deposits in Ghana. In 1956 Aluminium Ltd. announced plans for its French subsidiary, *Bauxites du Midi,* to develop a bauxite processing industry in French Guinea with an initial five year investment outlay of $100 million. Also under consideration was the establishment of hydroelectric-powered aluminum smelting plants in the same territory in association with Pechiney-Ugine, major French aluminum company, and other European producers.

And then there is the much discussed Volta River scheme in Ghana. First officially announced in 1952, it still remains on paper except for some incidental railway construction toward which ECA contributed $1.4 million. The close proximity of vast bauxite deposits and great potential hydroelectric resources, it is said, offers the possibility of producing aluminum here at a lower cost than anywhere else in the world. In 1952 it was estimated that facilities to produce and export 210,000 tons of aluminum a year— the dam, power installations, mines, smelter, railway, and a new harbor at Tema—would cost $403 million. However, a three-year study of the project released in mid-1956 indicated the cost had gone up to $865 million.

As originally planned, this cost was to be split three ways: about 30 per cent for the railway, harbor and other public works from the local government; another 30 per cent from the British Government for the hydroelectric scheme; and 40 per cent for the mines and smelter—in the equity of which the local government would have a yet unspecified minority share—from Aluminium Ltd., with the minor participation of the British Aluminium Company, which holds bauxite mining and prospecting rights in Ghana, Sierra Leone and Northern Nigeria.

The British Government would get 75 per cent of the Volta production and would thereby save many a dollar, for Britain now has to buy over four-fifths of its aluminum requirements from non-sterling sources (Jamaica, British Guiana, and Canada, though tied to Britain politically, are part of the dollar empire). But prospects of London being able to finance its share of the Volta project, especially with its enlarged budget, were dim. And so it was decided to ask the World Bank for help.

Aluminium Ltd. was not so much worried about the additional cost as about the security and profitableness of its prospective investment. The company is said to have wanted a 60 per cent cut of profits. In April, 1956, the president of Aluminium Ltd. told shareholders, anent the Volta project, that "private-risk capital is reluctant to venture into new areas unless the prospects of return on investment can be made to compensate for the increased risks assumed. These and many other problems will need to be solved before major investments can be justified."[3] There was also expression of concern, after Nasser's proclamation on the Suez Canal, that "the climate for investment in the Gold Coast" should continue to remain satisfactory.

On the other side, many criticisms of the project as planned have been voiced by Africans unofficially, particularly with regard to the inadequate degree of control which the Ghana government would have over the scheme as a whole and specifically over sectors other than that of the non-revenue-earning public works for which it is responsible. Will the Volta undertaking belong to and benefit the country's people, it is asked, or will the benefits mainly go to British, Canadian and United States interests plus perhaps a few wealthy Gold Coast investors holding minority shares?

Prime Minister Nkrumah has been sensitive to public feeling on this issue. His unofficial mouthpiece, the *Ghana Evening News,* said editorially, Feb. 13, 1956:

> . . . The Government is taking no chances, is leaving no stone unturned towards ensuring that when a decision on the [Volta] Project is arrived at it would be the best that could be taken in the interest of the five million people whose lives it would affect. Our memory is not so short as to render us oblivious of the various criticisms which have been made in connection with this Project. . . . We take this opportunity to assure our people that both our Prime Minister and Government are responsible and they will accept the scheme only when they are satisfied beyond all reasonable doubts of its thorough soundness and advantage to the country.

It was promised that when a satisfactory agreement had been negotiated, the matter would be put before the Legislative Assembly for full debate, and no agreement would be signed until after such debate—and after the end of British rule. Following independence it became known that three United States construction and investment firms were considering taking full charge of implementing the Volta project.

Uganda and Congo Attractions

Across the continent important mining developments are under way in Uganda. This East African colony came into the news not long ago, you may recall, when young Kabaka Mutesa II, king of the Baganda, was deposed and exiled from his country by the British for speaking out too plainly about independence. As the French authorities changed their minds and let the Sultan of Morocco return from exile, so did the British in the case of the Kabaka. The Colonial Office would indignantly deny it, but a deciding factor in this about-face was certainly the fear that great economic expectations for Uganda might be wrecked by internal revolt if the people's clamor for His Highness' return went unheeded.

There was the new hydroelectric power supply from the $62 million Owen Falls project (opened April, 1954), and British-sponsored textile and other industrial projects planning to take advantage of it. There was the railroad being built 209 miles westward from Kampala, Uganda's capital, toward Kilembe in the foothills of the Mountains of the Moon (Ruwenzori), where valuable mineral deposits were to be the object of a large-scale mining operation. There were phosphate deposits to the east around Tororo in the Sukulu Hills also to be developed. And with a smelter plant to be established at Jinja utilizing Owen Falls power, the prospect was for Uganda in the not too distant future to be exporting impressive quantities of copper and cobalt (with dividends for foreign investors) in addition to the cotton and coffee currently comprising over 85 per cent of the country's exports.

Top dog in the Kilembe and Sukulu mining operations is Frobisher Ltd. of Canada (headed by Thayer Lindsley of New York) whose other African interests include tin mines in South West Africa, copper and gold mines in Southern Rhodesia, and copper and iron mines in Mauretania, French West Africa. Frobisher put up 70 per cent of the $14 million capital for the Kilembe project and shares ownership of the Sukulu Mines enterprise with the Olin Mathieson Chemical Corp. of the United States and the Uganda Development Corp., a local government agency with investments in a variety of privately managed companies including Kilembe Mines.

It is expected that Kilembe will develop into one of the world's largest producers of cobalt, contributing greatly to United States requirements. And the production cost for its copper, it is said, will be below the average for the Northern Rhodesia mines—which is not at all surprising since the few Africans employed in Uganda's hitherto small mining industry were paid the equivalent of less than $5 a month in 1954, not even a third of the average Copperbelt monthly wage for Africans at that time.

One African country that the big American mining interests have been unable to penetrate except by indirect investment, and one of the most prized in mineral riches, is the Belgian Congo. The valuable piece of real estate that Leopold II promised to "open to civilization" has been kept closely guarded against intruders who might cut into the holdings of *Société Générale de Belgique,* the Belgian banking group which is big boss of the Congo and whose subsidiaries include *Forminière* with its diamonds and *Union Minière du Haut Katanga* (UM) with its copper, cobalt, and uranium. Both companies were established in 1906, 50 years ago, by Leopold's royal decree. The entire Katanga Province ruled by UM has been described as "in fact, a 'company town.' . . . Free enterprise in the Katanga, and in the Belgian Congo generally, does not go much beyond retail trade and a few manufacturing service industries of local scope."[4]

Deprived of the Congo and the wealth drained from it, what would be left of Belgian capitalism? In 1952 Belgian investments in Congo corporations amounted to $554 million, up from $219 million in 1947. Net profits of those Congo corporations during the six years 1947-52 came to $430 million, of which $250 million was distributed to shareholders.⁵ Union Minière's per share dividend payment rose steadily from $9.60 in 1948 when net profits were $19 million to $44 in 1955 when those profits had climbed to over $84 million.

The only recent direct access of American investment capital to a share of the lush Congo mining profits, specifically in UM, came about through the medium of Tanganyika Concessions, a British company which came on the African scene in 1899 and holds a 14 per cent interest in UM, 90 per cent ownership of the Benguela Railroad linking Central Africa with the west coast, and various other assets. In 1950 the Bank of England sold 1,667,961 shares it then held in Tanganyika Concessions (worth about $5.6 million) to a group of British, South African and Belgian finance houses. It was stipulated in this sale that 600,000 of the shares should be resold to a finance group in the United States representing Rockefeller interests. This transaction was duly consummated.

United States requirements in strategic metals are well supplied from the Congo, but the supply source remains under Belgian control. UM's closely guarded Shinkolobwe mine in the Katanga Province is widely known as the main producer of uranium for the United States during and since World War II. However, it should not be forgotten that from UM mines has also come this country's main supply of another substance associated with weapons of mass destruction, cobalt. Over $30 million worth of it was shipped to the United States in 1955, this representing about 30 per cent of the value of all Congo exports to this country in that year—excluding uranium.

The last United States agreement with Belgium signed in 1955 gave the Combined Development Agency (which buys and allocates uranium to the United States, Britain, and Canada) an option on up to 90 per cent of the Congo's uranium and thorium output in 1956 and 1957, and up to 75 per cent in 1958 and 1959.⁶ By then uranium production in South Africa, which is somewhat more hospitable to United States mining interests, will be at top level.

Much has been written about the contrast between African labor policy in the Congo and that in South Africa and other territories where the worker's job is strictly determined by his skin color. The change from the wasteful migrant labor system to a stabilized labor force began in the late 'twenties in the Congo as mechanized production advanced. During the depression period the number of white workers employed by UM fell from 1,951 in 1930 to 591 in 1934, and as production revived management found it expedient to keep down the number of white employees as much as possible by putting Africans in their skilled jobs at a fraction of their wages. By 1936 Africans were already operating railway locomotives and performing other skilled tasks in the Congo's industries.

Why did such developments occur in the Belgian Congo and not in South Africa? There was, of course, a much smaller white industrial labor force to draw upon in the Congo. But further, unlike the situation in South Africa, the Congo corporations and the Congo government (which participates in the control of UM and the other large concessions) are instruments independent of local white control, deriving their authority from Belgium, and policy is dictated by the interests of investors in Belgium, not those of the white settlers in the Congo. Somewhat parallel is the status of the American-dominated Rhodesian Selection Trust.

The opportunities for African self-development and advance in Congo industry have their price.[7] Aside from a wage system that wrings extra profits from both skilled and unskilled black labor, a revolting paternalism denies the Congolese political rights, functioning trade unions, or free access to knowledge. What of the social amenities for Africans that the Belgians boast of? The Abako, a Bacongo cultural association, in August, 1956, had this to say:

> What they call social works are in reality reinvestments of profits, a budgetary balancing. . . . One can build hospitals, schools, social centers . . . but one does not dare add a cent to the salary of the unfortunate Negro for fear that the treasury will be ruined. Naturally, one must be stupid not to understand that these social works are first and foremost for purely political ends . . . to distract the tourists and to mislead the visitors.

"There can be no question of paying in the Congo to a qualified native workman the same salary as paid in the Congo to the European specialist doing the same job," Belgian authorities state flatly.[8] The Belgian Congo wage formula is the one that Sir Ronald Prain of Rhodesian Selection Trust would like to apply in the Copperbelt mines. He explains it this way: "If, for instance, a [white] carpenter earning £100 a month in Africa would be paid £60 in England, that would be considered the standard rate. An efficiency ratio would then be applied, which would perhaps evaluate the

African carpenter's monthly wage at £30."⁹ In other words, the white worker gets a bonus of two-thirds over the metropolitan rate simply for being *in* Africa, while the other gets a 50 per cent cut for being African. Even if the latter eventually achieves efficiency meriting the "standard rate," his wage will still be 40 per cent below that of his white peers!

Of the 25,726 Africans employed (with 1,816 whites) in the UM mines in 1954, 12 per cent were in skilled and élite categories and received a basic wage equivalent to 82 cents to $2.66 a day, 32 per cent were in semi-skilled categories and got 42 to 60 cents a day, and the rest, 56 per cent, got an unskilled worker's daily wage of 22 to 28 cents.¹⁰ Here is the explanation of UM profits, of dividends of $39,400,000 in 1952, for example, when the total wage bill for Africans *and* whites was $23,680,000.

To return to the matter of United States investments in the Congo, if they have not been welcomed into the inner circle of the mining industry, they have made a little headway in the fringe of secondary industries that have been developing since World War II. The International Basic Commodity Corp. (Rockefeller), for example, has a 30 per cent interest in a textile plant at Albertville. The Pacific Iron and Steel Co. owns a metal fabricating plant at Leopoldville. The United States Plywood Corp. is getting veneer wood from the lower Congo. And there are others, not to mention the various branch plants and agencies of such firms as Singer Sewing Machine and International Business Machines.

But it was for more than this, surely, that the group of American financiers headed by Winthrop Aldrich of the Chase National Bank were looking when they discussed with Belgian authorities early in 1950 the promotion of American investments in the Congo. In 1951, the year following the Tanganyika Concessions transaction, there were loans of $70 million from the World Bank and $15.5 million from the Eximbank toward promoting Congo production and exports. But the private investments that followed after this pump-priming were primarily Belgian, not American.

One possibility of a big break-through has been hopefully considered and not yet altogether abandoned. It concerns the development of what is called "the greatest hydroelectric power site in the world" at Inga Rapids on the Congo River between Leopoldville and Matadi, and the industrial development of the nearby Moanda Plateau. Inga Rapids is said to have four times Niagara Falls' volume of water flow, and if harnessed would yield ten times the power production of the Grand Coulee Dam. All this would cost about a billion or a billion and a half dollars.

An American FOA mission headed by William M. Rand, former president of Monsanto Chemicals, inspected the Inga Rapids area in February, 1954, reporting favorably but emphasizing the magnitude of the undertaking. The Belgians understood quite well what that implied. While the Belgian Colonial Minister, M. Buisseret, favored going ahead with the project, with United States help, financial circles in Brussels including top officers of *Société Générale* and *Union Minière* frowned on a too massive investment of American capital.[11] The Belgian interests in 1956 formed their own syndicate to prepare plans for the project. The nature and extent of American participation remains uncertain.

A Summary of U.S. Postwar Trade and Investment in Africa

Exports from the continent of Africa in 1955 were about five times greater in value than in 1938 and about 46 per cent more than in 1948 (Table 12). And African exports to the United States were more than eleven times greater in value in 1955 than in 1938, 56 per cent greater than in 1948. Since 1950-51 the rate of this increase has tapered off, one reason being that the production and export targets forecast for Africa in the optimistic dawn of Marshall Plan aid to Europe were in many cases only partly realized.

TABLE 12. UNITED STATES SHARE IN AFRICAN EXPORTS AND IMPORTS, 1938-1955[12]
($ millions)

	1938	1948	1950	1955
African Exports				
Total	1,021	3,630	3,770	5,213
To the United States	55	394	494	619
% of total to U. S.	5.4%	10.9	13.0	11.9
% of total U. S. Imports	2.2%	4.9	5.1	5.4
African Imports				
Total	1,570	5,150	4,330	6,322
From the United States	118	785	344	588
% of total from U. S.	7.5%	15.2	7.9	9.3
% of total U. S. Exports	3.8%	7.6	3.6	3.8

As a market for American exports the African territories show a varying pattern. In the continent as a whole, the sharp upsurge in the supply of United States goods that developed during and immediately after World War II gave way to a sharp decline in 1949 as London and Paris moved to curb dollar-buying in the colonies and European industry began reclaiming those areas. With the Korean War boom in African exports, imports from the United States rose again in 1950-51, levelling off thereafter.

The four main suppliers of African exports to the United States in 1955 were the Belgian Congo ($109 million), South Africa ($95 million), Rhodesia ($66 million), and the Gold Coast ($50 million). These represented 23.5 per cent, 9, 13, and 18.6 per cent of the value of total exports from the respective countries. United States imports ranging between $25 million and $40 million also came from each of the following in 1955: British East Africa, Nigeria, Angola, French West Africa, Egypt, Ethiopia, and Liberia.

The greatly increased supply of foreign goods to Africa is the object of sharp international trade competition. This is seen, for example, in the see-sawing tilt between the United States and Britain for dominance in the South African market and for second place after Belgium in the Congo market. The Union of South Africa, which has been and remains by far the continent's largest importer (to the amount of $1,352 million in 1955), got almost one-fifth of its 1955 imports from the United States; in 1948 the proportion was over one-third. The Belgian Congo and Egypt received close to 15 per cent of their 1955 imports from the U.S.A., and Angola nearly 12 per cent. On the other hand, the British territories in Africa restricted their American imports to between two and four per cent, and the French territories took only a slightly larger proportion.

With regard to capital investments, from available statistics it is next to impossible to secure an accurate accounting of the total amount held in Africa by United States corporations and individual shareholders. The figures given by the Department of Commerce are, in the first place, based upon the *book* value of investments, which are acknowledged to be generally much lower than the market or replacement value. Secondly, the figures do not take into account all of the American capital invested in non-United States corporations registered in Canada, Europe, or African territories such as South Africa or Rhodesia. Notwithstanding these reservations, it may be assumed that the investment statistics in Table 13 provide at least an approximate picture of the growing stake of American private capital in Africa.

TABLE 13. DIRECT PRIVATE UNITED STATES INVESTMENTS IN AFRICA, 1943-1955[13]
($ millions)

	1943[a]	1950	1951	1952	1953	1954	1955[b]
South Africa [c]	50	140	157	194	212	216	257
Earnings		25	33	35	40	43	56
Liberia	17	82	104	140	186[d]	230[d]	261[d]
Earnings		15	35	48	35	18	31
Egypt	17	39	44	46	46	54	72
Earning [e]						6	3
British Colonies [f]	27	41	54	66	77	45	56
Earnings		5	21	20	27	15	14
French Colonies	13	31	32	36	37	44	45
Earnings		7	6	5	4	5	6
Rest of Africa [g]	6	19	19	22	26	73	83
Earnings		6	7	10	6	17	19
Africa, Total	130	352	410	504	584	662	774
Earnings		58	102	118	112	104	129

[a] As of May.   [b] Preliminary.   [c] Including South West Africa.   [d] Of which $135 million in 1953, $178 million in 1954, and $205 million in 1955 represented oil company investments, primarily in tankers sailing under the Liberian flag.   [e] Earnings included with Rest of Africa through 1953.   [f] Omitting Northern and Southern Rhodesia and Nyasaland in 1954 and 1955.   [g] Including Northern and Southern Rhodesia and Nyasaland in 1954 and 1955.

Especially noteworthy, apart from the steady rise in investments in most areas of Africa, is the high rate of profit returned. In 1951, when profit-taking reached its zenith, earnings on private United States investments in the continent as a whole reached 25 per cent, as compared with a rate of 17 per cent on the total of such investments in all areas abroad in the same year. In 1955 the earnings on all United States foreign investments was 14.3 per cent, compared with 16.7 per cent in Africa, or 22.6 per cent if we deduct the $205 million for the Liberia-registered oil tankers. With similar deductions made on the total investments in 1953 and 1954 it will be seen that the rate of earnings for the whole of Africa has ranged between 21 and 25 per cent every year since 1951.

Profit-taking at its rawest is seen in the 1951 earnings of 40 per cent in the British colonies (which means here mainly Northern Rhodesia) and 34 per cent in Liberia. The consistently high earnings in South Africa, Liberia, and the British territories contrast sharply with the smaller yields in Egypt and the French colonies.

Africa in 1955 was the recipient of just about four per cent of all direct private foreign investments from the United States. But while over-all American foreign investments in that year were two and a half times the 1943 figure (and about 70 per cent concentrated in Canada and Latin America), those in Africa were six times greater than in 1943. Despite this increase, however, both American and European private investments in most sections of the continent have lagged far behind what Washington, London, and Paris assumed would be attracted by the pumping of public funds into projects for the opening up of Africa for private enterprise.

As regards American capital, the investment "opportunities" in Africa publicized in recent years by the Department of Commerce and other United States agencies have often proved to be more of an American wish than a reality. European and South African capital are still dominant in the continent and while they may be willing to *share* some of the spoils with American capital, they will not voluntarily step aside and let the Americans take over.

American investment interests have made gains, of course, on several African fronts. But with the notable exceptions of Liberia and Rhodesia, these advances are yet largely in the nature of bridgeheads and infiltrations. Whether they will be widened and consolidated does not depend finally on the attitude of European and South African corporate interests. These and the Americans, too, have to reckon with African claims for the repossession of what is theirs by historical right. And the reckoning may quite likely be not so very remote. Suez was the beginning.

Part Three: Issues and Prospects

~~~~~~~~~~~~~~~~~~~~~~~~~~~~~~~~~~~

13. Design for Eurafrica

"AFRICANS ARE NOT opposed to economic, industrial, commercial and political development. On the contrary, this is welcomed. But they would rather forego all the benefits of these developments if they bring in their wake political and economic domination by outsiders."

Such was the view expressed by a delegation from Uganda which came to London in December, 1953, to intercede for the return of the deposed ruler, Kabaka Mutesa. Economic expansion, they pointed out, had not brought peace or well-being to Africans in South Africa, nor did imposition of Federation for the sake of the same objective promise anything good for Africans in Rhodesia and Nyasaland. There was concern, the delegation stated, lest with the economic schemes under way in Uganda—the Kilembe mines and other projects—"Africans . . . will wake up one day to find that they are dominated by powerful factors over which they have no control."[1]

From various sections of the continent comes evidence of a wide-spread bitterness, often erupting in action and not only words. Hungering for a new way of life, the African hears and sees economic expansion schemes talked about and developing all around him. His relationship to them is about like that of a poor man looking through the window of a rich man's restaurant. Except

DESIGN FOR EURAFRICA

that the African is not just an onlooker; he is compelled to give his labor for projects which he knows full well are aimed at the white man's benefit, not his, and point to the prolongation of the white man's domination, not to African freedom. Says Professor Harry R. Rudin of Yale University: "It is ominous"—a stronger word might be used—"that, just when the West needs Africa most, Africans are demanding greater freedom and better economic opportunities for themselves."[2] In this fundamental conflict of interests there is dynamite.

The Economic Squeeze-Play

A prominent member of the Malan-Strijdom regime in South Africa, Dr. T. E. Donges, Minister of the Interior, in 1951 put it very succinctly: "Regarded from the point of view of Europe and America, the answer is still the same—that Africa must be kept within that orbit. Its raw materials are the complement of the highly industrialized Europe and America."

Echoing Dr. Donges, the Chief of the Africa Division, United States Foreign Operations Administration, asserts: "Africa is important economically to both the United States and Western Europe inasmuch as this area is one of the most important producers of certain scarce raw materials in the world today. . . . The concern of the United States is that the various areas of Africa develop into modern societies *and remain in association with the West* [our emphasis.]"[3]

What is the nature of that economic association with the West? It consists, above all, in the promotion of African raw material exports to the outside world and in particular to the dollar market. The dollar surplus thus produced is held in European banks and government accounts. In Britain these funds are called colonial sterling balances; they rose from £446 million ($1,249 million) in June, 1945, to £1,446 million ($4,049 million) at the end of 1955. The importance of the colonial sterling balances to Britain may be judged from the fact that at the end of 1955 the sterling area's gold and dollar reserves stood at only $2,120 million.

"Britain is living on the dollar earnings of the colonies, who are prevented from freely converting their sterling into either goods or dollars, and must willy-nilly run up their balances," said Mr. Oliver Lyttelton (now Lord Chandos) criticizing the policy of the Labor Government in 1951.[4] But he and the Tories continued the same policy. The London *Daily Express* editorialized (June 5, 1954): "To her own colonies this country owes far more than she does to America. . . . There is a further difference from the money owed to the Americans; the balances which are due to colonies are money lent by the poor to the rich."

In view of the often-mentioned financial "help" given by Britain to her colonies through the Colonial Development and Welfare Fund and other government agencies, it should be mentioned in passing that, according to the report of Eden's Economic Secretary to the Treasury (May 14, 1956), in the six years 1950-55 the colonies added £700 million in sterling balances to Britain's finances while London was providing £300 million in government grants and loans to the colonies. One further footnote: the larger portion of such loans went to the white-settler territories in East and Central Africa whereas by far the largest contribution of sterling balances came from the West African colonies, notably Nigeria and the Gold Coast.

The other European powers also profit from the same poor-help-the-rich formula. The Governor of French Guinea, West Africa, noted with pride that that territory's 1952 exports of iron ore, bauxite and diamonds had earned over one billion colonial francs ($5.6 million) in foreign exchange. The Congo's trade provides Belgium with a surplus of many millions of dollars yearly not only with the United States but also with the rest of western Europe. Coffee, cocoa, sisal and other exports from Mozambique and Angola earn considerable sums for Portugal.

The continuation of this arrangement whereby Europe is kept in spending money by control of the trade in African raw materials rests on two assumptions. First, it is assumed either that Africa is and will remain a "passive" continent subject to direct European domination, or that even with the necessity of granting political concessions sooner or later in various areas, the economies of these "liberated" countries, as well as the rest of the continent, can be controlled as before by the metropolitan powers. The second assumption is that the era of go-it-alone colonialism is ended and that there is now required an increasing amount of international collaboration for the control, planning, investment in, and marketing of African raw material production.

Reference, of course, is to international collaboration *outside* the precincts of the United Nations, through various agencies in Europe or Africa, such as the Commission for Technical Cooperation for Africa South of the Sahara, with restricted memberships excluding what South Africa's Minister of External Affairs once spoke of as "so-called do-gooders from outside." In Washington, London and other European capitals this type of collaboration is termed "international responsibility"; in Cairo and elsewhere it has been called "collective colonialism." This new collective approach to the problem of colonial markets was widely discussed during the 'thirties, some proposing it as an answer to Hitler's demand for *"lebensraum."* It was dusted off and embodied in the "Strassbourg plan" which came out of the meeting of the 14-member Consultative Assembly of Europe in September, 1952. The authors of the plan, laying special emphasis on Africa, ordained among other things that there should be an "open door" in the colonies for the business interests and nationals of all member states, whether colonial powers or not, and the coordination of investment programs, region by region and product by product.

Further discussion of these matters took place at the Consultative Assembly's meeting in October, 1955. Committees of experts were set up to make a detailed study of the problems involved. A Franco-German Committee in May, 1956, considered joint action by interests in the two countries in establishing African rubber plantations and other projects. Also in 1956 M. Faure projected a "six-nation common market" in which France and Belgium together with their colonies would be integrated with West Germany, Holland, Italy, and Luxembourg. (British authorities were reluctant to sacrifice their exclusive sterling area benefits for the uncertain advantages of a European common market). The French scheme was formalized in a treaty signed in Rome March 25, 1957. Agreement was reached (subject to parliamentary ratification by the member countries) on the creation of an economic Eurafrica, a principal feature of which would be the development of African oil, mineral and other resources, particularly in France's colonies, by means of a $581 million investment fund pool for the first five years, France and Germany each putting up $200 million.

The Role of the United States

And the United States, what is its relation to this collective planning? Much of it, in fact, stemmed from prodding by the United States. We have earlier referred to the Organization for European Economic Cooperation, which was set up by the ECA early in 1948 bringing together Britain, France, Belgium and Portugal to plan how their colonies could help in the rehabilitation of Europe—with incidental benefits to America. One commentator says of the United States:

> Its world power position manifests itself in Africa in terms of interests in every territory, originating not only from investments but also from Marshall Plan and Mutual Security commitments. From these vantage points, the United States pushes for closer collaboration among the empires of Africa, particularly among those colonies that perform complementary activities required for getting strategic raw materials into American stockpiles. With so many connections, the United States cannot help becoming a principal arbiter in the affairs of Africa.[5]

True, there are finance groupings in Europe that would like to hold what they have in their colonial empires and keep the United States at least at arm's length. While we have seen some examples of the acceptance of the collaboration of American mining interests in Morocco, French West Africa, Nigeria, Rhodesia, and South Africa, a noteworthy development of the last two or three years is the emergence of a number of mining and other industrial projects financed by combinations of exclusively European capital. Thus we find Franco-German collaboration in the Mekambo iron ore fields of French Equatorial Africa and in various development projects in Morocco; and joint Franco-German-Italian investment in Southern Algeria and in hydroelectric power development in French Guinea. Also in the latter territory French, Italian, German and Swiss companies are contributing equal shares of capital toward the development of an aluminum industry. In the Congo there has been Anglo-Belgian agreement to invite West Germany's cooperation in supplying heavy industrial and transport equipment. It is doubtful, however, that this pattern of investment can extend very far without American participation; American capital is indispensable for the Europeans' bigger African schemes.

One of the most brazen schemes of investment in the "collective colonialism" pattern was the $20 billion African Development Co. proposed almost a decade ago in a British-edited Rhodesian journal.[6] The plan for this company, the editor said, had "been discussed in various influential quarters in Great Britain, America, and France and other countries of Western Europe." The description of the project was rhapsodic. "The whole Anglo-Saxon bloc," it was declared, "must go into profit-making development; something which is going to develop entirely new sources of wealth, provide new markets, and smash right through the whole idea of reduction and restraint. The solution is an African Development Company . . . it would be a commercial concern—out for profits—large expanding profits." And the United States government and its citizens would be welcome to join in. This was the great Capricorn Africa project.

African and world events have necessitated some trimming of plans. But the itch for African profits remains among Americans as well as others. "Our national self-interest, our need for raw materials and for new world markets," said the president of the New York Stock Exchange, Mr. Keith Funston, early in 1956, call for expanding American foreign investments during the next five years. If American investors answer the call, he said, "we can hopefully expect to see in the next twenty-five years a boom in underdeveloped countries such as the world has never known."[7]

Business Week (Oct. 31, 1953) also saw the vision and depicted the kind of world that would be achieved within the next quarter century during which the United States invested abroad $5 billion annually and got in return $20 billion worth of raw materials:

> Every businessman and every school boy will be acquainted with exotic new names. We'll talk knowingly of copper from Entebbe and Mufulira, of manganese from Amapa and Accra, of zinc from Perth and Bibao and Monterrey, of tungsten from O'okiep and Oruro . . . of oil from Kuwait and Maracaibo. . . . Americans will take longer vacations . . . most of the big hotels in the newer developments will be built and operated by familiar U.S. hotel chains. . . . And it's a safe bet that most natives on the tourist route will speak good Americanese.

Where is Europe in that dream picture? Where is anybody but America?

The Colonial Pattern of Production

The stress on raw material exports in the Eurafrica scheme has its counterpart in the checks on industrialization not directed to that end. What is sought ideally is a mining, plantation, and large-scale farming economy under European (or American) management and control, with allowance made for some processing of raw materials to reduce transport costs, for some light consumer-goods production, and for African-managed agricultural production in territories where there is little or no European settler population, provided the marketing of the produce in such areas is on European terms and remains under direct or indirect European administration.

The relatively higher degree of industrialization found in some of the white settler territories, South Africa, Southern Rhodesia, the Belgian Congo, and North Africa, does not mean that they are exceptions to the Eurafrica pattern. The deliberate exclusion of the mass of the indigenous population from full integration in the productive process in these countries results in a lopsided, unstable, and dependent economy just as in other non-white parts of Africa. There being no developed internal market, production is geared as elsewhere to the requirements of the external market. The well-known British economist, S. H. Frankel, points out that as a result of its Jim Crow productive system the Union of South Africa's economy "is still as dependent on extractive industry and on capital from abroad to finance it as it was at the beginning of the century."[8]

To continue the subordination of Africa's economy to that of the West, concentrating all major economic effort on maintaining and expanding African production for the requirements of European-American markets, is Point One of the Eurafrica planners.

European Immigration Schemes

Point Two is to populate Eastern, Central and Southern Africa, where European settlers have already gone, with as many more as can be secured and as quickly as possible, in order to fulfill the West's economic aims and insure its continued hegemony in the continent. In the pursuit of Point Two Europe's relationship to Africa is often likened to the opening up of the western United States. It does not matter that the analogy is false in several respects; the aim is the same.

"A hundred thousand Belgian colonists before ten years or the Congo may well no longer be Belgian," said the *Federation des Associations de Colons du Congo* in 1952, and others have set a target of 800,000 for the Congo's Belgian population in 50 years.[9] "We need a hundred thousand more Portuguese in Angola within the next ten years. Then there will be no nonsensical talk about African independence in this country," says a civil servant in that colony.[10] Sir Roy Welensky has declared that he wanted to see

DESIGN FOR EURAFRICA 165

a white population of 500,000 in Rhodesia within the next decade, and other Rhodesians even speak of the white population equalling that of the Africans by 1999.[11]

The actual number of immigrants is nothing like the figures so wildly talked about. The largest proportionate European population increase in the recent period has taken place in Southern Rhodesia. There the gross intake (not deducting emigration) came to 13,700 in 1955 and 17,119 in 1956 (it averaged 12,920 in 1946-1951.) And getting that number entailed considerable promotional work and expense. Most of the new Rhodesians in 1955, it is worth noting, came from South Africa—about twice as many as from Britain. Among the other immigrants were 81 Americans and people from 28 other countries as diverse as Brazil, Portugal and Yugoslavia.

In explaining its "policy of encouraging as many white immigrants to enter the country as it can absorb"—making the "white" quite explicit—the Rhodesian Government differentiates between unskilled work for which there is a "large potential supply of African labor," and "skilled labor and . . . technical, administrative and professional functions of practically all undertakings," representing the province of the "white settlers."[12] If it is implied that white immigrants are not to compete with Africans for their type of work, it is just as surely implied that skilled whites have nothing to fear from African competition.

And here we come nearer the heart of the matter. The technicians and others are not asked to come help train Africans to play their part in all phases of the expanding productive process. On the contrary, they are being brought in with the objective of trying to keep the existing economic relations between white and black permanently frozen.

Lord Malvern defined the pattern some 20 years ago when, as Prime Minister of Southern Rhodesia, he said, "in the European areas the black man will be welcomed, when, tempted by wages, he offers his services as a laborer; but it will be on the understanding that he shall merely assist and not compete with the white man."[13] In the present period, since it happens that Africans are increasingly "tempted" by wages to keep from starving, one finds the same idea voiced again and again by the upholders of the right of white rule. South Africa's Minister of Native Affairs, Dr. H. F. Verwoerd, for instance, states his opinion that "Natives" on farms are no more an integral part of the economy than the oxen, and that "South Africa can function industrially and commercially without economic integration being necessary."[14] In Kenya, Mr. E. A. Vasey, Minister for Finance and Development, explains, "Our economic structure developed in three horizontal layers: with the African providing the worker, the unskilled laborer, as the broad base; the Asian, the artisans and traders, as the middle layer; the European, with a few Asians, the executives and the administrators, the top layer."[15]

In 1954 the average income of male wage-earning Africans in Kenya's private industry was the equivalent of $165 for the year while that of the whites was $3,430 (the Asian receiving $1,134).[16] In the Belgian Congo in the same year the average per capita income of 25,700 employed whites was $7,620; for 1,146,000 employed Africans it was $190.[17] We have already noted the income of black and white mine workers in Rhodesia and South Africa. The economic Jim Crow pattern is found wherever whites have settled in Africa.[18]

There was a period in the 'thirties when South Africa had some 300,000 poor whites, about 15 per cent of the total white population, produced by agricultural dislocation, general economic depression, and the pressure of lower-paid non-white labor. The "poor white problem" was eradicated by the Government's "civilized labor" program. This consisted of such measures as substituting whites for non-whites in government and municipal employment at increased wages, establishing quotas of "skilled" jobs reserved for whites in building and other industries, awarding preferential contracts to firms that would guarantee all-white employment, and penalizing those that failed to employ a given percentage of whites.

Year after year the statutory wall between white and black labor in South Africa has been reenforced with new laws such as the Native Building Workers Amendment Act, making it illegal to employ Africans on skilled building work in other than "Native areas," and the Industrial Conciliation Amendment Act (1956) which gives the Minister of Labor authority to restrict any work in any industry, trade, or occupation to "persons of a specified race or persons belonging to a specified class."

The line between the African's permissible work and that of the white artisan is often very finely drawn. The managing director of a building concern in East London, South Africa, received a sentence of a £10 ($28) fine or 20 days' jail as a result of a government building inspector having come upon one of the concern's African laborers "with a trowel in his hand applying cement." The court ignored the excuse of the defendant's attorney that "my client gave his foreman strict instructions that the laborer should only use his fingers or a piece of wood to fill in the openings with cement, believing that it was legal."[19]

In South Africa they are at least honest, sometimes, about what they are doing. "Negroes can do skilled labor if trained for it; that is why we must never [train] them." In contrast is this lying bombast: "Rhodesians (i.e., whites) do not fear the black man. ... Even in 100 years' time no Native will be able to do the job I am doing today. You have only to look at America, where the Negro has had 300 years of association with the white man. How far has he got?"[20]

There is the testimony[21] of some Rhodesian employers who have allowed Africans to break through the racial barrier in industry. "Our African crane drivers [asbestos mine] are as good as any European crane driver." "Africans learn shoe machine work very quickly—sometimes more quickly, and better, than Europeans." "All our employees [agricultural machinery] start by knowing nothing. Some, after 3 months, can operate turret lathes costing £5,000." "The individual productivity of the African is equal to that of the European at all levels of jig operation." Obviously, it's not that the African can't do the job, and as well as the European, if given a chance; they just don't want him to— except, sometimes, at a lower wage.

The privileged position of the whites, derived from written and unwritten discriminatory labor codes, is the basis of white political solidarity in the settler countries of Africa. Even the lowliest European immigrant is made to believe that his superior station in life, as measured not only against the African's status but against his own former less prosperous condition back home, can be won and maintained only by supporting and preserving the *status quo* of white domination. In this light the importance of the immigration programs in relation to the Eurafrica design becomes quite clear.

Professor Rayford W. Logan of Howard University reports on the consequences of the rising number of French settlers in West Africa, particularly in the Ivory Coast: "Almost every plane and boat brings *'petits Français'* who compete with Africans for jobs. Some Africans received 6,000 West African francs, about $35, a month for doing the same work for which Frenchmen received almost four times as much. Sometimes Africans were discharged after training Frenchmen for a job. In the large department store, Pariscoa, in Abidjan, all salespeople were French girls."[22]

Rather than upgrade black mine workers, South African companies since 1948 have recruited more than 3,000 Germans, Italians, British, Dutch and other Europeans to be trained for skilled and supervisory jobs in the gold mines. As of November, 1955, there were 579 white South Africans as against 885 immigrants in the Government-operated miners' training schools. Meanwhile, white South Africans go to work in the Kilembe mines of Uganda or on the Kariba project in Rhodesia, for which several hundred Italian immigrant workers were also brought in.

The Northern Rhodesia copper companies are likewise concerned with maintaining their top layer of white miners. In March, 1955, the companies collectively put up something over $1 million to establish a technical college to give training to "young Europeans." A South African was selected to head the school. Applications for training were received from as far away as New Zealand and Singapore. Yet no technical training school for Africans exists in Northern Rhodesia, and not even adequate secondary schools. The necessity for outside recruitment of white miners in Rhodesia and South Africa arises from the fact that such work does not rate very high in settler prestige, and there is consequently a large turnover in the labor force as the whites, after accumulating a little capital with a few years in the mines, quit and buy a farm or a small business, or return home to Europe.

Another example of the demand for immigrants in industry is seen in the case of the Rhodesia Railways. With the expansion of the system there arose in 1954 an acute shortage of firemen, shunters and guards. Africans numbered 70 per cent of the railway employees but were barred from such categories of work. A proposal by an African representative in the Federal Parliament that the shortage be met by opening the jobs and training facilities to Africans was rejected by the Minister of Transport and Communications, Sir Roy Welensky, one-time locomotive engineer. But young Rhodesians did not want such work. Neither did young Britons, as strenuous recruiting efforts in England disclosed. So the search was extended up and down the European continent, and help was secured from the Inter-Governmental Committee for European Migration at Geneva. Early in 1956 the first results of these efforts appeared with the signing of 288 railway workers, mainly from Italy and Greece.

Nevertheless, the flow of immigrants everywhere remains inadequate to supply existing industrial demands. And as a result of this fact and the Africans' persistent pressing forward, it becomes more and more difficult, if not impossible, to prevent the Jim Crow labor code from being ignored in practice, even though still upheld in theory and law. With fewer than 4,000 new settlers coming to South Africa yearly and estimates of additional skilled and semi-skilled workers needed in the country running to 100,000 (January, 1956), it is to be expected that Strijdom and Company would be dismayed at the increasing number of Africans getting jobs hitherto restricted to whites in manufacturing industries (though not at the white workers' wages, of course). The new mines, too, find it necessary to run full-page advertisements in the popular African magazines with "Wages are good!" in bold type and pictures of "comfortable modern houses" for the black miners *and* their families. But the users of the largest proportion of African labor, the farms and most of the mines, continue to rely as usual on inexperienced migrant workers from the "native reserves" and outside territories. The same partial gains by black labor in the newer sectors of industry have occurred in other areas of white settlement, except for the Portuguese colonies where agriculture has few industrial competitors and slave labor conditions are consequently almost universal.

More Europeans Require More Land

Let us now glance at a few of the current land settlement schemes designed to accommodate additional European immigrants. In the Congo, settlers (Belgians only) are sought to take over a number of 1,235 acre farming plots in the Katanga Province. In Angola, to which the Salazar regime once exiled its political enemies, batches of Portuguese settlers have been arriving to establish farming communities on the high plateau of the southern Province of Huila. Some $40 million was scheduled to be spent for the development and preparation of this area for colonization. And in Mozambique 6,000 families from Portugal are being settled in the Limpopo Valley; the choice areas in the colony reserved for European settlement total more than 8,000,000 acres.

As though Mau Mau meant nothing, Kenya's European Settlement Board continues to invite English gentlemen with either big or little capital to come farm in the White Highlands, allocating large sums to assist them. Plots of from 500 to 1,000 acres are offered young tenant farmers with an unconditionally Government-guaranteed return of £5 ($14) per acre planted.

A Rhodesian announcement in June, 1956, stated: "Ranches of 15,000 acres, each manned by keen young Rhodesians, South Africans, or Britons, are being planned . . . [in] the emptiest well-watered land in Southern Africa. The northeastern third of Northern Rhodesia produces nothing except a bare subsistence for the 250,000 Natives who live there." The "bare subsistence" part is quite true, and for the simple reason that the able-bodied men have nearly all been drawn off to work in the copper mines and elsewhere. Are ranches for white owners the remedy? Another Northern Rhodesia project, backed by the Rhodesian Selection Trust, aims at settling nearly 3,000 European farms on reclaimed and irrigated land on the Kafue Flats. This scheme is linked with another large farming project in Southern Rhodesia.

These plans, it should be remembered, involve considerable governmental expenditure for purchase and clearing of land, loans to immigrant settlers, equipment, crop subsidies, technical assistance, and so forth. The keen young ranchers in Northern Rhodesia, for instance, are each to get 300 young breeding cattle on loan from the Government, returning them in five or seven years after their herds have grown to a thousand head. It is hardly necessary to say that Africans are far from pleased by the influx of Europeans to take over more land, and they certainly do not relish paying taxes into a public treasury which spends large sums procuring and aiding the new settlers.

But the Africans' greatest bitterness arises from the forced removal of scores of thousands of their people as a result of the immigration and "development" schemes which make up the Eurafrica design. The provision of more farms, plantations and ranches for whites has caused the uprooting of entire African communities. The expansion of white residential areas and industrial sites has meant the evacuation of Africans living on the outskirts of the towns to more distant parts. Hydroelectric developments such as the Kariba installations are planned without thought for the welfare of Africans whose land, the source of their sustenance for generations, is to be flooded; the people are simply moved willy-nilly out of the way. That an alternative hydroelectric project on the Kafue River would have involved the displacement of only a thousand Africans instead of 50,000 counted for nothing in the decision in favor of Kariba.

We have been told about some of the South African make-room-for-whites operations: about the pre-dawn arrival of 2,000 heavily armed police to enforce the evacuation of African families in February, 1955, from Sophiatown, seven miles outside Johannesburg, to a more distant site; about the current plans for the eviction of 100,000 African, Indian and Colored families from their homes and businesses in 16 of the principal towns and cities. But there have also been mass evacuations, not so widely publicized, in South West Africa, from a half dozen or more towns in Southern Rhodesia, from land "wanted for development" in the Cholo area of Nyasaland. In Tanganyika, where 400,000 acres of customary Masai land were handed over to Europeans for ranching and dairying, and where the Meru protested to the United Nations against being brutally driven off their land, a South African company recently applied for a 99-year lease for a 60,000-acre sugar cane plantation. There were strong African objections; the project was dropped—inadequate rail facilities was the explanation given.

Another more subtle method of wiping out traditional African land holdings and simultaneously augmenting the labor supply has recently come into vogue in some territories. It is typified in the operation of Southern Rhodesia's Land Husbandry Act (1951), which, according to Prime Minister R. S. Garfield Todd, would "turn 300,000 African communalists into capitalists" by substituting individual ownership and sale of land for the customary system of communal tenure. The new plan, Mr. Todd affirms, will make the Africans "farmers in their own right, on their own land, land they can sell or will as they please." To implement the scheme costs $19.6 million, $11.2 million of which is to come from the African farmers themselves. (Their cash income was estimated at $9.8 million in 1955, about one-third that of white Rhodesian farmers.) Originally planned as a 40-year program, it was decided in 1955 to complete the change-over within *five* years.

Similar plans have been proposed in Uganda. In Kenya the consolidation of African land holdings—begun with the Kikuyu as a "security" measure and then extended to other tribes—is to be followed by the registration of individual land titles. All this is in line with the view that free land exchange is the key to prosperity in Africa, as expounded by the British East Africa Royal Commission. That body strongly urged that "The traditional policy of 'land reservation' and of safeguarding sectional interests, whether of Africans or non-Africans, must be abandoned in the interests of the community as a whole."[23]

An apt comment on this precept is given by an Oxford don who writes:

> The protection of the European Highlands [in Kenya] is equated wth African tribal reservations and thus a sort of seeming balance is achieved by demanding the abolition, in principle and impartially, of all restrictions on land sales safeguarding "sectional" interests. This apparently would ensure "mobility" and "development." Both Whites and Africans should henceforth be equally free in principle to dine at the Ritz. . . . On precisely the same grounds, the British (mindful of the "success" of the second enclosure movement at home) laid the foundation of despair and stagnation by introducing private ownership first in Bengal and then elsewhere [in India]. . . . Far from encouraging full production, private ownership of land has encouraged speculative sterilization of land in Kenya.[24]

There have been no signs of the relaxation of barriers to African possession of land in the sacred white precincts of Kenya and other territories. It is only the Africans who, either voluntarily or involuntarily, are to abandon their traditional land holdings. Most of those in urban employment in Rhodesia and other settler countries still regard their collectively held land as "home," because their wages, based on the "cheap" migrant labor scale, simply cannot permanently support them, let alone their families, in the towns. A decent living wage is required before these workers are asked to embark on private ownership of real estate and give up what is left to them of their security in the land. The African knows what a bird in hand is worth as well as anybody else.

It is true that since the war there has arisen a small number of more prosperous African cash-crop farmers in East and Central Africa who are eager to enlarge their land holdings and have already done so in areas where freehold rights are permitted. They, of course, stand to benefit by the break-up of the traditional land tenure system. Many of them now qualify as Prime Minister Todd's "capitalists" to the extent that they are employers of labor on their farms. But it is a morbid kind of joke to talk about turning 300,000 "communalists" into "capitalists"! Yet it is revealing. For one thing on which the white ruling circles in this part of Africa stake their chances of staying on and holding what they have is for there to be quickly developed a black elite class reasonably satisfied with their own personal station in life who will dissociate themselves from revolutionary African demands and join with the whites in opposing the claims of a dispossessed and landless proletariat.

The European immigration schemes and their consequences are generating African antagonism. It can be seen and heard on all sides. Now and then white voices are heard, too, as in the case of Bishop Seabastiao de Resend of Mozambique, who has warned of the danger in alienating all the best land for white occupancy.[25] An American commentator, Dr. William O. Brown, Director of the African Research and Studies Program at Boston University, predicts: "As permanent European dwellers increase in urban areas of French West and Equatorial Africa and in the rural and urban areas of Portuguese Africa, the probability of race conflicts will be enhanced, even conceding the wide tolerance of the French and Portuguese in matters of race contact."[26] In British areas the probability of conflicts is multiplied by Anglo-Saxon intolerance.

The Question of Political Control

Africa and its people must be kept in the Western orbit, politically as well as economically. On that the foreign interests and rulers in that continent all agree. But when it comes to the question of How, they go their several ways. There are many differently shaped political mansions lining a one-way street in Eurafrica.

At one end is the Dominion of South Africa with a program of depriving Africans, Indians and the Colored of even the slightest participation in the affairs of government—"Either the white man dominates or the black man takes over," said Herr Strijdom. Next door is Rhodesia with its white population impatiently waiting for dominion status and allowing some token political representation, at least for the present, to Africans. In their neighboring colonies the Portugese deny that any question of political rights for Africans exists. The Belgians said the same about the Congo until recently, but now talk differently. In the British East African colonies, where plans for developing another white-ruled dominion went awry, varying and complex forms of political concessions are being tried in an effort to stave off the full rights and dominant control demanded by Africans.

At the other end of the street there is a different architectural pattern: "independence with interdependence"—within the French

Union in the case of Tunisia and Morocco, within the British Commonwealth for Ghana and Nigeria. This pattern, forced upon the French by their disastrous experience of attempting to "assimilate" unwilling peoples, is also designed for sub-Sahara lands. That the British decided their course in West Africa before African pressures reached the crisis stage of full revolt is most likely due to London's eagerness not to jeopardize the valuable economic assets represented by that area's exports, and to the fortunate absence of white settler complications there.

The *Nigerian Tribune* (June 18, 1956) comments on the passing of "the ancient romance of Crown and Empire," observing that "The problem of modern British Imperialism is one of fields of investment and business expansion, and experience has shown that this new imperialism does not require the political subjugation of backward nations. America is an example of the new world force. All Britain requires today is a guarantee that power is transferred to those who will make the free colonies a safe field for British investment." So likewise with the new French interdependence.

In both the Tunisian Neo-Destour and Moroccan Istiqlal parties elements favoring the retention of ties with NATO, Franco-American policies, and non-interference with French investment interests (currently estimated at $8.5 billion in Morocco) won ascendancy over other elements (called "extremists" by the French) represented by Salah ben Youssef in Tunisia and Allah el-Fassi in Morocco, who desired less dependence on France, curbs on French economic control in their countries, and closer ties with Cairo and the Arab world. But with France still fighting to hold Algeria, and with 100,000 French troops yet maintained in Morocco and more thousands in Tunisia, "moderate" leaders in the new North African states, under pressure from their people, were compelled to adopt an increasingly hostile attitude toward the government in Paris and to echo popular support of the Algerian cause. "It is inconceivable," declared M. Bourguiba in March, 1956, "that Tunisia on one side and Morocco on the other should enjoy their independence while Algeria, which lies between them, remains under the colonialist yoke."

Then came the astounding French action of kidnapping five top Algerian leaders flying on a peace mission from Rabat to Tunis aboard a Moroccan-registered plane as guests and under the protection of the Sultan of Morocco. And a few days after that event, which was October 22, 1956, came the Anglo-French invasion of

Egypt, provoking still further hatred of France in North Africa. Can Africans be expected to listen seriously to further French talk of "independence with interdependence?"

The policy of colonial self-government to which the British claim devotion has been ironically but not too inaccurately defined as "self-government at the right time, in the right place, and by the right people." One recalls the sudden military intervention in British Guiana in 1953 to oust the popularly elected government of the People's Progressive Party, whose policies were considered inimical to British and American interests. Shortly thereafter Gold Coast's Prime Minister Nkrumah found it necessary to suspend two prominent labor leaders from membership in the Convention People's Party because of their alleged identification with the World Federation of Trade Unions. Mr. E. C. Turkson-Ocran, one of those expelled, had organized the strikes which set off the Positive Action campaign in 1950 and led to Nkrumah's rise to power. The Prime Minister also found it necessary to make public statements giving reassurances to foreign investors, and announcing the barring of "persons who are proved to its satisfaction to be active Communists" from employment in the Government's public services. The latter action and the banning of foreign "subversive" publications in the Gold Coast were shortly followed by parallel decrees by African authorities in Nigeria. Even the more conservative organs of British opinion were led to express satisfaction with the course of self-government in West Africa.

Although the political institutions and stated aims of government vary widely throughout the continent, the ultimate *means* of maintaining political authority is always and everywhere the same —force. It is only when a blow-up occurs, as in Kenya, that outsiders are reminded of what the rule of force in Africa means. But it operates silently, too, and without cease. The Belgians once boasted of the absence of conflict in the Congo, but they did not mention the several thousand "political" and "dangerous" exiles (*rélégués pour motifs politiques, rélégués dangereux*), sent to confinement in isolated villages. One seldom hears of anything at all happening in Portuguese Angola but there, too, "objectors" are regularly sent to penal settlements on the southern coast or to the island of Sao Thome.[27]

It is logical that appeals for the cooperation of other powers in the organization of a continent-wide military apparatus should come from that country's rulers who have the greatest vested interest in perpetuating white domination over Africans and who have built up the most elaborate and ruthless system of rule by force within their own borders. Again and again have South African Premiers, from Malan down to the present, called for the formation of a pan-African "defense" scheme along the lines of NATO and SEATO. This ambition remains as yet still-born, but the South African Government did prevail upon the United States and Britain in 1952 (two years after the uranium agreement) to provide it with a large supply of weapons of war—partly to be used, the agreement stated, for "internal security." South Africa's Minister of Defense isn't quite sure whether the "master design" of the "potential aggressor" is "to arm Black Africa" or "conquest by subversion;" but he is certain that "for the West the battle for Africa has begun. . . . What the West now needs more than ever is a Southern African bastion."[28]

Alongside this one must place a new development in South Africa's foreign policy. The attitude of unconcealed contempt and hostility toward the new African-ruled states has been officially discarded. African officials of Nigeria and Ghana have lately been invited to receptions given by South African officials in London and Washington—and they attended! (Will it happen next in Capetown?) The apparent objective of the new policy is two-fold: from the Dominion's point of view to guard against the new African governments coming to the aid of their oppressed brothers in South Africa (we don't bother you; you don't bother us); and, in the larger context of British Commonwealth relations, to establish the basis for Ghana and Nigeria to cooperate even with South Africa in the pursuit of Eurafrican aims (we must all plan together for our common good). One suspects British and perhaps American promptings off-stage. There is obvious incongruity between this diplomatic line and the Defense Minister's mouthings quoted above, but look again at his last sentence.

Up to the present time United States diplomatic and economic support has been provided for the maintenance of European power in Africa wherever it was firmly in control or for as long as it could hold on. But as soon as self-government approached realization, the State Department gentlemen have performed a quick turnabout and rushed to embrace newly found friends. There are French charges that the Americans did not even wait in North Africa, but played both sides of the street at the same time.

Ambassador Dillon in Paris hails the new "interdependence"

between France and Morocco and Tunisia as "a relationship which we can count upon as one of the bulwarks of the free world," and then goes on to say that the problem in Algeria "is quite different and the solution must undoubtedly be different . . . the United States stands solidly behind France" there.[29] Yes, with American-made helicopters, too, it might be added. In Rhodesia Mr. L. V. Steere, the American consul-general, endorses the principle of the Africans' advancement but states his belief that it will be "several decades or generations" before they are sufficiently developed to play a role of full partnership in the Federation.[30] He takes his cue from those in power who say that in the distant future (Sir Roy Welensky puts it at 100 or 200 years' time) the Africans may earn the right to "become equal partners."

In the summer of 1956 the retiring South African Ambassador, Dr. J. E. Holloway, called at the State Department in Washington to say farewell. Mr. Dulles, after remarking that "a nation such as South Africa which produces men of character will always solve its own problems," said that he regretted he knew so little about the Ambassador's country. The reason, he explained, was that he only went to areas where there were problems, and he had no problem with South Africa.[31]

No problem with South Africa—the uranium production program is going all right, and the country is safely on the "free world's side." What else to worry about?

The fatal defect of the Eurafrica plans and calculations is that they under-estimate—if they do not entirely omit—the African.

14. They Won't Stand for It!

AFRICA IS IN REVOLT. It is in revolt, in the final analysis, against a status of inferiority imposed for non-African economic objectives, usually through direct or indirect alien political domination. America hears only fragmentary reports of the armed conflict and major strikes and protest demonstrations, yet the struggle goes forward in a variety of unrecorded manifestations of non-acceptance of subordination. Sustained, disciplined, organized action grows. But in the face of repression and provocation people will fight even with stones. The degree of mass organization and the way in which organized demands are answered determine the pace and form of the people's forward movement.

There is a remarkable identity between the smoking ban and boycott of European merchandise by both North African Arabs and Kenya Africans. During the height of the Mau Mau revolt in 1953-1954 not only the Kikuyu but all Africans in the area of Nairobi stopped drinking the white man's beer, wearing his hats, and puffing his cigarettes. A total boycott of the buses continued for months despite government intimidation of picketers and guarantees of safety to riders. The people readily joined in this form of reprisal in Kenya just as in Morocco or Algeria. Particularly in the latter country, as Americans have been told, "the attitude toward the native people sometimes approaches that of many whites toward Negroes in the United States in slavery days."[1] (Those slavery days, unfortunately, are still with us so far as attitudes go.)

A quality which undergirds African resistance to alien overlordship is the way people act together. It was evident, for example, in the response to the general strike call in Algiers marking the 126th anniversary (July 5, 1956) of French conquest: the city completely paralyzed, streets and cafes, shops and government offices all deserted. It is manifested, too, when a whole community will remain mute and suffer barbarous collective punishment to protect one of their own. Although there were the usual stool-pigeons and traitors during the Kenya war, the whites out of their fearful uncertainty of distinguishing "loyal Kikuyu" from Mau Mau drove 50,000 men, women and children in one sweep ("Operation Anvil") out of Nairobi into detention camps. Wherever the scene of conflict, it is the same: in the countryside non-combatants smuggle food to combatants; in a city street skirmish a gun is passed from hand to hand until someone escapes with it.

With such rock-like solidarity there can be no such thing as submission. Algerian prisoners jeer at their captors and spit on the ground. Black South African demonstrators being taken off to jail sing their songs of national liberation and lift their arms high with the raised thumb salute of freedom. In Kenya's Mau Mau detention camps the prisoners conduct sit-down strikes, refusing to labor at assigned tasks.

South African and Rhodesian Tinder Boxes

The white settler population below the Sahara is most largely concentrated in the Union of South Africa and the Rhodesias (as in Algeria above the Sahara), and in these territories employs the most direct and blatant forms of racial domination. But repression can boomerang. The recent advances in the Africans' organizational strength and unity in Rhodesia followed from the imposition of political federation with enlarged settler control, and in South Africa they resulted directly from the ruling Nationalists' spate of self-serving legislation.

The African National Congress in South Africa (ANC) came of age as an organization of mass struggle when it launched the Campaign of Defiance of Unjust Laws on D-Day—D for Defiance —June 26, 1952. The ANC and South African Indian Congress (SAIC), which joined in the campaign, had written Prime Minister Malan early in the year demanding repeal of the Pass Laws and other of the more oppressive edicts and forewarning him of the plan of defiance unless this was done. The Government responded with threats of full reprisal "for inciting subversive activities."[2]

Long months of intensive educational and organizational preparation throughout the country led up to D-Day. On a Sunday in early April great assemblies were held in all the major cities where a solemn pledge to support the campaign was taken. The *New York Times* (April 7, 1952) reported how "several thousand non-whites marched in Fordsburg Freedom Square [Johannesburg] to the tune of Paul Robeson songs played over a loud speaker."

The defiance volunteers were carefully selected and instructed. They went forth in groups to enter the "Reserved for Whites" sections of post offices, railway stations, and other public places, and to act in defiance of pass law and curfew restrictions. And when arrested, they went to jail without protest. In cities and towns all over the country batches of volunteers went into action. Women marched along beside the men and were of key importance in the success of the campaign. The people came from all walks of life, African, Indian, Colored, and—near the end of the campaign—some whites. All went to jail in defiance of unjust laws. By the close of 1952 over 8,000 participants in the campaign had been imprisoned.

The reaction of South African whites was at first one of shock. It was inconceivable to them that Africans were capable of such planning, organization and discipline. Then shock turned to alarm as wild rumors of the imminence of violent revolt began to spread, fanned by the news of the Mau Mau in Kenya. Riots that occurred were attributed to the Defiance Campaign, although not a single instance of violence occurred during the volunteer actions and arrests, special safeguards having been taken against provocation or irresponsible conduct.

The atmosphere of near-hysteria suited the Government's purposes. Even before the campaign started there had been a number of arrests of African, Indian and other progressive leaders, and a newspaper supporting the resistance movement and the cause of African freedom had been banned. As the campaign developed momentum, the sentences (including floggings) handed out to the arrested volunteers increased in severity. The entire leadership of the ANC and SAIC was called to stand trial. The Minister of "Justice" issued orders to the police to "shoot first" when there was trouble with "Natives." Then in February, 1953, with the Defiance Campaign as the stated reason, two laws were rushed through Parliament, one (Public Safety Law) enabling the Government arbitrarily to declare a "state of emergency" and assume absolute dictatorship powers, the other (Criminal Law Amendment Act) providing penalties of up to five years imprisonment, a $1,400 fine, and 15 strokes of the lash for participation in or support of defiance actions such as had been going on. These laws made continuation of the campaign impracticable.

The campaign failed of its objective of winning equality and justice, but it nevertheless achieved much in laying a more solid foundation for continuing the fight. The ANC became firmly based on wide popular support as never before, a younger and more militant leadership was elected to guide the Congress, unity of action toward democratic goals embracing all national and racial sections of the population was cemented, and tremendously important lessons in organization were learned.

The Defiance Movement spilled over into Northern Rhodesia. In 1953 the African National Congress of that country began a Challenge the Color Bar Campaign in the main towns. As crowds of Africans watched, "defiers" entered post offices, shops, cafes and public bars customarily reserved to whites. They also included one or two churches. In succeeding years the campaign shifted to the use of the boycott. Butcher shops and other stores were thus taught the necessity of serving Africans over the counter side by side with whites instead of on the outside through special hatches as had been done. European and Indian-owned shops have also been picketed for over-charging Africans. The campaign during 1956 was in part directed toward stopping Africans from buying anything but bare necessities in the stores, it being charged that prices in general were far too high in comparison with African wages.

A law was passed to bar the boycotting weapon, but the court upheld the right. The police were quick to intervene anyway wherever it could be charged that the picketers were resorting to force. But the use of force by whites to eject Africans from Jim Crow establishments went unnoticed. Mr. Dixon Konkola, president of the African Railway Workers Union, a member of the Congress national executive, and now president of the Northern Rhodesia Trades Union Congress, was arrested and sentenced to six months at hard labor in 1953 as a consequence of leading an orderly anti-Jim Crow demonstration.

In January, 1955, the means was found of sending to jail the secretary of the Congress, Kenneth Kaunda, and its president, Harry

Nkumbula, who was educated at Makerere College, Uganda, and the London School of Economics. They were charged with possessing prohibited publications in the form of books and pamphlets issued by the Communist Party of Great Britain. The magistrate in the case acknowledged that the publications were harmless if read by persons of intelligence and experience, and he admitted that the defendants were educated and intelligent. All the same, he maintained, the publications were illegal and "what is important is that both the men and the books are political."[3] And so the defendants were sentenced to two months' imprisonment at hard labor.

A Rhodesian newspaper, describing the preparations for the release of the men at the end of their sentence, tells much about the political temperature of the country:

NKUMBULA RELEASE: N. R. POLICE STAND BY. . . . All day tomorrow two police riot squad platoons will be standing by armed with sten guns, rifles and tear gas to prevent any outbreaks of violence during the celebrations and demonstrations by the African National Congress to mark the release of Harry Nkumbula from jail. The celebrations begin with a parade in which it is expected several thousand Africans will pass through part of the European township. A program has been planned for the whole day, including dancing and addresses by religious leaders and officials of the African Congress.[4]

It was the Africans' day. Whites stayed out of the way and the police show of force curbed not one song or speech.

In the Legislative Council of Northern Rhodesia an ex-missionary representative in August, 1956, warned that Nkumbula and the Congress represented the same kind of subversive threat to the country as did Jomo Kenyatta and the Kenya African Union on the eve of the Mau Mau "emergency." "We do not ask for the Congress to be proscribed, but for legislation to deal with it." (There were the same assurances at the beginning of the Kenya war that the KAU was not being outlawed, but Kenyatta and other leaders were promptly hustled into detention; proscription came a year later as an official stamp on an accomplished fact.) About this same time the copper companies appealed to the Government for help in stopping the series of strikes which had been taking place on the mines, the answer of the N.R. African Mine Workers Union to company efforts to undercut it by building up the African Staff Association as the sole representative for workers in the upper job-brackets. In Southern Rhodesia there were also rising demands for "firm action" by the Federal Government to halt the "disruptive" antifederation "agitation" in the northern territory.

The outcome was the proclamation of a state of emergency in Northern Rhodesia in early September, 1956, attended by police and troop reenforcements air-lifted in from Southern Rhodesia, and the use of police clubs and tear gas to disperse African pickets at the mines. It was charged that the Union was in subversive collusion with the Congress and striking for political ends. More than 70 leaders were summarily jailed, including the entire leadership of the NRAMWU with the sole exception of the president, Mr. Katilungu. Eleven days after the emergency proclamation in the Copperbelt, Southern Rhodesia followed suit with its own "emergency" as African railway workers, bitter at receiving only one-eighth of a pay increase demanded, went on strike. There, too, the police moved in as strike breakers, and the workers' leaders were arrested. That accomplished, the state of emergency was ended there after four days.

But not so in Northern Rhodesia. As the clamp-down continued there month after month it became evident that the aim was to cripple the NRAMWU. Union leaders were banished from the Copperbelt. The companies in fact asked the authorities to limit the number of the Union's paid officials and cancel its registration for engaging in an "illegal" strike. The law requires a trade union whose registration is cancelled to be immediately dissolved. Thus the African copper miners faced a show-down fight to retain their hard-won organizational gains.

In the case of South Africa the authorities have thus far proscribed only one organization opposed to its policies: the Communist Party of South Africa was legislated out of existence in 1950 with the Suppression of Communism Act. But this legal weapon the authorities have found quite satisfactory for beating all non-conformists over the head. Under this Act the Minister of Justice can among other things ban any objectionable publication, institute search and seizure of property, and issue orders to individuals to sever all relations with their organizations and/or remain within a specified town or area and/or refrain from participation in any gatherings. By this means and with other legal instruments Government has sought to stifle popular opposition by inactivizing the principal leaders of the ANC, SAIC, and labor and other organizations, whatever their racial composition, which stand for democracy in the country.

Up to March, 1956, 604 persons had thus had their liberties taken away, according to the Minister of Justice. They included 75 trade union officials (35 white, 21 African, 12 Colored, 7 Asian) and 529 others (237 African, 198 white, 54 Colored, 40 Asian). Along with this wholesale cancellation of civil liberties has gone phone-tapping and snooping, tampering with mail, constant attendance of police and notebook-in-hand detectives at meetings (if and when they can be held), and repeated police raids and searches of the homes and offices of leaders of democratic organizations—over 900 such search-raids during 1955.

Still, in spite of all, the work for democratic rights went forward. Then in December, 1956, having collected its "evidence," the Government struck, arresting 156 men and women, practically everyone of any consequence who stood uncompromisingly for African rights. There were melodramatic pre-dawn raids in making the arrests and the charge was—treason. Among the hundred Africans carried off to jail were the president of the ANC, Chief Luthuli, and Professor Z. K. Matthews, an internationally known educator. As the trial opened, police fired into the crowd of thousands who had gathered to demonstrate and voice support of their leaders. And so the rulers of South Africa hasten the coming of their own Nemesis.

The Fight for a Living Wage

The expansion of a foreign-controlled productive system in Africa means the coupling of twentieth century industrial techniques (the latest mechanical equipment and large-scale power facilities) with a general labor force paid and living by nineteenth century standards. The Liberia Mining Co. (Republic Steel and Lansdell K. Christie) digs up the iron ore with electrical shovels and uses a long conveyor belt to load it on ships at the rate of 3,000 tons an hour, filling a freighter every other day. Meanwhile, its African workers get less than 50 cents a day and their families scratch the earth with primitive tools trying to grow enough rice to keep alive.

Sisal growers in Kenya have imported hundreds of migrant workers from Ruanda-Urundi, the trusteeship territory under Belgian Congo administration, since they can't get enough Africans in their own colony to work any longer for a shilling or so a day. Twenty-one thousand of those recruited for Kenya's sisal farms in 1955 deserted either on their way to their employers or before completing their contracts. Yet to handle the large export of sisal, much of it to the United States, hundreds of new freight cars have been put in service and new dock-side cranes, forklift trucks and other equipment costing over $3 million have been installed at East African ports.

The consequence of this kind of economic "development" everywhere is a rising *national* income—from $45.9 million in 1945 to $294 million in 1954 in Northern Rhodesia, for example—out of which the African worker receives a steadily *diminishing* proportionate share. The high prices and profits on the increasing volume of exports swell the income of the owners of the mines and plantations. They also bring a higher cost for food and other consumer goods, which falls most heavily on the lowest paid workers. The African has to pay for somebody else's prosperity. "I warn Government that trouble is coming, and may easily come in the urban areas if something is not done about the cost of living," says a white member of Kenya's Legislative Council. "One of the greatest imports into this country has been inflation," says the Federal Minister of Finance in Rhodesia.[5]

There is ample evidence proving that, despite the rising output of export commodities, the urban African worker's standard of living is falling. A recent investigation[6] into the cost of living for Africans in the vicinity of Johannesburg, South Africa, revealed that those employed in the engineering and motor trades industries had received no increase whatever in their minimum basic weekly wages between 1950 and 1954, and the equivalent of only $1.68 or $2.16 increase in their *monthly* cost of living allowance. Those in the building trades and distributive industry fared only slightly better. During the same period, from 1950 to 1954, the cost of mealie meal, the main staple of the African's diet, rose 63 per cent, and his meat ("almost anything remotely connected with animal life") 58 per cent. Minimum food requirements would have taken 94 per cent of the family income if actually purchased. In order to provide for other needs, they starved themselves. In general, it was found that while the family income of the largest wage-earning section of urban Africans was estimated at 72.4 per cent of the cost of their minimum essentials in 1950, it was down to 63.4 per cent in 1954—a marked deterioration.

The health officer of the Northern Rhodesian Government described conditions under which urban Africans were living in 1952 as "horrifying." The Commonwealth Health and Tuberculosis Conference held in London, 1955, was told that "Tuberculosis was comparatively rare among the African population of Rhodesia until the thirties. Now it is sweeping through their ranks with a speed which we have no means of gauging but which we know to be alarming."⁷

The Kenya African Union complained of the rise in the cost of a 200-lb. bag of *posho* (corn flour) from just above a dollar in 1939 to $7.80 in 1952: "There is nothing that has hit the African worker so hard as this fantastic increase in the cost of his staple food." A Kenya welfare officer estimated that a family of five living in Nairobi needed an income of 200s. ($28) a month to live decently; the East African Royal Commission in 1955 found that only 5 per cent of the African workers in Nairobi earned that much, and that "the conditions of life for ... the majority of the Africans in the towns have been deteriorating over a considerable period. ... Moreover, their deterioration has not yet been arrested."⁸

In two African townships at Brazzaville, French Equatorial Africa, 74 per cent of the workers in one and 42 per cent in the other earned less than 60 francs a day in 1953, although French authorities calculated that a minimum of 120 francs (70c) a day was required to subsist.⁹ In Dakar the official cost of living index stood at 379 in 1953 compared with 100 in 1945. In Morocco, Tunisia and Algeria inflation has struck harder than anywhere else in the continent. More than half of all Tunisian families, it was reported in 1956, had to spend more than 90 per cent of their income for food.

The workers in non-settler territories are caught in the same vise. Liberia's spiraling living costs and the "perceptible squeeze on the wage earner" there were the subject of official comment in 1953. High prices, exorbitant rents and overcrowding in living quarters are a serious problem in the fast-growing West African towns much the same as in other sections of Africa.

The increasing impoverishment of masses of African workers at the mercy of an economic juggernaut spells hunger, disease, high infant mortality rates—all the common ills of subject peoples. It is a *killing* system. When these workers strike for higher pay they are in truth struggling for a wage that will allow them and their children to *live*.

Black workers in South Africa refuse to be stopped even by a maximum penalty of three years in jail and/or £500 ($1,400) fine for striking. Herr Strijdom and Company notwithstanding, strikes of African workers are on the increase; by official count there were 22 in 1953, 33 involving 3,853 workers in 1954 (the strike of 4,000 dock workers at Durban seems to have been overlooked), and 72 involving 8,083 in 1955.

There was the case of some striking textile workers in the South African township of Roodeport in 1956 who were each sentenced to a £10 ($28) fine and a month in jail. Though most of the sentence was suspended, they didn't have money to pay even the $7 fine that remained and went cheerfully off to jail. The employer spent the weekend searching the township for experienced workers, even some he had fired for alleged theft. He did not get one. On Monday morning he was at the jail with the fine money. A week later another batch of workers from the same factory appeared before the same magistrate on the same charge. This time the *whole* sentence was suspended. But it doesn't always happen that way.

In Southern Rhodesia, where black workers are also debarred from twentieth century labor relations, there was the strike of 9,000 African coal miners early in 1954 at the Wankie Colliery, another one of the many Anglo American Corp. properties. The miners demanded an increase of about 50 cents a day in their wages which averaged only $10.60 monthly. Railway workers, domestic servants and others came out in support of the coal miners. Troops were rushed in to break the strike; only a fraction of the wage increase demanded was won. Troops were likewise required at Mombasa, Kenya, in March, 1955, to deal with the strike of 7,000 dock workers who called for 2s. (28c) a day increase in the £1 ($2.80) wage received by most of them for a 50 hour work week. Here, too, a general strike threatened as other African workers joined in the walk-out.

In North Africa the trade unions sparked the general revolt. Below the Sahara their determination and strength were evidenced in the general strike throughout French West Africa which forced the French National Assembly in November, 1952, to approve the Labor Code for Overseas Territories, embodying the most advanced labor policy yet achieved in Africa and placing the rights and status of workers in the colonies on a par (though not yet in wages) with labor standards in France. M. Abdoulaye Diallo, one of the outstanding young labor leaders of French West Africa, has described the general strike that took place on November 3, two weeks before the National Assembly voted:

> Not one train ran. Not one boy made a bed. Not one cook boiled water for his European master. The faithful, in their prayers in the mosque, supported the action of the workers for a just cause. . . . The announcement by the employers in Abidjan that an air squadron would bomb the strikers made the workers smile. They were thinking that "the bombs would need eyes to distinguish the whites from the colored people of the town." Everywhere the Africans coolly and firmly avoided provocation, to the great disappointment of the colonialists. . . . What was the dominating idea which guided the workers in preparing and carrying out their strikes? It was to *fight against racial discrimination* wherever it occurs.[10]

The West African territories experienced wide-spread labor unrest during 1955 and 1956. Of many strikes in the pre-independent Gold Coast that of 37,000 mine workers lasting three months was most notable. Nigeria witnessed strikes by 42,000 workers in the tin mines, by 40,000 building trades workers, by workers in various categories of government employment—including even teachers. In Sierra Leone the difference between the 21 cents increase asked by the workers in their 52 cents a day pay and the 3 or 4 cents offered by employers led to a bitter strike of the Artisans and Allied Workers' Union.

There have also been demands for something better from the agricultural wage-workers, who are as everywhere the lowest paid and least organized. The more politically developed industrial unions, such as those in French West Africa and newly independent Sudan, have emphasized in their programs the importance of unity with farm workers and have given significant support to their struggles. Even without such help effective strikes have been conducted on Uganda's sugar and tea estates, on government-operated banana plantations in British Cameroons, and elsewhere.

Tired of Being Cheated

A few years ago, in 1953, when he was Governor of Southern Rhodesia, Lord Malvern himself acknowledged that "one criticism against 'colonialism' which had substance . . . was that raw materials had been taken away for the industries of distant countries at a price which did not leave enough in the country of origin for the provision of adequate health, education, and other social services."[11] He immediately added that this was now being changed with the development of secondary industries in the country. But a year and a half later we find him saying, "It is the abject poverty of the masses which is the cause of the trouble. We have not the money to educate them and elevate them." And still later, in 1956, after all the appropriations for the Kariba Dam, railroad expansion and other capital works, there again came the refrain of "our inability to raise the funds reasonably required to develop . . . the African population"—this time from Southern Rhodesia's Prime Minister, Mr. R. S. Garfield Todd.

Well, let us see. A European member of the Rhodesian Federal Assembly, the Rev. Andrew B. Doig of Nyasaland, remarked recently, "I find amazing the number of people [white] in the Federation exempt from payment of any income tax. I do not think it wise or right in face of the large sums we are hoping to get from overseas." White Rhodesians pay no income or other direct tax unless their income is $1,120 (if single) or $2,240 (if married). The few Africans who earn that much come under the same schedule. Only about 30,000 of the 250,000 white population in the Federation pay such a tax, yet the other 220,000 also make use of all the public services available for the whites, including *free education*. In addition, they get government subsidies for building their houses, running their farms, and so forth.

What of the African? He alone is called upon to pay an annual tax from the time he is 18 years old, regardless of what he has or hasn't earned—a £1 poll tax ($2.80). And he himself pays the major part of the cost of whatever social services he receives. The African's child "will have no education of any kind in the rural areas unless he, the parent, provides all the necessary capital expenditure on classroom and teacher accommodations of more than at least 90 per cent of the rural schools. Besides, he has to provide all the equipment for the school, the child and, partly, the teacher. Even some of the Government primary schools for urban African children are subsidized by the parents who provide some of the equipment."[12]

There were accommodations for only 20,558 children out of an estimated 50,800 in Northern Rhodesia's urban African schools in 1954, and for fewer than a quarter of the 21,750 children in one area. Thus it happens that a Copperbelt mine worker out of his slim wages will have to pay $56 or $70 a year for the education of each of his children at one of the mission schools, which carry the responsibility for most of the education—a responsibility most governments in Africa have been quite satisfied to leave to them. In all three Federation territories only one-third to one-half of the children of school age are receiving any education, and most of these get three years or less of continuous schooling.[13]

"We have not got the money. . . ." Why? The Rhodesias are certainly not to be classed among the poorer countries of Africa. The reason is that the African is *cheated.* He is cheated first by the copper companies and other employers who would rather pay extra taxes on their profits to the government than give their African workers more money. He is cheated a second time by a government which spends its revenues thus received to provide facilities for the further expansion of the copper and other business interests and to promote the size and welfare of the white population. The whites get educational and other services equal to those in England, live far better than they could afford to do there, and yet pay absurdly light taxes compared with schedules in Britain, other European countries, or the United States. The Africans, on the other hand, are expected to shift for themselves, carrying most of the financial burden of their education and general social advancement on their own backs. "We have not got the money. . . ."

An instructive contrast could be drawn between the progress in educational services provided in the Gold Coast since Africans became responsible for internal affairs of government (prior to the achievement of independence) and what was done there before that change-over of administration, or what is done now in settler countries like the Rhodesias. That analysis cannot be made here, but at least one or two points of interest can be mentioned in passing. Mr. Todd deplores the fact that too few Africans in Southern Rhodesia (under 1,700) yet receive secondary education (there is only one Government secondary school, 14 mission-run) and *hopes* that by the end of 1960 another thousand can attend a two-year secondary course; under African administration of an "Accelerated Development Plan for Education" in the Gold Coast, between 1951 and 1955 the number of secondary schools rose from 13 to 31 and the number of secondary school students from 2,709 to 7,711. Mr. Todd deplores the lack of an African technical school in Southern Rhodesia; in the Gold Coast during the four year period two new technical institutes were opened at Tarkwa and Takoradi, two more were nearing completion at Kumasi and Accra, and enrollment in technical institutions rose from 606 to 1,756. In the Rhodesias there is the often heard complaint of the lack of qualified teachers; in the Gold Coast five new teacher training colleges were built, four more were doubled in size, and 2,500 new certificated teachers were trained in four years. Africans know that it *can* be done—if there is the *desire* to do it.

The state of African education in Rhodesia is typical of that in all settler-ruled territories, though perhaps somewhat better than in some. In Algeria, for example, only 300,000 out of 2,000,000 Arab children of school age get instruction; in secondary schools were 6,000 Arab as against 28,000 European pupils in 1956. In the Portuguese colonies the number of Africans receiving any education ranges from two per cent of the population in Angola to four per cent in Mozambique: the whites in these territories consequently have no worry of being outnumbered by the few Africans (4,555 in Mozambique in 1955) who qualify as *civilizados* or "assimilated" and are thereby entitled to equal privileges with them. Neither have the whites much worry on this score in the Belgian Congo with its *matriculés* (numbering about a hundred in 1955) and its *evolués* comprising the African elite.

A Belgian commission which surveyed the Congo's schools not very long ago reported how African children supposed to be getting some primary education were found to be spending their time attending to the coffee, peanuts and other crops grown for the market by the missions on their extensive land holdings.[14] Elsewhere the children are put to work without even the pretense of educating them. On Kenya's European farms in 1954 there were officially reported to be 39,784 "juveniles" employed, most of them on monthly contracts and the rest as day laborers, resident laborers, or domestics. A Rhodesian newspaper reports: "Many industrial and commercial firms make use of child labor in and around Salisbury. The age of the children in some cases is about six to seven years... Many of them look miserable... Not a few show signs of malnutrition.... Nearly all these children are illiterate and have never seen the door of a school."[15]

The white supremacists lay stress on what African children should *not* learn. For the plainest expression of this it is difficult to surpass Dr. Verwoerd, the South African Minister of Native Affairs. "There is no place for him [the African] in the European community above the level of certain forms of labor... For that reason it is of no avail for him to receive a training which has as its aim absorption in the European community," he said, in explanation of the Bantu Education Act which became effective in 1954 despite loud

African protests and boycotting of government schools. And again, "Natives will be taught from childhood that equality is not for them. . . . I will close down any school which preaches inadmissible doctrines." To the same effect was the warning given a conference of African teachers in Northern Rhodesia: "If the African is keen on politics, he is unable to resist the temptation to express his views strongly when teaching a class. . . . The Government will not be prepared to pay the salaries of disloyal people who oppose its laws and plans for promoting progress."[16]

Authorities, especially in settler territories, are suspicious of African efforts to establish and conduct independent schools of their own in order to remedy the inadequacies of both government and mission education. Such action in itself is assumed to imply insubordination. A memorandum of the Kenya African Union to the United Nations in 1948 called attention to the manner in which officials in Kenya, where Africans began organizing their own schools in 1925, had obstructed and closed institutions established by the African Independent Schools' Association, intimidating and even imprisoning some of its teachers.

The author of the memorandum on behalf of the KAU was Mr. Mbiu Koinange, who after studying in the United States, receiving the M.A. degree from Columbia University, returned home to become founder and principal of the Kenya Teachers' College and Secretary of the African Education Council responsible for 300 independent schools unaided by the Government. He was in London presenting a Land Petition when the Kenya war broke out in 1952 and so escaped the general arrest of African leaders. But his father, then 90 years of age, a retired senior chief revered by his people, was arrested January 31, 1953, and despite acquittal of the charges against him, he was ordered held in detention for the duration of the "emergency." The assault upon the KAU was the signal for closing the independent schools. Some were demolished, some were turned into police stations, and "jails and guillotines were set up in some. 35,000 innocent school children were deprived of educational facilities altogether," writes Mr. Koinange.[17]

To Determine Their Own Destiny

It does no good for the Right Honorable Viscount Malvern of Southern Rhodesia to rant: "Economic development can do a thousand times more to advance the Africans than franchise laws or cries for social equality." Or for that country's Minister of Native Affairs to rave: "Black nationalism and its filthy consequences would be excluded by development." For too many Africans, not only in Rhodesia but elsewhere, have come to realize that this "development," as the Rev. Doig has said, "does not put their good very high in the list of priorities."

Symbolic of the way the tide is running was the action of the Kabaka's Ministry in producing and publishing its own development plan for Buganda early in 1956 without consulting the Governor of Uganda about it and without the Governor's local representative even having heard of it. According to the London *Economist's* report on it, the first sentence of the Ministry's plan, which was curiously omitted in British newspaper accounts, stated that the first objective is self-government for both the province of Buganda and the country of Uganda. It was added that divisional officers would be appointed with full responsibility to administer the plan, clearly implying that the services of British officials would not be needed and they might just as well get ready to leave.

Mr. Harry Nkumbula speaks to his Congress followers in Northern Rhodesia, saying, "You and I are determined to be free; you and I are determined to have a word, and a big one at that, in determining our destinies. We must have the right to earn a decent living according to our capacity and not according to our color."

A leader in French West Africa, Mr. Gabriel D'Arboussier, declares, "We want production for the needs of human beings, not human beings broken on the wheel of production."

And in East Africa, when the people used to gather in tens of thousands for the Kenya African Union mass meetings, they expressed it in song:[18]

> *Our fight for the land will never cease.*
> *It was ours, and it will be ours, forever and ever.*
>
> *We do not fear those who speak behind our backs;*
> *If they scorn us, they will not be here forever.*
>
> *We look for the day to arrive*
> *When great jubilation will reign everywhere,*
> *And the children of black men throughout the world*
> *Will know happiness in the return of their rights.*

15. Freedom Road

ASKED ON AN Edward R. Murrow television interview in April, 1956, what he thought was Africa's most urgent need today, Prime Minister Nkrumah answered without hesitation, "I think the first essential thing is political emancipation, because once they are politically emancipated, they are in the position to develop their own country in a way in which they think fit." Africans' agitation for immediate self-government and independence signifies, for one thing, their refusal to let their lives be ordered according to other people's economic theories and blueprints. What they demand is Africa for the Africans!

Self-determination begins with a people holding the power to make independent decisions, to exercise full political authority. This is what is demanded everywhere by articulate Africans. For them neither the presence of non-African minorities in their midst nor their participation in a French federal or British commonwealth system implies any restriction upon their claims to self-determination. As regards the independence-with-interdependence systems, once political power passes to the indigenous peoples, their relation to the former ruling power as equals or unequals will depend in the final analysis not upon signed agreements and declarations of principles but upon life.

A much more immediate and weighty problem is posed by the settler populations in Africa. The course of the bloody struggle throughout all North Africa and the extremity of the repressive measures required to maintain white power in eastern, central and southern Africa make it evident that a most bitter and possibly world-shaking conflict is probable and imminent in the latter areas. It can only be avoided by the speedy adoption of a radically changed approach to the question of the rights of Africans in settler countries by the responsible European officials, and likewise by the American State Department, and their insistence—by effective methods of economic persuasion, if need be—that the settler barriers to African freedom be removed.

One Man—One Vote

Force cannot hold them down. That much we should have learned from Asia. There were indignant protests in West Africa over the sending of 30,000 Senegalese to help the French fight Algerians. Some of the Senegalese surrendered and changed into uniforms of the North African Army of Liberation, which in turn pledged solidarity with all Africans in their struggle for independence. "Thus we ourselves manufacture the poison that is in-injected into our own veins," was the bitter comment in *L'Express,* a Paris newspaper. Just as Moroccan and Algerian troops sent to Indo-China by France became the hard core of North Africa's resistance, the paper said, so are the West Africans sent into Algeria bound to become sooner or later the leaders of a new rebellion in the heart of Africa.

And half-way, compromise measures only add to Africans' resentment of being treated as less than equal. They scorn being granted a minor token share in administrative responsibility, tricky franchise measures which make some people's votes count for more than others' and disqualify some from voting at all, or "parity" arrangements and other devices which guarantee that the non-African minority will never be outvoted by the African majority. Such concessions might have been accepted ten years ago as *beginning* steps toward something better, but not today. Too much has happened and is happening. Full political rights and majority rule is what they ask for, nothing less—and *now.*

Algeria: In this war-torn colony which French (and United States) officials maintain is an integral part of France, and where, as *Life* magazine (June 4, 1956) affirms, an Arab's vote counts for only one-ninth of a French *colon's,* the first point in the plan of settlement advanced by all sections of the National Liberation Front is a Free Algeria—recognition of the people's sovereignty and independence.

French Cameroons: In 1949 the people's organizations in this trusteeship territory petitioned the United Nations for independence by 1956. In 1954 M. Ruben Um Nyobe, general secretary of the *Union des Populations du Cameroun* (UPC), urged United Nations' support for the election of a legislative assembly by universal suffrage preparatory to self-government. At last in April, 1955, Cameroon organizations called for termination of the trusteeship status and the convening of a constituent national assembly. A month later came the Government's reprisal: a campaign of brutal assault, terror and killing against the petitioning organizations and their leaders.[1] Nyobe was killed in 1958, but the struggle continued.

French West Africa: At an important public meeting in Dakar in 1956, called to unite four Senegalese political parties, the keynote struck by the chairman was: "We want to create an *entente cordiale* of all Senegalese, whether by birth or adoption, devoted to the struggle for the complete autonomy of our territory."

Belgian Congo: An African paper, *Conscience Africaine*, in the "Manifesto" set forth in its special issue of July-August, 1956, declared, "The Belgians should understand now that their domination over the Congo will not be forever. . . . We will never agree that a Belgo-Congolese federation be imposed on us without our free consent or that this may be made the condition of our political emancipation."

Kenya: A mass meeting of the Kenya African Union in 1947 unanimously resolved that the political objective in Kenya "must be self-government by Africans for Africans," with safeguards for the rights of minorities. In 1956 the Kenya Federation of Labor headed by 27-year-old Mr. Tom Mboya demanded "complete democracy, one man, one vote, and an increase in African representation within the next year which would reflect the relationship of the African community to the other races in the colony."

Uganda: The Uganda National Congress voices the outright demand for self-government at once, rejecting the government's 1956 promise that in 1961 members of the Legislative Council might for the first time be chosen by direct elections on a common roll, *provided* satisfactory arrangements were made regarding the qualifications and disqualifications of voters and candidates, and regarding "adequate representation" of the Indian and white minorities.

Nyasaland: Mr. M. W. K. Chiume, speaking in the Legislative Council, asserts that "the composition of the Legislature should reflect that of the population. Instead, three million African owners of this country are represented by only five Africans, while other people equivalent to one five-hundreth of the African population are represented by 17 or 18 members. . . . We cannot run away from giving the vote to every African."[2]

South Africa: "The people shall govern! Every man and woman shall have the right to vote and to stand as a candidate for all bodies which make laws. All people shall be entitled to take part in the administration of the country. The rights of the people shall be the same, regardless of race, color, or sex." So reads the Freedom Charter adopted by delegates to the great Congress of the People in 1955.

It is important to recognize that the almost universal African demand for an unrestricted franchise is not simply a matter of abstract democratic principle. One man-one vote means protection and advancement of the interests of the people *as a whole;* it means getting rid of the system whereby individual Africans or special categories of them are selected as "spokesmen" and "representatives" of all the people—in short, it means getting rid of the overlords, stooges and collaborators.

A white member of the Rhodesian Federal Parliament, Dr. Alexander Scott, once remarked that Lord Malvern's "beau ideal" of the African was a sergeant-major who controlled underlings but who was himself controlled by his superiors. An African teacher in a Catholic secondary school in Southern Rhodesia writes:

> In Africa, every African who is held in high esteem by the Europeans and especially by the authorities is at once looked at with great suspicion. Those who are branded agitators by the white authorities are held by Africans in high esteem. The reason is plain and simple: the so-called agitators speak the truth and in politics the Europeans do not seem to appreciate plain speaking from an African, especially on things political.[3]

In March, 1956, the five African unofficial members of the Nyasaland Legislative Council, formerly nominated by the Governor, were for the first time elected by the three African Provincial Councils. The victors were four prominent members of the Nyasaland African Congress and an ex-member. Naturally, Congress officials acclaimed this triumph and voiced their determination to "battle relentlessly toward self-government and the contracting of Nyasaland out of the Federation." Was it simply a coincidence that less than a month thereafter came police raids on the homes of the Congress officers, followed shortly by the trial and sentencing of the president, Mr. J. S. Sangala, and the secretary, Mr. T. D. T. Banda? The charge: being in possession of a seditious publication (that is, one banned by the Government) and committing a seditious act (that is, sending a statement to the Governor and to a local white newspaper "calculated to bring the Government into hatred and contempt, to cause disaffection . . . and to promote ill-will and hostility between different sections of the population").

No, the Sangala's and Banda's won't qualify as Lord Malvern's sergeants-major. But there are others, a few almost everywhere and not only in Africa, who do. They are the ones who can be depended upon not to fight for the masses of their people but to concentrate instead on getting themselves and their own elite group or class integrated into the white's world.

The Belgians and Portuguese have for some time systematically enlisted their *matriculés* and *civilizados* in the apparatus of colonial rule. The French, too, have encouraged many a colonial subject to feel that France came before his own native land, and some of them, it must be acknowledged, have risen to great heights in government and the professions, which is not the case with the Belgian and Portuguese colonial elite. Today, however, the Congolese are beginning to ask their overlords embarrassing questions; and in the French territories, political candidates will likely be examined more closely with reference to their stand on French *vs.* African interests. It is noteworthy that there has been no black administrator in France's African colonies since the death of Felix Eboué, Governor of French Equatorial Africa, in 1944.

In the British settler territories there are many whites who have lately come to think that perhaps something like the assimilation policy of their European neighbors, even though on the way out in French circles, might be the answer to their own problem of mounting nationalist demands. There is much talk of a "developing African middle class" with its "vested interest in change which is reasonable, gradual, and ordered, not drastic and dangerous." It is thought that if only this class of Africans can be drawn into some form of political and economic alliance with the whites, some concessions to that end being granted, then the future may be saved. Here is the familiar divide-and-rule strategy once more, on the class level this time instead of the tribal or racial level. When this prospectus is presented to the public, the interests of the dominant classes in the country become the interests of the country as a whole: "We must all be loyal Kenyans (or Rhodesians, etc.) and work for the good of the country, forgetting our racial differences."

Such is the door opened to the more educated and prosperous

Africans by the British Capricorn Africa Society and similar organizations which make a special point of inviting the membership of all races. But at the same time the door of *general* African political advancement is slammed shut. The Capricorn Society, for example, says, "We reject the idea that the vote should be exercised without qualification. In the special circumstances of East and Central Africa . . . universal suffrage would give rise to the danger of irresponsible politicians . . . being elected to the legislature on grounds irrelevant to the common good." It accordingly advocates (1) limiting the franchise to those who have completed Form II of the secondary school course or its equivalent, and (2) granting extra votes up to six to those who satisfy other stated qualifications of income, public or professional service, and so forth.[4]

One African's answer to such proposals is: "Racial tension in Central Africa can only be averted by a true partnership which concedes the right of self-government to every man and woman irrespective of race or so-called degree of civilization. Any sort of franchise loaded on racial, educational or property qualifications can only lead to a conspiracy of the voters against the voteless."[5] Another African spokesman, Mr. Chiume of Nyasaland, says, "Africans in this country cannot exchange colonialism and imperialism for Capricornism. They will not be impressed by catchwords and slogans which are . . . a tricky way of deviating Africans from realizing their right to self-determination for their respective countries."

The Capricornists apparently forget that Africans in their area have their eyes on North Africa; on the Sudan, Ghana, and Nigeria. Even in France's colonies below the Sahara with their settler populations, the people have won victories in the abolition of the dual electoral college system (which guaranteed a special political status for the white minority) and the removal of restrictions on universal adult suffrage. Is it expected that the British settler territories, or the Belgian and Portuguese colonies either, can remain isolated islands of white political privilege in the midst of the surging sea of African liberation?

African Self-Government and Non-African Minorities

Capricornism is one form of black-white cooperation; it has the blessing of government authorities. On a different level are the efforts toward promoting a united movement embracing all sections of the population in support of full political rights for the African; this kind of cooperation is attacked by both government and Capricornists. A white person who aids the African National Congress causes is regarded by the great majority of his fellow-whites as a renegade, an outcast. The Rev. Trevor Huddleston followed the Rev. Michael Scott out of South Africa, not to return. And there have been many others.

There was the case of Mr. Simon Zukas, who had lived in Northern Rhodesia most of his life and served with the Rhodesian forces in World War II. When the Federation issue arose, he threw himself courageously into the struggle on the side of the Africans. His work won him election as a vice president of the N.R. African Congress. He served on the editorial board of Congress' *Freedom Newsletter.* His articles in that organ opposing Federation were seized upon as a basis for his summary arrest, trial, and deportation in 1952. He was a white man. And he was "dangerous to peace and good order." *Freedom Newsletter* commented bitterly, "When an African helps a European, it is partnership. When a European helps an African he should be deported."

The greatest dread of South African authorities is a coalition of black and white democratic forces. There is a constant war against these forces on either side of the color line, but the Government's full weight is thrown against those who join hands *across* the color line. The "treason" trial of the 156 leaders of the democratic coalition vanguard is the latest instance. In sentencing Dr. Y. M. Dadoo, president of the SAIC, Mr. Moses M. Kotane, member of the ANC National Executive, and others under the Suppression of Communism Act in 1952, the magistrate in the course of his judgment said:

> It is common knowledge that one of the aims of Communism is to break down race barriers and strive for equal rights for all sections of the people, and to do so without any discrimination of race, color or creed. The Union of South Africa with its peculiar problems created by a population overwhelmingly Non-European is fertile ground for the dissemination of Communist propaganda. This would endanger the survival of Europeans, and therefore legislation must be pursued with the object of suppressing Communism.[6]

Thus, under South African law anyone opposing racial discrimination is thereby guilty of propagating Communism and liable to prosecution. This legal doctrine rests on the official dogma that (a) white domination in all spheres is proper and necessary to the country's social order, (b) only agitators or outside trouble-makers seek to change the existing system, and (c) they do so solely for the purpose of stirring up racial conflict. White supremacists in the United States pursue the same upside-down manner of reasoning, of course.

Both major political groupings in South Africa, the United Party as well as the Nationalist Party, support the principle that the white man alone must rule. They differ only in that each holds that it can maintain white supremacy better than the other. There is no greater difference between the Dutch-derived and British-derived sections of the population as a whole. But there has existed and still exists a small but sturdy band of whites, both Afrikaaner and British, industrial workers, university students, and men and women in various professions, who take their stand for democracy side by side with the ANC and African trade unions.

Some of these white allies may be Communists, certainly many are not. That they are ready to support Congress demands is what matters; on that basis they are welcomed as fellow-soldiers in the fight for freedom. The same principle applies to members of the Congress. But the Government takes the position (echoed by some professed supporters of the Africans' cause) that because of its association with white and Indian organizations and the presence of Communists in these organizations and in its own ranks, the Congress is "Communist-dominated"—though the mere fact of its opposition to Government policies would entitle it to that label in any event.

In answer to this sort of attack ANC leaders say that they are building a broad people's movement in which there must be room for everyone who believes in a democratic South Africa regardless of race and regardless of political party. In an organization such as the Congress there is necessarily a wide diversity of views. "People seem to be alarmed at the fact that there may be a so-called right wing, center, and left wing in the Congress," says its leader, Chief Luthuli. "To me it is a healthy sign in any organization when people freely express their points of view." Another ANC leader, Professor Z. K. Matthews, has said:

> I resent the suggestion that the African people require Communists to teach them to defend their rights. Ever since the Bantu encountered the Europeans on the banks of the Great Fish River long before the Communist Manifesto was even thought of, they have struggled for equal rights in the land of their birth. They will continue their struggle, and not allow themselves to be browbeaten by smear tactics in their determined fight for their liberation.

The present close ties between the ANC and the SAIC, representing the Indian minority in South Africa, developed from working together in specific campaigns toward common objectives. For a long period Indian leaders considered it sufficient and proper to concern themselves solely with problems of their own group. But during and immediately following World War II Dr. Y. M. Dadoo and other young leaders came to the fore who recognized and stressed the need of promoting unity with the African majority. This tendency was furthered by the cumulative weight of anti-Indian and general racist legislation—the latter also affected the Colored population in the Cape and some of their organizations were likewise drawn into united action. The urgency of closer Indian-African understanding and cooperation was heavily underscored when Africans suddenly launched riotous and murderous attacks upon Durban Indians in 1949, goaded on by European-fostered hatred of the Asians and by bitter African resentment of exploitation at the hands of Indian traders and property-owners.

The Government itself laid the basis of united African-Indian opposition to its policies by dispelling Indian illusions of their having a favored status above the African. Moreover, South African Indians, most of them descendants of indentured laborers brought over between 1860 and 1911 to work the Natal sugar estates and for other jobs, are predominantly of the working class and accordingly have common interests with African labor, despite occasional competition for unskilled and semi-skilled jobs.

The situation is different with the Indian minorities in Kenya, Uganda and Tanganyika. Though their forebears were in many instances also indentured workers imported for such tasks as building the East African railway system, they won representation in the territorial governments even before the Africans because of having advanced to positions of importance in the commercial life of these countries. Although actually granted an intermediate status below the whites, East African Indians nevertheless usually tend to indentify themselves with the white ruling circles rather than with the Africans and to ignore Nehru's injunction that Indian migrants must always remember they are guests of the African in his country. Indians in Kenya have given financial assistance toward the Africans' independent schools and for overseas scholarships, and there has been occasional voicing of support for nationalist demands. But one finds growing African-Indian friction in many areas of East Africa. Particularly is this so in Uganda where the unscrupulous Indian middleman has incurred the hatred of African cotton growers. In such instances the African cannot be expected to differentiate between European and Indian trespassers.

Returning to the question of minorities in South Africa, a central problem is the powerful pressures preventing the alliance of white and black workers and now driving them farther apart. Since the disastrous Rand strike of 1922 when white mine workers demanded a for-whites-only brand of socialism, much had been done toward combatting racism in the labor movement. White labor organizations in 1939 and repeatedly thereafter urged full legal recognition of the African trade unions. But with the coming of Malan-Strijdom rule, these advances toward labor unity were all but cancelled out. Even some of the previously liberal white unions bowed to the Government's order prohibiting any but white members in recognized trade unions. Yet there was resistance to the racist code. When a new trade union center excluding African organizations was established in October, 1954, with official endorsement, the dissenters answered by organizing the South African Congress of Trade Unions the following March, embracing 42,000 workers without restriction as to race.

"The key question is, can real trade unions survive in South Africa?" writes Mr. Alex Hepple, veteran labor leader and representative of the South African Labor Party in Parliament. He puts it squarely up to the white trade unionists:

> Only the workers can answer that. If white workers persist in swallowing the propaganda that the non-European worker threatens their existence, and as a result, support reactionary policies, their unions will degenerate into artificial forms. On the other hand, despite discouragement and repressive laws non-European trade unions will rise and become powerful. That is the lesson of history. . . . Working-class unity is needed now. Workers should no longer allow themselves to be duped by cunning appeals to racial prejudice and cries of "Communism." They should stand together and help create trade union unity. If they fail to do that, they will surrender themselves to slavery.[7]

One of the younger ANC leaders, Mr. Joseph G. Matthews, a lawyer, the son of Professor Z. K. Matthews, expresses it this way:

> The unit of the African nation which inhabits South Africa is the key to democracy in this country. The most comprehensive freedom in South Africa is the freedom of the African. In the emancipation of the African nation is involved the emancipation of all the minorities—the Indian, the Colored, and even the European![8]

It is customary for imperialism's apologists to assert that African nationalists aim at driving out the whites, or that African self-rule would mean the oppression of non-African minorities. If we are talking about the political programs of organized African movements, and not about what may be said or done in the heat of spontaneous retaliation against one's oppressors, there is not an iota of evidence supporting this thesis of the traducers of African nationalism. On the contrary, in North Africa, in the Kenya African Union, and in the various Congress organizations there have been repeated declarations guaranteeing the security and rights of all minorities within the framework of majority rule.

"Africans are not asking for Europeans to be sent out of the country, but European domination must go," says Mr. Tom Mboya of the Kenya Federation of Labor. And concerning Algeria a competent authority writes, "It has been wrongly stated that the Algerian nationalists are trying to force the French *colons* to leave the country. This is not true. The Algerians want the French to live with them as equal citizens. . . . It is FRANCE, not the *colons*, that they want to leave. They want France to recognize the separate character and individuality of Algeria."[9]

The Northern Rhodesia ANC in its 1956 statement of aims proposed guaranteed political representation for minorities at the outset of African self-government: "When no race any longer has reason to fear domination by another race the policy of reserved seats for minorities can be ended and the Legislative Council will be a truly democratic expression of the majority of all citizens." In Italian Somaliland, preparing for self-government in 1960, ten of the Legislative Assembly's sixty seats are reserved for the non-Somali communities—the Somali Youth League holds all but one of the remaining seats.

European *domination* must go, not the European. But if he insists upon trying to retain or regain his privileged position, then naturally such a person must be dealt with as a menace to the people and their government. The Moroccan Government, within a few months after assuming direction of the country's affairs, was compelled to deport 64 members or close sympathizers of the reactionary *colon* organization, *L'Union pour la Présence Française*, for conspiring to incite a Berber revolt.

French West Africa within the past few years has also become infested with *Présence Française* and Poujadist groups with their racist, imperialist propaganda. A French newspaper in Dakar, *Les*

Echos d'Afrique Noire, carried on its front page, February 21, 1956, a large picture of the paper's editor, M. Maurice Voisin, speaking at a Dakar Poujadist Movement meeting, and above the picture this bold banner headline: "NON, A L'AUTONOMIE! *L'A.O.F. est* française!" (No, to Self-Government! French West Africa is *French!*). These developments are seen by one commentator as clearly indicating "dangers that the weakening of French power in North Africa may lead to 'realism' and 'toughness' in West Africa; and make it much more difficult for West African politicians to follow the policy of collaboration [the French word] with the administration to which most of them are at present committed."[10]

In the British settler territories there are likewise groupings which scorn even the Capricornist formula as too soft and conciliatory, insist upon not yielding an inch to African franchise demands, and rail against the alleged "liquidation of the Empire" by the London Government (which capitulates all too readily, like the Paris Government, to settler pressures). Yes, there will very probably be required the deportation of some irreconcilables like those in Morocco from other sections of Africa. But that has to wait for self-government, for London and Paris are in the habit of jailing or exiling African "extremists," not the settler die-hards. And in the meantime? "If the franchise is not given it will eventually be taken, in forms and under conditions not so acceptable to the European population."

And what of South Africa, where white power stands insolently and smugly defiant? One may cite the opinion of Mr. Leo Marquard, president of the South African Institute of Race Relations, a predominantly white organization of liberal persuasion, favoring a *gradual* extension of franchise rights to Africans. Addressing a white audience in Southern Rhodesia recently, Mr. Marquard said that the question was not so much *whether* Africans would achieve political power in South Africa—he had no doubt that this would happen—but how and when they would do so. One way was by peaceful evolution, but there were powerful forces opposed to this. The other way, he said, was "by revolution, which may take the shape of many unsuccessful and isolated revolts that will be ruthlessly suppressed, but will triumph in the end. During the course of this it is quite possible that civil disorder will reach such dimensions that foreign countries interested in the value of our strategic position and raw materials rather than in our political morals, will intervene to keep order."[11]

The United States and Britain are of course the "foreign countries" most directly interested in South Africa's strategic importance and exports. The question is on whose side they will intervene in the life-and-death clash between the forces supporting African libration and democracy and those determined to maintain the present racist autocracy. By what they have done and what they have failed to do, Washington and London have thus far stood on the side of the ruling minority in South Africa, giving it consistent aid and comfort, and endorsing in effect if not in fact a form of rule that is evil, utterly decadent, and doomed. There is little time left for the great Anglo-Saxon powers to make a change and start moving with the tide of history instead of against it.

After Political Independence—What?

The achievement of political emancipation is the indispensable first step toward full emancipation. But it is important to emphasize that it is *only* the first step. The franchise and self-government are not ends in themselves; they are the necessary instruments for making decisions and executing plans for the social-economic emancipation of a people. Political freedom does not automatically open all other doors. Many self-governing countries in Africa and elsewhere, including this hemisphere, have dependent colonial economies no different in form from those of politically subject lands. The process of their full liberation awaits completion.

The winning of economic emancipation does not mean the severing of trade relations with the former ruling power or other highly industrialized states any more than political emancipation means the expulsion of European settlers. It *does* mean the transformation of economic relations as speedily as is practicable to provide for more equal terms of trade, with the newly freed state no longer concentrating all its efforts on the supply of raw materials for world markets while remaining more or less completely dependent upon outside sources for manufactured goods and often even its food requirements. If we are striving for world-wide economic stability and the general levelling upwards of all living standards, then there can be cooperation between economically advanced and retarded countries in terms of the latters' development of a more industrialized, balanced and self-sufficient economy. But if it is maintained, as in the Eurafrica scheme, that Africa must remain simply the raw-material servant of European and

American industry, then there is obviously a fundamental conflict between this brand of interdependence and the goals of African economic independence.

United Nations reports point out that the percentage of the world's population that is undernourished continues to increase, and that the gap between "developed" and "underdeveloped" countries, even in *agricultural* production, continues to widen—the rich countries becoming relatively richer, and the poor ones relatively poorer. What the poorer countries require, the world organization's economic experts state, is simultaneous advance in the modernization of agricultural production and in expansion of industrial production:

> While industrialization in the broad sense is impossible unless agriculture is modernized, agricultural progress will be frustrated unless there are industrial openings to absorb the manpower released from agriculture and unless the supplies and services essential to modern agriculture can be obtained at least in part locally. . . . Industrial development will expand the markets for agricultural produce and for new imported manufactured goods.

As applied to Africa this would mean revolutionizing the present agricultural system in which the great mass of the population is compelled to devote its energies to either primitive production for self-subsistence or uneconomic growing of export crops. It would mean reorganizing use of the land, especially in the case of foreign-controlled estates and plantations, to effect the proper balance of production between what a country requires for its own needs and what is to be exported, and to provide a decent and secure livelihood for those who work the land. It would mean eradicating the migrant labor system with all its evils and promoting the development of a stable, efficient working force in both agriculture and industry along with proper provision for their social well-being. And the common aim of these measures would be the building of a sound economy geared to industrial growth and diversified production.

Needless to say, there can be no uniform blueprint for the implementation of these objectives in all African states. How to proceed, how to relate the new and strange to what is traditional and customary in African society, is the heart of the problem. This is of course for the people themselves to decide, after all the advice of the experts has been weighed. But on one general point there can be little difference of opinion. There is the pressing, universal African need to escape from the slavery and stagnation of complete dependence on the fluctuating, externally-controlled revenue from one or two raw material exports, and from dependence on the little that comes the African's way from the white man's economic enterprises in Africa. This is the case in Rhodesia and Kenya just as in Ghana and Nigeria, in Morocco and French West Africa as well as in Liberia and the Sudan.

In the settler territories there will necessarily arise special problems, particularly with reference to the distribution and use of land. In Algeria, where the French farmer possesses all but 50 of the 1,300 largest farms and has an annual income of $4,200 a year compared with $70 a year for the Arab farmer,[12] nationalist leaders place agrarian reform as the third essential point in their program, following (1) the achievement of independence with a government, an army and their own foreign policy, and (2) the election of a constituent assembly. It has been frequently proposed that abolition of the "white reserves" should precede everything else in Kenya, the *New Statesman and Nation* for one suggesting in 1954 that the British Government "buy out the settlers and allow democracy to develop in an African Kenya." As for South Africa, the voluminous reports of the Tomlinson Commission (1955) and its numerous predecessors have resulted in no change in the continuing deterioration and famine in the "Native reserves," from whence slave-wage migrant workers are regularly drawn by the white farmers and mine owners. Only a government truly representative of the African majority will do away with these rural ghettoes or change the system whereby, as a South African writer (*Fighting Talk*, May, 1956) has indicated, white farmers were helped with $314 million in government funds while black farmers got about $2 million during the years from 1910 to 1936.

Some Problems of the Emergent African States

Thus far African nationalist movements have been compelled to concentrate on the overthrow of European *political* domination—the first liberation task. But mass demands for a better existence, for freedom to mean something more than just the right to vote and govern themselves, press upon the nationalist leaders. As the transfer of political power becomes an accomplished fact and the fight against alien overlordship recedes, the full force of the demands for economic deliverance must be faced. The newly freed countries of Asia and Africa cannot afford to let long intervals intervene between their political and social revolutions. They want to catch up with the industrially advanced countries and enjoy the same social standards they have—and without waiting 50 or 100 years. It is to be expected, therefore, that the drive for popular social-economic objectives will quickly develop a compelling momentum in the new African states.

There is no smooth, easy road ahead, however, even in the countries with no settler problem. For in addition to external pressures toward maintaining the social-economic *status quo*, internal obstacles must be overcome. A common characteristic of colonial liberation struggles is that the unity of the forces working together toward political emancipation is broken by divisive influences once that goal is achieved or nears achievement. Tribal, class, and sectional interests come to the fore as the control, form, and aims of government come to be decided. The united anti-imperialist front gives way to political parties contending against one another.

This disunity is in large part the legacy of colonialism. The opposition to the central government of Ghana by the Ashanti and Northern Territories, or the contention between the parties and leaders of Eastern, Western and Northern Nigeria, reflects the gratuitous bequest of the departing overlord. Mr. Harold Cooper, formerly with the British Colonial Administrative Service and now a lecturer on African Affairs at the School of Advanced International Studies, Johns Hopkins University, cites[13] the background of this bequest:

> Our adoption of the device of "indirect rule" had its origin in two worthy enough motives: to reduce the cost of administration and to preserve what was good in the institutions which had been built up, before our coming, by the Africans themselves. Where we made our mistake was in preserving those institutions like specimens in a bottle rather than as living plants which needed to be given elbow room for healthy growth. . . .
> As time went by, the chiefs leaned more and more on the administration as the buttress of their power, while the administration turned more and more to the chiefs for comfort and reassurance in face of the gathering unrest among the detribalized elements in the urban centers. . . . We made courtiers and aides-de-camp of the chiefs, who were our friends, and politicians of the nationalists, who were our foes . . . the British, as they pack up their polo helmets and get ready to pull out of West Africa, are leaving a good deal of unfinished business behind them. . . . Imperialism at the center is being dismantled, but lesser imperialisms formerly tributary to it survive.

Tribalism has been defined as "a socio-cultural antagonism to political and economic domination by the predominant national group (be it racial or linguistic-cultural) in a given African society." While this social feature obviously impedes political solidarity in the emerging African national state, it should not be regarded as foredooming the realization of a democratic state structure with an effective central authority. After all, there have been many states comprising heterogeneous societies formed in other parts of the world; they had their difficulties, too, and overcame them. Centralized authority is essential for the planning and execution of state-wide economic programs to which all will contribute and from which all will benefit. At the same time, cultural autonomy must be protected and fostered within the state; here the positive values of tribal resistance to domination will be seen in the preservation of a diversified cultural tradition.

As tribal exclusiveness tends toward vertical segmentation of the body politic, so growing class stratification tends toward horizontal segmentation. Both are important factors in the composition of the major political parties of Nigeria, for example. Here and in other countries, such as Ghana, the Sudan, French West Africa, Tunisia and Morocco, the dominant political parties are under the leadership or dependent upon the financial support of the more well-to-do elements of the indigenous society. These include the wealthier businessmen, merchants and traders; the rich farmers or farm operators; the higher categories of civil servants; and the overseas-trained lawyers and other intellectuals.

The corporation known as Zik Enterprises Ltd. embraces 12 subsidiary companies representing the varied commercial interests of Dr. Nnamdi Azikiwe, head of the National Council of Nigeria and Cameroons and Prime Minister of Eastern Nigeria. Chief Festus Samuel Okotie-Eboh, one-time treasurer of the NCNC and now Nigerian Minister of Labor and Welfare, is a rubber and timber magnate and owner of a chain of schools and various business enterprises. He smiles when the opposition calls him "Capitalist Minister." Mr. Louis Philip Ojukwu, another figure high in NCNC circles though not an active politician, operates a country-wide transport business and is a director of half a dozen British and African corporations in Nigeria and a member of another half dozen government corporations and boards.

In the NCNC,, whose power is based mainly on the Ibo people in the East, as well as in Mr. Obafemi Awolowo's Action Group in

Western Nigeria, where the Yorubas are dominant, there are numerous other men of similar financial standing. In the Northern Region of the Hausas, the Northern People's Congress represents the interests of the emirs, sultans and other hereditary feudal rulers who have reason to fear the loss of their own power when the British go.

It should be understood, of course, that men such as Chief Festus and Mr. Ojukwu by no means represent the average West African businessman. Trade and commerce remain dominated by the big European firms, with Syrian, Lebanese and Indian merchants occupying an intermediate status. But some small gains have been registered by the African entrepreneur, who brings up the rear. In Nigeria, for example, African buyers were handling over 18 per cent of the country's cocoa and nearly seven per cent of its palm kernels and peanuts in 1953 as compared with less than one per cent of these crops a decade earlier.[14] The growing demarcation between big and petty traders is illustrated by the establishment of an all-African Gold Coast Chamber of Commerce, and by a meeting of local merchants in Lagos in 1955 at which the small traders complained of being at the mercy of both European and wealthy Nigerian businessmen, and shouted "Capitalist! Capitalist!" at an African speaker who proposed that Government should restrict the issuance of import licenses on the basis of a trader's initial capital and the number of houses and cars he owned.

Back in 1950 soon after the CPP had won its first victory at the polls, Nkrumah warned his followers in words that merit current re-emphasis:

> We see daily the consequences of the love of money, and Western civilization is tottering on its foundation because Mammon and all that it stands for is making a last desperate effort to be the supreme ruler of the world. . . . As a young race now looking forward to freedom and all its responsibilities, we must be careful how we imitate, blindly, the evils of greed which have done so much havoc to Western civilization.
>
> Already today there are signs that we are disregarding the African way of giving and sharing with each other. Today, Africans turn out Africans from their houses because foreigners will pay a higher rent. Today, many Africans join with foreigners to undo and harass other Africans. We cannot allow these degenerate Africans to flourish in our midst and we look on all such people as liabilities to the liberation movement and fifth columnists and Quislings.[15]

It is evident that the European corporations operating in Africa seek to maintain and strengthen their position by taking the wealthier African business men into the family. These firms have heeded the advice given by a former British Colonial Secretary, Oliver Lyttelton (now Lord Chandos). "What you really want to do," he told them, "is to build up a feeling that the foreign capital and the local inhabitants are engaged in a trusteeship" by appointing local directors and giving opportunities for local share capital investments, however small. Besides making room for individual African investors and directors, foreign firms in such countries as Nigeria, Ghana, Liberia and Uganda have also provided for investments in their enterprises by local governments or government corporations—investments short of majority control, that is.

Another tactic is illustrated by the United Africa Co. increasing the number of Africans in its management staff from one-twelfth of the total in 1939 to one-quarter by 1954. Early in 1955 two Africans were for the first time appointed to the board of UAC in the Gold Coast. A commentator reports: "There has been in recent years an effort to transfer up-country retail trade to African supervision or even to full African control. This is a maneuver which, to use a military metaphor, can be described as 'removing the visible occupation.' Its major advantage is that it promotes prosperity and contentment among that huge class of middlemen from which political parties draw most of their funds and a portion of their leadership." There is this additional observation made: "Favorable as the climate may seem for the foreign investor, some of the old animosities are still pulsating only a little way below the surface of events."[16]

With the issue of political independence holding the center of the stage and with the necessity of attending to first things first, there has clearly been an effort by the nationalist leaders in Nigeria and the Gold Coast (prior to the achievement of independence this year) to avoid any direct clash with the foreign economic interests in these countries which might jeopardize or delay the grant of self-government. The same consideration might account for their repeated assurances that there would be no nationalization of the mines or other private enterprises.

In earlier days, before the British made any formal commitments about West Africa's political future, criticism of the parisitic foreign monopolies was open and vigorous. There was at the same time suspicion of any kind of fraternization by Africans in public office with British personnel "except on purely official relations." "What imperialists failed to achieve by strong-arm methods, they will hope to bring off by cocktail parties," said the Gold Coast's CPP; and Nigeria's NCNC warned that ceremonial parades and other such "official clap-traps tend to soften our nationalism and make stooges of otherwise dynamic nationalists."

That remains the prevailing sentiment in places like Kenya or Rhodesia, where Mr. Dixon Konkola calls on the workers to demand nationalization of the copper mines. But in the British West African countries times and tactics have changed. There was, for instance, nothing whatever out of order to mar the recent visit of Her Majesty to Nigeria, most dazzling of all the "official clap-traps." Certainly it is appropriate that an atmosphere of harmony should attend the transfer of political power, if at all possible. Nevertheless, it must be said that there have been some disquieting signs on the West African economic scene while awaiting that event.

Reassurances to foreign investors may be good diplomacy in the circumstances, but what of the excursions abroad by West African leaders in search of more European and American investors? And what of the new recent concessions? British rubber and tea planters who no longer found the Malayan climate very healthy have now turned to West Africa, and been welcomed. In the Cameroons, adjacent to and politically integrated with Nigeria, tea and cocoa (Cadbury) plantations have recently been granted. And a Dunlop rubber estate concession with full British ownership rights has lately been obtained in Eastern Nigeria, whose Prime Minister, Dr. Azikiwe, once declared that "the plantation system owned and worked by white men with foreign capital is unacceptable."

It is quite understandable that it would have been diplomatically unwise for Dr. Nkrumah's Government in 1956 to have dug down to the basic question of the validity of the place occupied by the European mining companies in the Gold Coast's economy, although that would seem to be the fundamental issue raised by the wage dispute which the Government was called upon to settle between the gold mining firms (whose annual production is worth about $28 million) and the mine workers (whose wages, an inquiry board found, were not even enough to feed them adequately). Assuming that a thorough-going examination of the problem had to be side-stepped at the time, one yet wonders whether there was no other recourse for the Government except to award a $560,000 two-year subsidy to the gold mines so that they might make some small wage increase for their workers (short of the Union's demands) and thus keep the mines operating—and dividends continuing to British shareholders.

The most disturbing thing about these developments is that they may make it more difficult for the African governments to proceed on the right economic road when they *have* achieved full self-government and *can* make their own decisions.

The CPP, let us remember, stands pledged "to serve as a vigorous conscious political vanguard for removing all forms of oppression and for the establishment of a democratic socialist society." The NCNC in Nigeria has expressed similar aims. And in French West Africa the *Bloc Démocratique Sénégalais*, headed by M. Senghor, which merged recently with the new unified *Bloc Populaire Sénégalais*, voiced the objective of "eliminating classes and castes by the conquest of power and the socialization of the means of production and exchange." Do these expressions imply the intention of seeking the achievement of socialist goals by revolutionary methods? No. As Mr. Thomas Hodgkin, a close student of African nationalist movements, notes, "Both Dr. Nkrumah and M. Senghor are well acquainted with Marxism, but they and the parties which they lead are committed, for the present, to policies of gradualism. The fact is rather that any African 'mass' party, if it wishes to gain popular support, must speak the language of modern radicalism."[17]

And if it is to retain that popular support, we would add, it must strive to meet the needs of the people with a specific program for lifting them out of the bondage of colonial dependence. "What is our next united task?" asked Dr. Nkrumah in October, 1956, following the announcement of the coming date of Ghana's independence. It was, he said, "the achievement of economic justice: freedom from want, and freedom from disease, filth and squalor."

After Suez—What?

The issue of the right of once subject countries to exercise sovereign control over their resources was flung smack into the center of world attention by President Gamal Abdel Nasser's nationalization of the French-British privately owned Suez Canal Co., July 26, 1956. That act marked the culminating stage in the long struggle for full Egyptian independence.

Persia in 525 B.C. was one of the earlier invading overlords to seize Egypt, whose national history goes back more than six thousand years; Britain, arriving in 1882, was the last. "They always said they were on the point of leaving, and always found an excuse to stay," says Nasser of the British. London was forced to grant limited independence in 1922 and yielded further rights in 1936, but the British garrison remained in the Suez Canal Zone and British dictation of Egyptian policy was all too crudely manifested during World War II. The postwar upsurge and the Nasser-Naguib coup and ousting of Farouk at last compelled Britain to agree (February, 1953) to self-government for the Sudan and (October, 1954) to military evacuation of the Suez. The last British soldier carried away the last British flag five days before the deadline of June 18, 1956. But the Suez Canal Co. remained. And Mr. Dulles set the stage for its demise, the act of nationalization coming just one week after the State Department's "calculated risk" retraction of the offer of United States help in building Egypt's Aswan Dam.

The income from Egyptian operation of the Canal, said Nasser, would be used to build the Dam and fulfill the development of the country's economy. (The Company's receipts from ship tolls in 1955 amounted to $98.6 million, yielding dividends of $30.5 million—9,500 francs on each 250 franc share; Egypt got $9.5 million, including taxes.) He pledged that shareholders in the defunct company (registered in Egypt and subject to Egyptian law), whose 99-year lease would have expired November 16, 1968, would be fully compensated at share prices in the Paris Bourse as of July 25.

In the heady swirl of charges, conferences, proposed plans, and debate that followed Nasser's declaration, the one thing to emerge clearly from the statements of the British, French and American diplomats was their common insistence on regaining *control* of the operation of the Canal—by force if necessary, said Eden and Mollet; by peaceful means if possible, said Dulles. They yielded reluctantly at last to public demand that the matter be brought to the United Nations. When Egypt still refused to submit to dictated terms, the British and French created an excuse to apply force, with a humiliating fiasco as the outcome.

The objective of control was sometimes slightly disguised under a rather curiously inept appeal to principle: "One man, one nation must not control an international waterway!" This, as one writer comments, is "Pretty cool, considering that Britain controlled it alone from 1882 to 1952 . . . expressly rejecting internationalization under the League of Nations in 1924 (when the Egyptian Premier Zaghul proposed it to Ramsay Macdonald): considering too how Britain has opposed international supervision of the Dardanelles."[18] Not to mention the closer-home instance of the United States and the Panama Canal.

The Suez issue brought into sharp contrast the old world principle of imperial power and the new world concept of the sovereign equality of nations. During the negotiations prior to the invasion of Egypt it was NATO *vs.* Bandung and the Soviet Union. Even countries usually allied with the West backed away from efforts toward pressuring Egypt into submission. And when it came to the actual use of military force, the United States went over to the side of Bandung and the Soviet Union—a significant new departure, even if short-lived, in American policy and international relations. With both of the world's foremost powers aligned against them the would-be conquerors ceased their blustering and beat a hasty retreat from Egypt.

Before the invasion the Tunisian and Moroccan governments had voiced popular support of Nasser's stand, conceding his right to nationalize the Suez Canal Co. despite French views to the contrary. The Sudanese government said that Egypt has exercised her sovereign right and wished her all success. Dr. Azikiwe of Nigeria declared, "We [Africans] regard the Suez Canal crisis as something that was inevitable because sooner or later those of us who had unequal treaties imposed upon our grandfathers must react like Nasser."[19] One can forecast with fair certainty, as a consequence of Suez, increasing mass demands for an economic New Deal coming from the peasants, industrial workers, small traders and businessmen, and the new rising generation of students up and down the continent. In other African countries, as in Egypt, the people will not be satisfied with less than full independence.

The pressures from below were swelling up even before the Suez crisis. The secretary-general of the Tunisian trade union movement (UGTT) warned the pre-Neo-Destour regime in 1955 that "If the new government does not establish an action program, we shall have a free hand regardless of who the new cabinet and its head may be." Though the trade unions are hostile to the Bourguiba Government's social and economic policies, the principal labor leaders in the name of national unity have striven to postpone a showdown. But some sections of the labor movement refuse to shelve even temporarily their demands for a socialized economy.

With the deterioration of their relations with France during the latter half of 1956, the Tunisian and Moroccan government leaders turned more and more toward the United States. Suggestions of the need for American financial aid were coupled with diplomatic reminders that the United States air bases in Morocco had never received the Sultan's sanction. One Moroccan spokesman summed it up: "The United States can save North Africa for the West if she helps us now." But at the same time Moroccan labor raised stronger demands for protective measures against the foreign monopolies and a start in nationalization of the predominant French-held enterprises in the country.

French West Africa had the dubious distinction of representation in Premier Mollet's Cabinet at the time of the 1956 Suez crisis. The representative was M. Felix Houphouet-Boigny, a wealthy cocoa and coffee planter, the first African in France to hold full ministerial rank. We have referred earlier to his role as head of the RDA and to the split that occurred in the organization. It has been pointed out that "Although it was the Right (*tendance Houphouet*) that retained control of the political machine, the Left was by no means eliminated: *tendance D'Arboussier* still has influence ... among the students, in the trade unions, and in the local party branches."[20] At the unity meeting held in Dakar in mid-1956 an officially recognized (Houphouet) section of the RDA and an expelled (D'Arboussier) section both joined in the all-Senegalese political entente. Such current trends within the country, the growing strength of the African labor movement, and the impact of events in North Africa and Egypt all point toward the resurgence of militant nationalism in the French sub-Sahara territories. The recent enlargement of African political rights in those colonies will not suffice to satisfy rising demands for full equality of status.

In British West Africa, along with a developing middle class there is also evident the growth of class consciousness in the ranks of labor, particularly in Nigeria. A special relationship exists in Nigeria and other British West African countries between labor and government in that the government departments are the direct employers of the great majority of wage workers. Labor spokesmen in Nigeria complain that politicians who once championed labor's cause, particularly at the time of the 1945 general strike, have become indifferent upon assuming power.[21] There has been continuing agitation for the organization of an independent labor party in Eastern Nigeria, and the formation of a United Working People's Party has been announced. Such are the trends at present, although as yet no working class party has become a factor in Nigerian politics.

The All-Nigeria Trade Union Federation (ANTUF), which advanced from 53,000 members in 1953 to 181,000 in 1955 (nine-tenths of all organized workers and about one quarter of all wage-workers in the country), is a force for national unity and progress. At its third annual congress, November, 1955, ANTUF called for the development of heavy industry, mechanization of agriculture, and the extension of cooperatives, and reaffirmed labor's demand for Nigerian independence and a unitary form of government.

Another West African problem is that of the tens of thousands of poorer cocoa and other cash crop farmers, many of them heavily debt-laden. The improvement of their lot requires that the new African governments disencumber themselves of the colonial legacy of the single crop economy and the attendant inevitable exploitation of the peasant producer. One of course hears of plans for the development of new industries in the various territories, but there has as yet not been found any substitute for the customary colonial expedient of financing such projects and government expenditure in general primarily on the basis of revenue from exports of peasant produce. Since such revenue depends on the margin of difference between the price of cocoa or palm oil in the world market and what the African farmer gets paid for it, it is obviously in the government's interest to keep the farmer's price for his crop down to the lowest possible level. That it is an African instead of a European administration that does this in no wise alters the harsh consequences upon the cash-crop farmer. As long as the old system continues, one can look for further trouble such as has arisen lately among angry Sudanese cotton growers and Ashanti cocoa producers.

The problem of financing development expenditure out of current revenue raises again the question of the very substantial sterling balances belonging to Ghana and Nigeria held in London banks. And belonging to other African countries, too: Dr. Muwazi of the Uganda National Congress asked in 1955 why capital from the United States and Canada should be required for the Kilembe copper mine project when Uganda had some $78 million available for investment in her cotton, coffee, and maize funds. The Gold Coast's overseas balance at the end of 1955 was £215 million ($602 million). One view of this matter of the sterling balances, a sensible one it seems to us, is as follows:

Rather than maintaining the foreign confidence by which the Government sets such store, on the basis of large, inactive and, with the steady rise in prices, depreciating real value of the reserves, it might be better for it to rely for this confidence on a soundly contrived expansion and diversification of the economy as a whole. A country such as the Gold Coast, verging on independence, should be able—and ought—to insist that it dispose of its sterling balances in the manner in which it conceives to be in its own best interests.[22]

So we come back to the original question of what is required after political emancipation to achieve complete African freedom. "The index of economic independence," writes a young Nigerian, "will be measured not by pretentious economic plans or the amount of foreign capital that is attracted, but rather by the pursuit of calculated economic development programs based upon a definable economic doctrine that reflects the needs of the people."[23]

The accomplishment of this goal will bring the improvement of the cocoa farmer's income and existence, the raising of the mineworker's wages, the provision of consumer goods at a fair price for the mother, free and adequate education and health services for her children—all the concrete things for which Africans aspire when they demand "Self-Government Now." But getting these things requires that the government leaders, supported by all sections of the population, come to grips with and remove the obstacles that stand in the way, particularly the alien-controlled corporate interests that grow fat on Africa's natural wealth and the toil of its people. Political freedom must open the way to economic, social and cultural freedom. That is what many millions of Africans expect and demand. Truly has Dr. Nkrumah said, "In everything we say and do . . . we must . . . avoid getting isolated from the people."

Some five years ago a member of the Nigerian House of Representatives, the central legislature, spoke these words:

For the first time in the history of this country the humble peasant has, thanks to the struggle of the people of my party, come to play the most significant role of electing those who legislate for his country. Probably over eighty per cent of us in this house hold our mandate from those humble poor in our remote villages. . . . I can still see the earnest faces of those peasant electors from Akpabuyo, Uwet, Okoyong and Odot: the very incarnation of poverty and illiteracy and bad health. . . . The rural people, the disinherited masses, must now come to the focus in our policy. They have a real bargaining power in our economy. We do not have to wait till they agitate before we turn the scale of history in their favor. We are here as their brothers and servants to meet their needs.[24]

16. New Horizons: The Worlds of Bandung and Socialism

AT THE FIRST London Conference on the Suez crisis, September, 1956, the Soviet Union's Dmitri T. Shepilov and India's Krishna Menon tried earnestly but without success to impress upon the gentlemen of the West that their endeavors to override Egypt's sovereign rights and impose their own dictates were dangerously out of date in the present-day world. It is one thing for the gentlemen of the West to disavow colonialism and declare it dead; it is quite another thing for them to abandon the habits of colonial masters.

Freed from foreign rule, nearing it, or looking toward it, and united by a common contempt of second-rate status, the peoples of Asia, the Middle East and Africa are no longer amenable to the gunboat-diplomacy of another day. Nor can they be forced to bend the knee by economic strangulation, for they now have an alternative to Western markets in the socialist sector of the world.

The Alternative of Socialist Assistance

Time was when economically backward countries desiring industrialization had to accept the plans and terms of European or American investors, or do without outside help. Like it or lump it. But times have changed. The unindustrialized countries, as Walter Lippmann has indicated, are no longer "dependent upon us because [in the socialist countries] they now have an alternative supplier of capital and technical aid. . . . The emergence of the

Soviet Union as a competitor is one of the great historic events of our times."[1] The monopoly by monopolies has been cracked.

The Soviet Union's heavy industry has now advanced to the stage where it can meet domestic requirements, help build up the industrial plants of other socialist countries, and provide a surplus of capital goods for export to non-socialist countries that want it. And they can also supply the technicians and engineers to bring industrialization and mechanized agriculture to such countries: build a plant for turning out farm tractors, let us say; train people to operate the plant; and show them how to make the best use of the tractors. Former U. S. Assistant Secretary of State William Benton reported in January, 1956, that the Soviet Union was turning out 50 per cent more engineers and more experts in certain technical specialties than the United States. Seven months later a member of the U. S. Atomic Energy Commission, Dr. Willard F. Libby, said the Soviet Union was graduating more than twice as many engineers as this country.

Not only the Soviet Union but other Eastern European socialist countries and China are now in a position to export the steel and machines for heavy industry and the technical know-how to go with them. They have been doing so. It was not much of a problem for China, for instance, out of an output of 2,850,000 tons of steel in 1955 (more than double its 1952 production), to sell 60,000 tons of it to Egypt, or for Hungary, prior to the upheaval there in 1956, to provide the equipment and technical aid to build an electric power plant in the same country.

Soviet economic aid programs to less developed countries throughout Asia, the Middle East and parts of Africa perhaps exceeded those of the United States in quantity, a U.S. Senate subcommittee reported in July, 1956. The *kind* of assistance given is of more significance than the quantity of it. The socialist countries do not normally make direct money loans, so assisted governments do not have the problem of heavy interest rates or of being restricted to spending the money as the lender directs. Neither are socialist countries seeking export markets for manufactured consumer goods or secondary industries of their own in poorer countries. Their assistance takes the form of barter transactions that will enable the countries to industrialize themselves, Burmese rice for Soviet heavy industrial equipment, Egyptian flax for Czechoslovakian agricultural machinery.

A World Bank mission to India advised the Government that

the solution to its financial problems was to lower the barriers to foreign investment. But India's former Minister for Commerce and Industry, Mr. T. T. Krishnamachari, said:

> In a country with a low standard of living, very high marginal rates of profits are not possible in any industry, much less in a consumer industry. . . . Owing to these reasons India might remain for quite a number of years unattractive to venture capital. . . . We hold steadfast to our determination that we shall not sell our freedom, no matter what may be the temptation. The real test of international interest in India is not the giving of doles but in the sharing of technical knowledge and helping India to industrialize. . . . We accept help from whatever quarter it comes so long as it is not tied to any political strings.[2]

One example of foreign aid that meets this test is the Soviet Union's construction of a one million ton capacity steel plant at Bhilai in Central India.

"The backward countries have been greatly disappointed by word from the United States that the use of reactors to produce electricity in underdeveloped areas is still a long way off," wrote Thomas J. Hamilton of the *New York Times* (March 3, 1955). The offer to train technicians to operate the reactors "when they are ready," he said, fell far short of Asian expectations. However, in August, 1956, a group of Egyptian scientists left Cairo to study at Soviet atomic research institutions in preparation for the establishment of a nuclear laboratory in Egypt, with the aid of Soviet technicians and materials, toward the use of atomic energy for peaceful purposes.

The Cold War vs. African Self-Determination

At the time of the great Soviet counter-offensive drive in the last war, Prime Minister Smuts, speaking in the South African Senate, paid tribute to "a feat of desperate bravery for which there is scarcely a parallel in all history. We may inveigh against Bolshevism, against Communism," he said, "but if these are the fruits of Communism they represent one of the most amazing things in all history. This is a fact, a fact to be reckoned with not only in our day but for generations to come."[3]

At the invitation of Premier Stalin a delegation from the British Parliament made a tour of the Soviet Union early in 1945. A member of the delegation, Col. (now Sir) Charles Ponsonby, gave a report of his observations at a meeting of the Royal Empire and

Royal African Societies, Lord Hailey presiding. He said in part:

In Russia I visited the Republics in Central Asia of Azerbajan, Uzbekistan and Turkmenistan, but I will take Uzbekistan as an example. . . . Twenty-one years ago the literacy in Uzbekistan was seven per cent. . . . There were only one or two small irrigation schemes on the Czar's estates—there were no factories and no hydro-electric plants. What is the situation after twenty-one years? Now 98 per cent of the population can read and write; there are 4,000 schools, two universities and several technical institutes; there are large, efficient factories; huge irrigation schemes; twenty hydro-electric plants, and, amongst other things, a wonderful ballet and opera, including in its repertoire *Othello* and *Desdemona*. . . .

When I visited these Central Asian States, and saw all this progress I was bound to make comparisons. . . . Could we have done what was done in Uzbekistan or Turkmenistan? Here is an instance. In 1924 a boy leading his flocks from one oasis to the next; in 1945 that boy a member of a collective farm (irrigated) and sharing in a bus to go to the principal city to listen to his favorite opera—*Hamlet*. Can you see that happening in East Africa?[4]

The French Colonial Conference at Brazzaville early in 1944 also decided to send a delegation to study Soviet methods of education. But Africans even more than their administrators were anxious to apply the lessons of Soviet experience to the problems of their own countries. There is wide evidence that there existed in 1945 the real basis for European-Soviet cooperation in promoting African advancement. But then the Cold War intervened. Now, after a decade, the Soviet Union has come forward and offered economic assistance to the independent peoples of Africa.

We and the Africans were told that a Soviet military invasion threatened that continent, and that an insidious campaign of Communist subversion and propaganda was under way to stir up riot and insurrection. NATO was extended to North Africa, American and European bases were hurriedly established, military conferences called at Nairobi and Dakar, a METO (Middle East Treaty Organization) added to NATO, Communist parties outlawed in North and South Africa, possession of Communist publications made a punishable offense almost everywhere, all the doors and windows tightly shut and locked.

But it seems we were misinformed. The "enemy" came by sea, not by land. He came offering trade deals and technical know-how. We and the Africans were not forewarned of that. It just wasn't expected in the Western capitals, any more than it was expected that the Soviet could make an atom bomb so soon. Nevertheless, this offer of economic assistance was also a threat to Africa and the "free world," we were then informed, "an acute phase of the Cold War." And Vice President Nixon was called upon to make a hurried trip around the world carrying the message that the price of such Communist aid was a "rope around the neck."

We have not yet been told how this alleged Communist noose differs from the made-in-America one that Walter Lippman alluded to when he spoke of the United States Government going "to great lengths in tying economic aid to the raising of local military forces in the countries we help."[5] A communique issued in February, 1956, by the Liberian Embassy in Washington, quoting an editorial in the *Liberian Age*, a Government organ, made note of the fact that "elsewhere the Soviet does not dictate how money is to be spent by recipient nations and is offering easy terms, and is not linking programs with military commitments as is America." While indicating Liberia's rejection of the Soviet offer of economic assistance, the statement at the same time pointedly asked, "But has America offered us worthwhile economic aid?" It would require quite a volume to quote even a fraction of the statements by Americans in and out of public office characterizing United States foreign economic aid—ECA, Point Four, technical assistance, and the rest—as an instrument for the accomplishment of United States political objectives, a Cold War weapon.

Let us recall one instance of this weapon's use, the case of the offer and subsequent refusal of United States (and World Bank) funds for Egypt's great project to develop the Nile Valley. When Mr. Dulles turned his back on the Aswan Dam scheme, the alleged unstable condition of Egypt's economy was given as the reason for the rebuff. But at a press conference about a month earlier Secretary Dulles had said that it was "unlikely" that the United States "would find it practical or desirable" to assist on the Dam if the Soviet Union had a share in it.[6] At the same conference he said that Egypt's recognition of the Chinese People's Republic was "an action that we regret." Over two years earlier, when the agreement on British military evacuation of the Suez Canal Zone was under discussion, the Egyptian Government was informed "that its current tactical flirtation with a policy of neutralism endangers its chances of obtaining United States economic and diplomatic assistance."[7]

Let us now hear the other side of the case, President Nasser speaking:

Our dealings with the Communist bloc have been strictly commercial. It has attached no political strings to any of its deals, including my purchase of arms from Czechoslovakia. Our cotton, on which our whole economy depends, was piling up. Britain was exerting economic pressure on us and the United States had its own surplus cotton problem. . . . We had to expand our trade so that we could build up new industry and wipe out the poverty of our people. If I had continued to allow our cotton to pile up simply because of a hypothetical fear of what might happen if we dealt with Communists, I would have been a fool.[8]

If countries must pass a loyalty test to secure United States economic aid, it is clearly not the case with Soviet offers of economic cooperation, for these have been extended to such countries as Pakistan, the Latin American republics in general, and two of the foremost bastions of the West in Africa, Libya and Liberia. The object, said Mr. Nixon, is to make them economic, political and/or military satellites of the Soviet Union. If so, is it conceivable that any sane government would go about it in such a wholesale fashion, including some of the toughest customers in the bargain? It seems more likely that what worries Washington is not so much the interests of the prospective recipients of Soviet aid as its *own* interests. What it fears is the weakening or loss of its *exclusive* controling influence in the countries concerned; it fears giving these countries the chance to make choices and decisions of their own.

It is this anxiety which underlies the so often repeated concept that Africa "is the potential prize of competing ideologies," or "promises to become one of the major economic and ideological battlegrounds in the struggle between the Communist bloc and the Atlantic Alliance." This view of Africa is widely current—even among that majority of the American people who support the cause of African freedom. It has become a commonplace like the fatalistic expression, "Another strike, so prices will go up again," something one repeats after others without pausing to analyze. But there are also certain people who know precisely what they are saying when they speak of Africa as the "prize," the "battleground." They mean that African freedom is all right in the abstract, but it is not for the people to decide for themselves what they will do with their freedom—they won't be *allowed* to make that decision.

Often the expression reflects the attitude (either unconscious or deliberate) of one talking about inferior people who *can't know* which way to go but must be pulled this way or that. This brings to mind the remark of a Belgian official cited by the Rev. George

W. Carpenter, an American missionary with long experience in the Congo. The official said to him, "We used to think the African's mind was an empty vessel, and that all we had to do was to pour European civilization into it. No one now would dare make such a statement, but our policies are still based on that idea. We must rethink everything."

In the twists and turns of American policy on how best to keep Africa in the Western camp there has been a wavering uncertainty between the view that the pace of liberation should be slowed down lest "dangerous political vacuums" be created, and the view that it should be speeded up lest the people turn toward others who *support* their struggles. Here, too, some rethinking is needed. For it becomes increasingly evident that the grant of independence is not the end of the matter. A correspondent of the New York Times (Aug. 19, 1956), has remarked that some Americans "assuredly are disillusioned with the idea that if only the one-time colonies get their independence soon enough they will become loyal friends and allies."

Nor will their minds be made up by what they are told in Voice of America broadcasts, in hand-outs from the continent-wide offices of the United States Information Service, and by a constant stream of visiting good-will ambassadors, white and colored. Nigerian newspapers may carry a dispatch from Washington announcing that "49 per cent of all Negro families [in 1950] owned their own automobiles." And they may print a Voice of America "Factual Survey of the American Negro," the first sentence of which reads, "Negro Americans, who comprise one-tenth of the population of the United States, are participating today in every phase of American life." But the African newspapers also report—and much more prominently—what is happening to Afro-Americans in Alabama, Mississippi and Texas, or the fact that the American State Department until overruled by the Supreme Court, did not allow Paul Robeson or Dr. W. E. B. Du Bois to travel abroad.

The prevalent African reaction to the Cold War mental diet fed them is perhaps summed up in a *West African Pilot* editorial (June 30, 1953):

> We know no more about Communism than what its American and British detractors have pushed across to us as propaganda. . . . But judging from what we see and experience from day to day, we feel that all this talk of the so-called "free world" and "iron curtain" is a camouflage to fool and bamboozle colonial peoples. It is part and parcel of power politics into which we refuse to be drawn until we are free to choose which ideology suits us best.
>
> For the time being, we shall judge every nation strictly on the merits of the attitude of that nation towards our national aspirations. We have every cause to be grateful to the Communists for their active interest in the

fate of colonial peoples and for their constant denunciation of the evils of imperialism. It is then left to the so-called "free" nations to convince us that they are more concerned about our welfare than the Communists, and in this regard we believe more in action than in mere words.

There are undoubtedly some wealthier indigenous elements in Morocco, Tunisia, West Africa and elsewhere who would welcome an alliance with American capital in keeping down their dissatisfied peasants and workers (called "Communists" to simplify matters). But the model of Liberia is too widely known throughout Africa for the acceptance of American "protection" to be popular among newly-liberated peoples.

And despite all the locking of doors and windows, Africans do somehow manage to learn something of what is going on in the non-Western parts of the world. Emperor Haile Selassie tells an American interviewer, "Communism has no hold on my people at present. But my people understand from listening to the radio that Communism has done a lot of good in certain countries."[9] The Information Service of India in Accra, Ghana, for instance, has provided public film showings of India's accomplishments since independence and of Nehru's tour of the Soviet Union.

The African press, though hampered by limited news sources, provides occasional uncensored reporting of events such as the welcome given by the Indian people to Premier Bulganin and Mr. Khrushchev during their visit (November, 1955) to India. The *Ghana Evening News* (January 17, 1956) devoted most of its front page to the report of the Soviet Communist Party on the new Five-Year-Plan, quoting the statement that Russia could "in peaceful economic competition in historically shortest time overtake and surpass—on population basis—the most developed capitalist countries."

The question-box editor of the *Nigerian Tribune* (Jan. 24, 1956) answered a reader's query whether Nigeria should reject an offer of technical and economic assistance like that extended by Soviet representatives to Liberia on the occasion of her 1956 inaugural celebration.

It may be quite true [the editor writes] that in attending the inauguration and in making the offer of aid Russia was trying to get a foothold in Africa. But whatever may be Russia's intentions, I think it is unwise for Liberia to throw away the offer either because she suspects Russia or because she is afraid of her godfather, the United States. . . . If and when Russia does make an offer to help us [in Nigeria] technically, economically or otherwise, I would vote for whole-hearted acceptance of the offer, always provided that no political strings are attached. A free Nigeria should welcome aid from any quarter.

The Meaning of Bandung

At the Asian-African Conference held at Bandung, Indonesia, April, 1955, the voices of the peoples of the two continents were heard in a united declaration of their determination to submit no longer to the dictation of others, but to chart their own path of progress, freedom and peace; to accept no longer an inferior status among nations, but to assert their right to cooperate as equals in the advancement of all mankind. The Bandung Conference, attended by the official representatives of 29 countries[10] embracing nearly a billion and a half inhabitants, marked a turning point. It represented the end of an historical era in which only white nations, with very few exceptions, could lay claim to the exercise of sovereign rights.

Bandung was a living demonstration of the practicability of coexistence. The delegates present represented practically every existing religious creed, political principle, and economic system; there were Christians and Shintoists, democrats and monarchists, communists and capitalists. Despite sharp exchanges of differences on some issues, they agreed unanimously on the final all-embracing Joint Communique. Said China's Premier Chou En-lai:

> The course which we peoples of the Asian and African countries have taken in striving for freedom and independence may vary, but our will to win and to preserve our freedom and independence is the same. However different the specific conditions in each of our countries may be, it is equally necessary for most of us to eliminate the state of backwardness caused by the rule of colonialism. We need to develop our countries independently with no outside interference and in accordance with the will of the people. The people of Asia and Africa . . . know that new threats of war will not only endanger the independent development of their countries, but also intensify their enslavement by colonialism. That is why the Asian and African peoples all the more hold dear world peace and national independence.

Such was the general common denominator of agreement. Said Indonesia's President Soekarno:

> What can we do? We can do much! We can inject the voice of reason into world affairs and mobilize all the spiritual, all the moral, and the political strength of Asia and Africa on the side of peace. . . . We can demonstrate to the minority of the world, which lives on other continents, that we, the majority, are for peace, not for war.

BANDUNG AND SOCIALISM

Bandung signalized the fact that in the traditional continental strongholds of colonialism, and particularly Asia, the anti-imperialist forces had advanced to the stage of taking in the whole world and not simply the boundaries of their respective countries as the province of their responsibility. It was the culmination of various Pan-African and Pan-Asian movements that first emerged after World War I, but which could not achieve full stature and unified form until solid gains had been made in the struggle for national liberation. It was at the same time the answer to an urgent need. Years before Bandung it was being said in South Africa, for example:

> Our nationalism must transcend the barriers of nationality and geography and discover in the peoples of Africa brothers in a common struggle to assert the dignity of Africa. . . . [It] is suicidal for us to think along different lines when the European powers and settlers are coordinating their thinking and their planning, and as far as possible pooling their resources.[11]

African nationalists, still on the lower rungs of liberation's ladder, have eagerly grasped the outstretched hand of their Asian brothers. The Africans' horizon has widened. The struggle of Indians for the freedom of Goa becomes a reminder to West Africans that they too face a coming fight to break Portugal's hold on her colonies in Africa, and they say, "The bonds of friendship between Asia and Africa since Bandung must therefore grow even tighter still. With the one great vision which unites us, the colored people, hand in hand with other races, must fight for a world free from such sporadic outbursts of imperialist violence and repression be they in Goa or Morocco, South Africa or elsewhere."[12]

"Freedom and peace are interdependent. The right of self determination must be enjoyed by all peoples," the representatives at Bandung declared with one voice. In striking contrast was the strong opposition of the colonial powers to the inclusion of the right of national self-determination in the draft covenants of the United Nations on human rights. After protracted delays and debates a vote was finally taken at the 1955 General Assembly on a draft article which specifically included colonial and trusteeship territories and which stated in part,

> All peoples have the right of self-determination. By virtue of this right they freely determine their political status and freely pursue their economic, social and cultural development. The peoples may, for their own ends, freely dispose of their natural wealth and resources. . . . In no case may a people be deprived of its own means of subsistence.

The vote was 33 in favor, 12 against, with 13 abstentions. Those in opposition were the United States, the United Kingdom, France, Belgium, Netherlands, Canada, Australia, New Zealand, Norway, Sweden, Turkey and Luxembourg. Shall we call these countries (adding South Africa, whose representatives were absent from the vote) the anti-Bandung minority of the world? Recent history has demonstrated that the more the Western powers seek to shore up their own economic and strategic interests at the expense of the "uncommitted" and so-called neutralist countries in Africa and Asia, the faster will their reputation and influence in those continents dwindle.

The term "neutralist," usually pronounced with a sneer by Cold War partisans, is not liked by leaders of the countries so designated because it implies simply a negative policy, one of non-involvement or aloofness. Yet President Eisenhower among others recalls that "We were a young country once" and for 150 years found such a policy of neutrality and non-involvement in European power conflicts necessary. Instead of calling it "neutralism," Prime Minister Nehru defines India's position as "the positive independent policy of a country trying to make friends with all and not hostile to any country." The critics of "neutralism," he says, are suffering from a hangover from old ways of thinking; they have not got rid of the old conception of Europe or America declaring what policy other countries should follow.[13]

And President Nasser's attitude in 1956 was similar. "What's a neutral policy? Neutrality is a term to use only in war. We adopt an independent policy, a policy of active coexistence. One-third of our trade is with the Western bloc, one-third with the Eastern bloc and one-third with the rest of the world. If our trade had all been with the West, we would be in a very critical position today. Thank God we had this policy."[14]

The Suez crisis that erupted in the summer of 1956 was the first head-on clash between Big Power domination and Asian-African self-determination following Bandung. That the issues could not be summarily resolved in the old ways of Western coercion and force, even though attempted, is proof of the existence of a new equation of world power. The abortive Anglo-French attack on Egypt indicated once again how desperate and degenerate the waning European imperialists are. It was a "preventive police action" to forestall Soviet aims and plans in the area, the aggressors said as a sort of after-thought. Does this foreshadow the shape of things to come? If the West's ideological and economic weapons cannot keep the African obedient to its dictation, will deadlier weapons be used, bombs such as fell on Port Said—all in the name of saving Africa from Communism?

Let us remember that the masses of Africans are not concerned with East-West differences and rivalries, that they *are* deeply concerned with winning their freedom, and that it is the continuance of Western domination in its various forms standing in the way of that freedom which will bring greater conflict and more war in Africa. The one alternative is the speedy grant of national self-determination, political and economic—freedom with no strings attached—to the continent's indigenous peoples.

17. "Who Is on My Side?"

THE MAIN OUTLINES of the present policy of the United States Government toward Africa, if it can be called a policy, date back to its entrance into World War II. In November, 1942, the same month that Lt. General Dwight D. Eisenhower landed in North Africa with 150,000 American troops, Dr. Emory Ross, general secretary of the Foreign Missions Conference of North America, wrote in the *Survey Graphic,* "In essence, our relationship to Africa today is a war relationship; our interest, a war interest. The relationship is not really *to* Africa; the interest is not really *in* Africa. In our present enterprise Africa is chiefly a base, a field, a terrain. Our major efforts there are to solve *our* problems."

Under the pressing urgency of concentrating on winning the war, such a self-centered policy at that time might be excused. *But has it changed?* General Carlos P. Romulo, certainly no leftist or enemy of Washington's officialdom, wrote[1] in 1955:

> The American attitude toward Asia and Africa is still colored by the same predominantly material considerations which originally motivated the Western approach toward Asia. In this view Asia is still primarily a theatre of the cold war, a potentially valuable ally in a shooting war, a major factor in global military strategy, a rich and populous region that must be kept in the camp of the democracies and on the side of the free world. Although this judgment may seem valid and sufficient for the purposes of the United States and the West, it does not seem so to the Asians and Africans themselves.

He stated that there must be a "revaluation" of American and Western relations to the peoples of Asia and Africa "before those relations deteriorate beyond repair." The same warning note has been struck by leading American anthropologists. Some years ago Dr. Melville Herskovits cautioned against continuing to "regard native peoples as groups for whom we must make decisions. . . . We must shed the assumption that if there is to be a world order it must be organized wholly on the European and American model."[2] More recently Dr. Ralph L. Beals has remarked:

> The discussions of applied anthropology in government shocked me by their complete acceptance of the view that the basic problem is how someone can do something to other people tacitly understood as inferior or subordinate. . . . It is time some, if not the primary, emphasis of applied anthropology should be on determining what people want and aiding them to get it rather than on how they can best be persuaded to do what is thought best for the dominant culture.[3]

The Africans' traditional practice of communal ownership and their ready acceptance of the modern system of cooperative enterprise would naturally seem to point toward the development of socialist rather than capitalist institutions. If so, what right have we to insist that they open up their countries to "free enterprise" or scrap the system of collective land tenure?

The emerging self-governing states require the materials and tools to modernize their agriculture and develop their own industries. Why should they not get such help wherever they can, provided it does not involve mortgaging their economic or political independence—a matter which they alone can and should decide?

If African governments seek to develop friendly diplomatic, trade, and cultural relations with all other states, by what authority can we say, "No—only with us and our allies!"?

"The Communists are very smart in their dealings in Africa and we are not," Congresswoman Frances P. Bolton told a Washington press conference upon her recent return from extensive sight-seeing in that continent. Americans there spent too much time denouncing Communists, she reported, while the socialist countries went about the business of selling goods to the Africans at prices they could afford.

A *New York Times* (April 9, 1956) survey of American foreign aid programs makes the following point: "The Soviet does not moralize about whether a country should have the arms it seeks or whether it needs the type of factory it wants. A result is that each deal creates much good will at relatively low cost. Carefully supervised loans and gifts, however lavish they may be, tend to leave the recipients with the feeling of the tramp who is required to sing a hymn to get a free cup of coffee."

Wanted: A Policy of Coexistence and Cooperation

The most certain way for America to "lose" Africa—to lose what is left of the Africans' friendship with this country and incur their enmity instead—is to continue the present methods of trying to "hold" it. The people of Africa have their future to build. The Cold War measuring-rod of United States objectives in that continent is out-dated and self-defeating. If "losing" Africa means its ceasing to be the special preserve of Western interests, then it is as certainly lost as Asia. The leaders of the West, let us hope, will face up to the reality of the relation of forces in today's world and resign themselves to the necessity of getting along otherwise than on the backs of the Africans.

An unnamed high European official is quoted as saying, "We'll simply have to work out a new way of living with the East—a way without special Western spheres of influence. It will not be nearly as good as the old ways but we haven't any choice."[4]

A fresh, new approach to United States-African relations will obviously require a simultaneous transformation of American-Soviet relations. Humanity demands this, it is sick to death of the dead-end stagnation and senseless armaments burden of a world divided into Western and Eastern camps. The cry is for coexistence and cooperation in place of antagonisms and conflict, for social reconstruction instead of atom bombs.

The West can make a try at this new way of living with the East in Africa. The reality of coexistence will develop out of the fruitful results of cooperation. Africa's great economic and social needs offer an extraordinary opportunity for practical East-West cooperation. Why should not the United States and the Soviet Union work *together* in helping to build Egypt's Aswan Dam, for example? Here is one path to a unified world of peace and progress; what is done in Africa should promote similar advances in other areas.

In the widespread reappraisal of foreign aid programs in the United States and abroad that has attended the Soviet Union's entrance into the field of assisting the economic development of non-socialist countries, there has been a pronounced emphasis on the need for giving the United Nations the necessary funds and authority for performing this function on a far bigger scale than it has hitherto done. It is properly said by Asian, African, and some Western spokesmen that such assistance has great advantages over unilateral aid programs in that it minimizes the danger of Big Power domination and the aggravation of spheres-of-influence politics. The support for such an enlarged United Nations program of economic aid for "underdeveloped countries" comes from an extremely wide range of church, civic, labor, foreign relations and other organizations of citizens in the United States and Britain.

The present governments of these countries, however, plead the impracticability of the project until progress has been made on disarmament agreements and reduction in expenditures for weapons of war. Certainly it is true that for other more important reasons than financial ones, little wholehearted or substantial support by the major powers for United Nations or other schemes of East-West cooperation in aiding needy countries can be expected as long as they give top priority to planning and spending for war. But the fact is—as admitted by all except Chiang Kai-shek, Syngman Rhee, and a few others of the same kind—that the war alarms have receded. Steps have been taken toward the reduction of armed forces in countries on both sides. And world-wide pressure continues to increase for a universal ban on the production, testing, and use of nuclear and thermonuclear weapons.

Therefore, even though much yet remains to be done toward promoting a secure peace, conditions are ripe for a new beginning in the sphere of international cooperation in the interest of the economic and social needs of less developed countries. Such a beginning, moreover, may contribute toward the resolution of political differences and the further reduction of armaments. On the other hand, with continued postponement of a fresh approach to this kind of international cooperation within or outside the United Nations framework, there is almost certain to come a multiplication of frictions and conflicts in Africa, Asia and the Middle East.

The United States is the main battleground where the fight for a constructive Western foreign policy must be won. Walter Lippmann is one of many who have pointed out that, "The military policy, as we now operate it, is incompatible with the kind of constructive economic aid that so many of us inside and outside the Administration believe is necessary."[5]

According to the testimony of Secretary of State Dulles before the Senate Foreign Relations Committee, April 30, 1956, 83 per cent of American foreign aid at that time was military and was contributed to countries allied with Washington in various "mutual security" pacts. Nearly half of all United States foreign economic aid in 1956 went to such Cold War allies as South Korea, Formosa, South Vietnam, Pakistan and Turkey—countries that Senator Allen J. Ellender of Louisiana has collectively called "bloodsuckers." One of them, South Korea, receives from the United States $300 million a year for economic support and another $300 million in military assistance. And add to this the enormous expenditure for the United States' own military forces. One item: $4 *billion* for 500 B-52 jet "stratofortresses" to carry hydrogen bombs.

An economic aid program which is primarily an adjunct of a military program is worse than none at all. It does economic harm to the recipient, gives the donor dangerous delusions of strength, and breeds international friction. The American people want a program of peace, as politicians at election time realize only too well; but their government's policies are shaped to military specifications. It is time that human values took precedence over strategic criteria in the formulation of American foreign policy.

Can the American economy weather the shift from war production? One might better ask where we are headed if there *isn't* such a shift made. The change-over from large-scale war production to peace-time production must necessarily, just like the reverse process, involve a measure of state planning and implementation. Surely America's productive plant and manpower can find ample scope for employment by helping to supply the immense quantity of capital goods and services required for the rapid raising of the living standards of two-thirds of the world's population, and by attending to the housing, school construction and similar needs of two-thirds of its own population, plus such other domestic necessities as adequate flood control and highway construction. The economic aid to other countries would bring a return (which guns and planes do not) in the development of new markets (but not *exclusive* ones) and increased trade for American goods (but not on the former unequal terms). Also to be remembered is the material savings to Joe Smith in taxes now flowing down the drain of war expenditures at home and abroad.

But, above all, when they stop working at making super-bombs and start turning out more tractors, machine tools, and the other material things that mankind needs, the American people will be contributing toward a United Nations world of freedom, equality, cooperation, mutual respect, and peace.

Questions for Americans

Aligned against the African are the white settler groups, the big corporation interests, and the military planners and policy makers in Western capitals who reject coexistence with the socialist sector of the world.

And who is on the African's side? One counts India, China and most of the rest of Asia and the Middle East, together with the Soviet Union and the Eastern European countries friendly with it. One counts also popular sentiment in many other countries of the world, and the present tide of world history.

Thus the outcome of the recurring clashes between the two mighty cross currents sweeping Africa appears clear. The preponderance of strength is on the side of the African liberatory forces. They will certainly triumph. But what of the United States? What of the American people? On which side are they?

The African stands strong and erect, his brow furrowed with mixed determination and earnest questioning as he stares ahead into the distance. "Who is on my side? Who?"

Perhaps his thoughts are about the workers of America.

"The American companies in our land—they are your bosses and our bosses too. That should mean something, shouldn't it? I wonder if you know how many months we have to work for the wages you get in one week. Do you ask, as we do, why this should be so?

"When we were out on strike for three months in the Copperbelt mines, generous donations came to us from workers in many European countries. It meant much to us, very much. Two of the struck mines belonged to one of your big American companies. So we would have welcomed some sign of solidarity from your trade unions. Maybe the news of the strike could not reach you from so far away.

"We know of your statements endorsing our struggle for political freedom. We are grateful. We have also heard that you want your Government to give us more economic help. God knows we need many things. But we are troubled. Why are we told that we must refuse help from those you call enemies? Are they really *our* enemies if they are willing to aid our advancement? We cannot help wondering if what you call help is not really a bribe. You must surely understand that our freedom is too precious to be bought.

"I implore you to try to understand and make your Government understand that we in Africa are eager for America's friendship and aid, but only if they are freely given without conditions. We in Africa want to try to help *end* the Cold War; *we will not be used to fight it.* If you in the ranks of American labor will unite with us on this one thing, then you are in truth our allies. That is the voice of your great body of organized workers that we are anxiously waiting to hear."

Or perhaps the African's thoughts, as he gazes searchingly into the distance, turn to the people of African descent in America. . . .

"Are we not bound together, my brothers, by more than ancestral ties? Are we not both in battle against the same kind of tyranny and for the same dignity and equality? Do we not both repudiate the fraud of gradualism and compromise? Our fight in Africa derives added strength from your advances. And your civil rights gains surely owe something to our freedom victories in Africa and Asia.

"Why, then, do we not stand closer together? Though only one-tenth of America, your power is much greater than that. You have your newspapers, your great church bodies. Your people are joined together in many organizations. The politicians scramble for your votes. Your united demand for your country to support our cause and stop aiding our enemies would be listened to. That is what we in Africa wait to hear.

"Some of you have raised your voices, we know. Some among you, whom we honor, have been punished for speaking out too boldly for African freedom as well as for the rights of black Americans. They could be singled out and penalized only because there was no united support among you for the truths they spoke. On one side it is said that racial oppression cannot be finally ended in America until it is conquered in Africa. But you have others who maintain that the future of the colored people in America is assured, no matter what happens in Africa. It is for you, not us, to decide which is right. But one warning I must give you: do not be misled by those who call us 'Communists' for demanding our rights or 'terrorists' for fighting to save our lives.

"I beg you not to let yourselves be silenced or intimidated or divided by false issues in your support of our fight—any more than in your own struggle for freedom. Let us stand together, brother. Let us walk together."

Yes, the Africans' freedom is certain. It can come more quickly, however, and with less violence and pain in the process for them *and for us,* if the United States wields its great influence to ease the transition to African independence. This requires that the concept of Africa as a European or American appendage be once and for all scrapped. It requires the implementation of entirely new Western aims that are in harmony with African aims, and paramount among these must be the immediate liquidation of white settler and colonial domination and the promotion of cooperation among *all* nations willing and able to assist in the development of Africa *for the Africans.*

Even though Europe yet has much larger stakes in Africa than the United States, and even though the Africans' immediate and direct adversary is European overlordship, it is still nevertheless true that the United States holds the decisive responsibility for either blocking or promoting the rapid and peaceful liberation of Africa. This is so because of the dominating influence of the United States and its economic power in the Western alliance, in the policy-making capitals of Europe, and in settler-ruled countries such as Rhodesia and South Africa. The question is whether America's authority will make itself felt in these places and in the United Nations on the African's side, or whether it will continue to be directed toward serving American strategic and profit-making prerogatives in the continent, utilizing and supporting the European systems of control or shifting to a go-it-alone policy in areas where Europeans are no longer in the saddle.

If a poll on this issue could be taken among the American people with the alternatives honestly explained to them, there is little doubt what it would show. American officials, indeed, have been at pains to explain abroad the difference between popular anti-colonial sentiment and official policy in the United States regarding Africa. The New York *Times* (Dec. 28, 1954) reported:

> It is believed that the Pentagon, like the European sections of the State Department, holds that American policies on Africa might make trouble for United States projects to increase the supply of strategic metals and could not possibly do any good. . . . It has been a long uphill fight to make those in authority in Africa understand that public opinion [in the United States unfavorable to African colonial regimes] is not Government policy in the United States and that basically the American policy in any political sense toward central, eastern and southern Africa is simply the absence of a policy.

The final responsibility lies with the American people. So long as their voiced or unvoiced opposition to continued imperialist domination in Africa fails to bring about any fundamental change in their government's policy in that continent, the people of the United States must to all intents and purposes be counted on the side *against* the African, no matter how many Americans, both black and white, may deeply resent being placed in that position. The continuance of such a contradiction between the American people and their government in the present critical period of African history spells grave danger for Africans and Americans alike. If only for the sake of their own best interests, Americans *and* their government are called upon to take their stand unequivocally along with the great majority of humanity on the side of *African freedom*.

POSTSCRIPT

THE AFRICANS' STRUGGLE for freedom has surged forward with increasing momentum during the two years since this book was first published. In one place, then another, the waves clash; the exploiters and colonizers on the one side, though forced to give ground in most areas, still determined to retain their control over this last great vestige of empire; and, on the other side, the various nationalist movements asserting and demonstrating their determination to cast off the yoke of the foreign overlords—and quickly.

Amid the rush of dramatic developments in Africa during the past two years one might single out as most significant the emergence of the Republic of Guinea, on September 28, 1958, as the ninth independent, African-ruled state, and the advance toward a new level of African unity of policy and action on both a regional and continent-wide scale as signalized particularly by the All African People's Conference held in Accra, Ghana, in early December, 1958. Guinea's declaration of independence, embodied in her emphatic answer of "Non!" to De Gaulle's constitutional proposals, gave notice to Britain's colonialist partners in Africa (France, Belgium, Portugal principally) that they, too, had better start packing their baggage. "Africa is a continent on its own. It is not an extension of Europe or any other continent," said Prime Minister Kwame Nkrumah in opening the Accra Conference. The truth of this declaration was pressed home to French and Belgian authorities a few weeks later, in January and February, when uprisings shook Brazzaville and Leopoldville.

The historic All African People's Conference represented the convergence of the maturing liberation forces of the continent. From 28 lands, extending from the Arab North to the Bantu South and from Dakar across to Zanzibar, came the 500 representatives of political, nationalist, labor, youth and women's organizations. They included delegates from hitherto voiceless lands such as Portuguese Angola. They unanimously voted to continue to speak and act together for the common objective of liberating the whole of Africa—"in our lifetime."

The main emphasis of this assembly was on unity. Dr. Nkrumah noted that the Conference had "helped us to discover the source of our weakness, that is, the division within our own ranks. Now we are resolved to eradicate these divisions and put an end to the traditional tactics of imperialism of 'divide and rule', which aim at pitting tribe against tribe, country against country, individual against individual."

In working to achieve national freedom and independence, the Conference took note of the necessity of combatting tribalism, religious separatism, and traditonal African institutions, notably chieftaincy, which "do not conform to the demands of democracy" and have "clearly shown their reactionary character." The second stage of political unification would be for the independent African-governed states, first, to secure the abolition or adjustment of the European-created frontiers which have partitioned people of the same ethnic group within two or more different states, and, secondly, to join together in five regional groupings: North, West, East, Central, and South. The Union of Ghana and Guinea marked the initial step toward a West African Federation. The third and ultimate objective of unification would be the establishment of a Pan-African Commonwealth.

The same compelling convergence of freedom forces led to the convening of the Conference of Independent African States (without the Union of South Africa, though it was invited), the first session of which was held in Accra in April, 1958, and the second in Monrovia, August, 1959. The same motivation brought about organization of the Pan-African Freedom Movement of East and Central Africa in September, 1958. It also led to the establishment of the Union of Workers of Black Africa under Sékou Touré's leadership, uniting African labor organizations previously divided by identification with rival metropolitan labor bodies. It likewise spurred the Trade Union Congresses of Nigeria and Ghana to establish together in September, 1959, the nucleus of a West African Federation of Trade Unions.

I had the great privilege of being present at the All African People's Conference and of traveling extensively for more than two months in Ghana, Togoland, Nigeria, Ivory Coast, and the Republic of Guinea. Among the rank-and-file delegates with whom I talked in Accra, and in conversations elsewhere with students, teachers and workers, I found an eagerness to get down to concrete questions of organization and action. It is this drive for organization and action that is causing such frequent alterations in the political map of Africa.

With the addition of Nigeria, Somaliland (under Italian trusteeship), and Togoland and Cameroons (both under French trusteeship) to the ranks of the independent states under African rule in 1960, the number of such states will advance to thirteen. And thanks to Nigeria's great population, largest of any state in Africa and conservatively estimated at 35 millions, the total number of Africans under their own independent governments will, after October 1, 1960, reach approximately 120 millions. This will mean that for the first time since the European conquest of Africa there will be more *free* Africans than under white rule, a slight majority of the total current estimate of 231 millions. The year 1960 thus marks a turning point.

There may be more. The four countries cited have advance commitments for freedom in 1960, but there are others knocking at the door. Senegal and French Sudan, two of the 12 African republics comprising De Gaulle's "French Community," have rather quickly decided that local autonomy is not enough. Modibo Keita and Mamadou Dia, Premiers of the respective countries, which jointly established the new Mali Federation in April, 1959, have informed De Gaulle that their states desired full independent status "as soon as possible." And in the British sphere, Sierra Leone in the west and Uganda and Tanganyika in the east are among the most forward in demanding the same. The Tanganyika African National Union led by Julius Nyerere has won both dominant control in the local government and the cooperation of the European and Asian minorities in pressing for independence. Yet Britain has thus far refused to say when Tanganyika, under its trusteeship, will have its freedom. Why independence for the other trust territories and not for Tanganyika? The answer is all too obvious —fear of the repercussions in other parts of the as yet solid belt of British-ruled Eastern and Central African territories stretching from Kenya down to Southern Rhodesia.

The Struggle for Power in White Settler Areas

As West Africa moves forward to freedom, the contrast sharpens with the complacent *status quo* posture of those controlling other parts of Africa, the areas where white settler interests are involved. In at least two instances, however, circumstances have recently forced some involuntary shifting of posture. The nationalist explosion in the Belgian Congo, shattering the myth of Congolese contentment, compelled the Brussels authorities to begin talking, if cautiously, about the Congo moving "towards independence without fatal delays but also without inconsiderate haste."

Algeria is, of course, the other case in point. The long years of attempted military suppression of the Algerian revolution having served only to deepen France's internal crisis and offend humanity, President De Gaulle, on the eve of the perennial United Nations debate on the Algerian question, came forward in September, 1959, with proposals for securing a peaceful settlement. But the prospects were clouded by certain reservations of French rights attached to the proposals and by doubts as to whether De Gaulle would in fact negotiate with the independent Provisional Government established by the National Liberation Front in 1958.

Elsewhere in white settler Africa the pattern remains about the same as in Mississippi, Alabama, and other southern areas of the United States, with a hardening of resistance to the black man's advancement and, above all, to his right to vote. The "emergency" proclaimed in Rhodesia and Nyasaland in March, 1959, on the pretext of the discovery of a plot to massacre whites, provided the excuse for outlawing the major nationalist organizations, jailing their leaders and members by the hundreds, and conducting a vicious campaign of police terrorization and killing. It made no difference that an official London-appointed commission of inquiry found the "massacre plot" to be non-existent and the Africans' grievances real; Dr. Hastings Banda, leader of the Nyasaland African National Congress, and Kenneth Kaunda, head of the Zambia African National Congress of Northern Rhodesia, remained in jail along with their colleagues, and their organizations continued banned. Meanwhile, South Africa has pushed its *apartheid* code to new extremes of racist tyranny in education and other fields. The South African Parliament is now no longer to make any pretense of representing anything but government by and for the benefit of white South Africans; even the token representation of Africans by a few white members of Parliament has been abolished.

The London *Economist* (Dec. 13, 1958) has expressed the view that "The fate of Africa in the next decade depends upon economic advance catching up with political advance in the 'Africanized' north and west and political reconciliation matching economic growth in the plural societies of the center, east and south." Whether this analysis is sound or not depends upon one's definition of terms. Do Morocco and Ghana want the kind of "economic growth" that goes hand in hand with a system of massive exploitation of black labor, that provides economic benefits only for foreign investors and a small minority of the resident population? It is to protect and maintain the lop-sided economy of profits from cheap labor that political rights are denied black people in countries such as Rhodesia and South Africa—just as in southern sections of the United States.

What, then, is to be the nature of the "political reconciliation" in the white settler countries? Does it mean something akin to Sir Roy Welensky's "partnership" in Rhodesia? Or is it perhaps what the London *Daily Telegraph*, ardent defender of the empire, is talking about when it says editorially that Africa can evolve without race war "only if there is a genuine and general readiness to recognize that almost wholly black states will be black, but parti-colored states (such as the Central African Federation and Algeria) where the white element has found a homeland cannot be subject to wholly black domination. The fact must surely be faced that the principle of universal suffrage cannot solve the problem of black and white in Africa, which in the final analysis can be solved peacefully only by a frank recognition of the harsh realities of power."[1]

Strange, isn't it, that the question of the validity of universal suffrage in "plural societies" appears to arise only when the pluralism is one of different skin colors? And isn't the *Daily Telegraph* simply saying once again that might makes right? It is, indeed, true that the weapons of force and violence are in the hands of the white rulers, and it is for them to decide whether to spill more African blood to delay the transfer from minority to majority rule.

Let it not be thought that it is the white settlers alone in Algeria, Rhodesia, or elsewhere who block the road to African freedom. It is not simply political control by itself that is at issue. In polite diplomatic circles the other part of the matter is not openly discussed. M. Jacques Soustelle, however, casts caution to the wind and bluntly states that France must hold Algeria "Because Algeria means the Sahara and the Sahara means oil. . . . That is why France must make sure of retaining free access to the Sahara and prevent it from falling under any other than French sovereignty."[2] And De Gaule himself stipulated in his proposals for breaking the Algerian deadlock that whatever decision the Algerians might reach as to their relations with France, the Saharan petroleum resources would remain French. In like manner, behind the "settler problem" in Rhodesia and South Africa is the question of British and American investments in and control of those countries' copper, gold, diamonds, uranium and other resources.

Which Economic Road for the New Independent States?

What of the all-black African states that have won or will shortly win their political freedom? Will they go on to achieve economic independence? Some American commentators are worried about the new states' tendencies toward economic planning with its socialist implications and with possible assistance from the Soviet Union and other socialist countries. A. T. Steele, of the New York *Herald Tribune*, representing another school of thought, thinks otherwise. Recalling the colonial powers' former resistance to American enterprise and investments in West African countries, he says:

> The picture has changed greatly in the last few years. The erstwhile colonial powers themselves seem eager to get the Americans in—up to a point. For the former it's a kind of insurance: get the Americans in and you'll have a strong potential ally in case the new governments get rough and rash with foreign interests in the future.
> Much as Africans may celebrate the advent of political freedom, it will be a long time before their independence will be as complete in fact as in name. The old economic dependence will continue for an indefinite period. Except at the grass-roots level, the commercial and foreign-trade structure in nearly all these countries is in foreign hands, and as yet the Africans have neither the financial resources nor the know-how to take it over.[3]

There was unfortunately too litttle said about economic problems in the speeches at the All African People's Conference, the emphasis almost throughout being on political emancipation. Nevertheless, many of the young delegates were thinking and talking privately about the dangers of continued imperialist exploitation in the newly independent countries. They were very glad to have the question brought out into open discussion in the message which Dr. W. E. B. Du Bois sent to the Conference setting forth the choice which the liberated African peoples must make between the blandishments of a dying capitalism and the security and progress of the socialist way of life.

Western imperialism, Dr. Du Bois warned, "offers to let some of your smarter and less scrupulous leaders become fellow capitalists with the white exploiters if in turn they induce the nation's masses to pay the awful cost. . . . Strive against it with every fibre of your bodies and souls. A body of local private capitalists, even if they are black, can never free Africa; they will simply sell it into new slavery to old masters overseas."

The visitor to Accra will be impressed by the new Ambassador Hotel, the new University College, and the new office and government buildings and department stores recently constructed or going up, but he will see little such modernization as yet under way in the housing of the city's poorer workers or in the countryside. In the exclusive Ikoyi section of Lagos the visitor will see residences of extraordinary sumptuousness in which senior officials and other members of the African upper strata dwell. He will see in the bustling city streets business-suited Africans with briefcases under their arms, beggars in rags with outstretched hands, and traditionally garbed men and women balancing enormous burdens on their heads. He will see a chauffeur-driven limousine contesting the right of way with a two-wheeled cart piled high with wooden crates and being pushed and pulled by four or five black men, their bent backs wet with sweat. In the larger department stores, staffed with African clerks but under non-African ownership, he will find anything from a hi-fi set to frozen chicken imported from abroad—at higher than London prices; while in the stalls of the African market-place there will be a variety of locally-produced food-stuffs, and cheap manufactured articles and cast-off clothing from overseas, along with a multitude of bright colors, pungent odors, and flies. Everywhere one sees incongruous contrasts between the two distinct modes of life, one based on European standards and the other on the level of existence of the African masses.

Will this gulf widen, or will it be bridged? One can, it is true, point to some positive accomplishments in Ghana and Nigeria, particularly in enlarging the facilities for education. And there is the new modern port of Tema being developed down the coast from Accra. But can it be said that there is as yet a serious effort to curb spending on non-essentials and concentrate all resources on raising the general standard of living? Government assistance to small business enterprises, building construction of the type mentioned, and the limited work thus far undertaken in the agricultural sector cannot effect any basic changes in the economy. There are, of course, larger plans like the Volta River hydro-electric scheme in Ghana and a similar project on the great Niger River in Nigeria, as well as some proposed basic industrial undertakings; but implementation of these projects, it is usually said, must wait on foreign investment capital. Be that as it may, the question remains whether the resources that *are* available within such countries are being effectively used toward lifting them up out of economic dependence.

Political leaders are dependent upon their more affluent compatriots for party funds, but they are also dependent upon the masses for votes. In Nigeria I found trade unionists critically examining their relationship to the major political parties they helped to build up, and tackling the problem of unifying and strengthening the Nigerian labor movement to serve the workers' interests better. The following extract from a three-part article on this subject in the *West African Pilot* may foreshadow future developments:

> On the political side, the Nigerian Trade Union Movement must find a way of removing the political-ideological weakness which makes it a prey to all labor opportunists. To my mind, first it must cast overboard firmly and openly (as it has been inclined to do in practice) the doctrine that unionism has nothing to do with politics. This does not mean that individual unions must start canvassing for this party or that. In fact the frustration and fragmentation which is bound to result from this will lead to a worse situation than the present. What I do mean is that the trade union movement as a whole must take active part in determining the political-economic complex which affects the conditions of their working lives. . . .
>
> This means in practice that the trade union movement must either ally itself with one political party in the country or take steps to organize one specifically around the interests of the working class. The first course seems ill-advised; the second seems to have won tacit approval within the movement itself, whatever outside advisers may do to confuse issues. There is no doubt that the Nigerian worker will welcome a workers' party with a real sigh of relief. . . .
>
> I have been told that it is because of lack of money that the Labor Party has not been organized. I think this is putting the cart before the horse. It is because of disunity that the money has not been found. And there are those, I insist, who have a vested interest in this disunity because they fear the might of a working class whose power they saw in 1945 and 1950 [the years of general strikes in Nigeria].
>
> On the ideological side, the position must be straightened out by discussion. As I see it, two steps are necessary: (1) The workers must make up their minds that no one will be allowed any more to break the unity of any section of organized labor with the shout of communism. . . . (2) They must decide whether they want militant unionism or Uncle Tom unionism. There is this fact, however. In underdeveloped countries militancy is not really a

matter of choice. In these countries a trade union *must* be militant if it is to be united and strong.[4]

Guinea Points the Way to Full Freedom

Conakry, capital of the Republic of Guinea, I found quite different from other West African cities. There were relatively few automobiles to be seen, no Coca Cola signs, and no multi-storied buildings except for one or two apartment houses and the one modern hotel built by the French before they knew they would be leaving. Government offices and official residences were modest.

There are some fundamental and significant differences otherwise, also, between Guinea and other West Afrcan countries. First, Guinea had no group of large-scale farmers, big traders, business men allied with foreign firms, high-salaried officials or other elements of an African middle class of wealth; President Sékou Touré and other important political figures in the country have a background of organizing and leading African workers. Secondly, while the country was yet under French rule and he held the post of Vice President of the Executive Council, Sékou Touré was able to abolish the chieftaincies on the grounds of their corrupt and inefficient practices, and to establish in place of the old tribal authorities an all-embracing network of over 4,000 village councils elected by universal suffrage. Thirdly, the *Parti Democratique de Guinea* (P.D.G.), operating through 4,000 local committees encompassing every man, woman and child in the country, determines national policy and, through the party's representatives in every village, town ward, office, and workshop, has the responsibility of seeing that agreed-upon policy is carried out.

These three circumstances—the assumption of political leadership by working-class rather than middle class elements; the clean sweeping out of the chieftaincies, props of French authority and enemies of national consciousness and unity; and the existence of a unitary political apparatus with its authority based upon the will of all the people—these circumstances go far toward explaining why Guinea chose independence and why its outlook for economic advancement is different from that of other West African countries.

"In underdeveloped countries human energy is the principal capital," says Sékou Touré. Concerning the Konkouré River dam project for developing hydro-electric power, which the French, prior to independence, had promised to finarce, he declares, "We shall build it with our own hands if necessary." Shortly after independence he addressed the people of Guinea in this fashion:

> They said of China that disaster awaited it because China lacked the means of satisfying the needs of its 600 million men and women. Those 600 million men and women have proved this false by constantly raising the living standards of the masses every year, to the great honor of the Chinese nation. If we lack the billions [of francs] to do such a thing, we have our men and our women, we have our will, our arms and our legs, and we should know how to work.... We will be the first African government to establish compulsory labor [*travail obligatoire*], I say it publicly. Compulsory labor will be established, we have no shame in saying it, since the work will not be for the benefit of M. Sékou Touré, nor for the benefit of the Government, nor for the benefit of anyone else; it will be for the benefit of the very same people who give their labor. Work will be assigned and, a year hence, one will no longer walk through a town and meet a thousand boobies in the streets chatting from morning till night. Six months hence one will no longer meet any young girl of Guinea, torso naked, carrying two bananas on a tray, going to engage in prostitution.[5]

To a great crowd which gathered to celebrate independent Guinea's first May Day in 1959 and to greet Dr. Nkrumah, who was visiting the country, President Sékou Touré announced:

> Since its advancement to national independence Guinea has made an appeal for human investment, and its people, responding grandly to this challenge, have already accomplished more than the leadership of the P.D.G. believed possible: 3,600 kilometers of vehicular roads, hundreds of new classrooms, dispensaries, markets and stores have been constructed, without the expenditure of a single franc from the national budget for all these accomplishments.

He went on to tell the people that Guinea's first three-year plan of economic development, costing ten billion francs ($40 million), would go into effect January 1, 1960, with the main emphasis on the total transformation of agriculture (*la révolution agricole*) to increase production and productive capacity. The liberation of the peasant classes from their bad working and living conditions was one of the major objectives of Guinea's revolution, he said, and the Party would also continue to strive for the emancipation of women and the proper development of the country's youth. "We shall collectively raise the level of our conscience," he declared, "to the height of the great destiny of our country—neither rich nor poor, neither privileged or exploited, but all for each other, we will join together in building a new nation which will be triumphant over enemies, treacheries, and betrayals."[6]

In relation to the African continent Guinea is a comparatively small country, though some 14,000 square miles larger than Ghana, with a population of only two and a half million. But it is safe to say that its influence will far transcend its size. It lies in a strategic position bordering on Sierra Leone and Liberia to the south, the Federation of Mali to the north, and the Ivory Coast to the east. Moreover, it is linked with Ghana in the development of a West African Federation which it is hoped will shortly include Nigeria and other newly independent states. The remarkable story of what Guinea has accomplished and is striving to achieve in its political and economic revolutions is not yet widely known in Africa or elsewhere. But the news will surely spread. In Guinea's experience Africans near and far may find inspiration and answers to some of their own pressing problems.

I left Guinea and Africa with regret, and with a feeling of certainty that I would be returning to the continent soon. I came away with my faith in Africa's future confirmed.

The United States and Africa

Before I left the United States at the end of 1958, a greatly expanded official apparatus for dealing with Africa was beginning to take shape in Washington. A little belatedly the State Department recognized the necessity of catching up with the pace of political change in Africa and with American investments there. A new bureau of the State Department was established in August, 1958, to deal exclusively with African affairs, formerly classified merely as a subordinate section of European or Near Eastern affairs. A new Assistant Secretary of State for African Affairs, Joseph Satterthwaite, was named to head the bureau's staff of 77 in Washington and its 274 Americans in embassies and consulates all over Africa. To man this expanding apparatus candidates for African service are being sent for special training to institutions such as Northwestern University and Boston University, which received a government grant of $425,000 for a three-year program. Others have been given a 60-day look-and-learn tour of ten African countries under a Ford Foundation grant. It comes as no surprise that Sékou Touré should be officially invited to visit the United States. In 1958 it was Dr. Nkrumah who was the President's guest, and in 1960 or the next year it will undoubtedly be the Premier of independent Nigeria.

It is noteworthy that over a third of the $14 million budget increase requested by the United States Information Service (U.S.I.S.) and Voice of America in 1958 was for African services. This means such things as the installation in Liberia of a new super-powerful transmitter for the Voice of America broadcasts, and enlarging the ideological campaign being waged by the U.S.I.S. to win over African minds.

To get an idea of the nature of this campaign you might join me in thumbing through a copy of the *American Outlook* (November, 1958), published by the U.S.I.S. in Accra. On the first page we see a striking picture of a young Nigerian who is studying in the United States and who was a featured drum soloist at the Radio City Music Hall in New York. To the right of the masthead is a boxed quotation from Nehru, "Communism has definitely allied itself to the approach of violence." On page two, among other items, are "Ike Calls for a 'Great Peaceful Crusade' Against Poverty" and "'Peepholes Seen in Iron Curtain." Page three features pictures of a gift of corn from the United States to relieve food shortages in the north of Ghana and the opening of a new U.S. consulate office building in Lagos. The main article on the next page is headed "Dulles Reaffirms U.S. Support of Self-Government Principle," but most of the article, it appears, concerns his views on the dangers of "international communism." The center-spread is captioned "Liberia-U.S. Cooperation Accelerates Development of Liberian Resources." Next we come to "Purchasing Power of U.S., Soviet Workers Compared," "Ghana Trade Unions Welcome Foreign Investment Aid," and the second of a series of three articles "describing the vital role that foreign capital played in helping the new American nation [the United States, that is] achieve its political and economic goals." Among other items in this issue are a story on Pasternak's refusal of the Nobel literature award, citing a comment by Howard Fast, and another story quoting singer-actress Lena Horne as saying, "Particularly outside the arts I think the Negro's progress has been tremendous. I never thought in my time I would see public school integration." Readers of this paper are advised that "Material which appears in this publication may be reproduced without cretit to *American Outlook*." Indeed!

All the money spent on these propaganda services could be saved by Washington simply taking a bold and forthright stand on Algeria, South Africa, or the Portuguese Government's absurd insistence that its African colonies are integral parts of the metropolitan country and no business of the U.N.—not to mention the citizenship rights of black Americans. Lacking such proof in *deeds*, no amount of propaganda can persuade Africans that the United States Government is concerned with their freedom and welfare.

In one of the papers presented at last year's American Assembly, held under the auspices of Columbia University and concerned with the topic, "The United States and Africa," it was stated that in the African areas dominated by white settler populations

> the nationalist ambitions of Africans clash directly with the interests of our allies and friends and with their established formulae for political and economic control. The fact that we do little to help erase racial discrimination alienates the African and Asian groups. . . . Justifiably or not, our inaction and our policies become prime targets for hostility from the new nations. They keep the United States on the defensive.
>
> Another factor which might affect our disposition to act—and one about which little is known—is the chance that a politically significant segment of the American Negro population would press for a different policy. This has not happened yet, but apprehension concerning it reinforces our defensive posture.[7]

The latter paragraph brings me to the final point of this postscript. It is necessary to report that I was asked time and again, wherever I went in Africa, why Americans and particularly Americans of African descent were not doing more to try to reshape their Government's policies to coincide with the interests of struggling Africans. "Why doesn't your N.A.A.C.P. link up its fight with ours?" I was asked. "Why didn't the N.A.A.C.P. have delegates at the All African People's Conference?" "Why is it that the organizations of black Americans do not sponsor visits of our African leaders to your country?" These are all valid questions. They must be answered not with elaborate explanations or excuses but with *action*.

Africans regard the freedom of all oppressed people of African descent, wherever they may be, as their responsibility. They have said so at the Accra Conference, in the General Assembly of the United Nations, and elsewhere. Let us not be fools! Let us not be cowards! Let us at last say it is so that all the world can hear, "Yes, brother, we will stand together with you! We will walk together!"

(*October, 1959*)

David H Anthony, III

Afterword: To now sing the praises of the formerly *Unsung Valiant*

W. Alphaeus Hunton was part of a vanguard of AfricanAmericans who stood firm to form a phalanx against racist and classist oppression, locally and globally. Their internationalism was not merely rhetorical but active and engaged. We are only beginning to discover who these people were and what they attempted.

In the post-Second World War years this was especially evident in over 50 African territories still writhing under the crushing weight of colonialist and imperialist hegemony. Most of these nations contained activist workers and students involved in organizations seeking reform or radical, even revolutionary change to liberate them from the oppressive classist status quo. These processes were not only witnessed but often assisted by key allies who came to join them in their protracted campaigns for justice, rights, and freedom.

Alphaeus and spouse Dorothy spent time in exile in Conakry Guinea, Accra, Ghana, Lusaka, Zambia, South Central Africa. A frontline state (formerly colonial Northern Rhodesia), Zambia's capital was home to a myriad of expatriates and freedom fighters lending varying levels of support to the widely ramified continental, transnational movement to overturn minority rule established by the racist regimes of late imperial Portugal, breakaway Southern Rhodesia, and *apartheid* South Africa. Alphaeus had followed the progress of these movements assiduously since the outbreak of the Second World War in Europe and had made this known in speeches, pamphlets, and articles, especially through the auspices of the International Committee later Council on African Affairs, which produced *New Africa*.

Huntoncorresponded with Ghana's Prime Minister Kwame Nkrumah, statesman Dr. Ralph J. Bunche, India's Jawaharlal Nehru, and Walter Sisulu, leader of the African National Congress, and

Afterword

South African Communist Party. These and other writings were deposited posthumously in the William Alphaeus Hunton Papers at the Schomburg Center for Research in Black Culture.

Alphaeus Hunton came from an extraordinarily illustrious family. His father and namesake was a giant in the history of the Young Men's Christian Association which in the time of the social gospel movement created space for conscientious people of faith who sought to struggle for progressive social change in the here and now. It was one of the late 19th century antecedents of the later liberation theology that became so important in the history of the Latin American Revolution of the 1960s and seventies. His mother, Addie Waites Hunton, and Kathryn Johnson, worked alongside segregated African American troops in France during World War I. They subsequently wrote and published *Two Colored Women with the American Expeditionary Forces* chronicling a little known saga of the Great War. His spouse, Dorothy Hunton, wrote a moving and thoughtful memoir, *Alphaeus Hunton: The Unsung Valiant*, whose intimate portrait of her life partner insightfully revealed a man of many parts, as only a devoted companion could. Hunton's nephew, legal scholar, Professor Stephen Carter, is an accomplished author of a series of highly acclaimed, best-selling books on ethics among other topics.

Alphaeus Hunton's footprints led in many directions, both within and beyond the confines of North America. As has been true for many AfricanAmericans who lived in exile, Hunton met and impressed others fleeing political persecution. Internationalists came to know him from many vantage points, including in places he was unable to see at first hand such as South Africa, a land for whose liberation he labored from afar, like countless others. Those who survived to see the first stages of the disengagement from apartheid, the release of political prisoners, and unbanning of the ANC, Communist Party and other organizations in 1990, the first all-race elections of 1994, and the climax of the half century spent fighting the odious system of "separate development" included people who had met Hunton in exile. In that sense, *Decision in Africa* reappears at a most opportune

Afterword

time to permit us all to now sing the praises of the formerly *Unsung Valiant*.

After having been invited by President Kenneth Kaunda to live there, Alphaeus Hunton died of cancer in Lusaka, Zambia in January 1970. Each place in which he and Dorothy Hunton made their homes outside of the U.S. was chosen in consultation with and at the invitation of the head of state. They knew his worth.

Now we have an opportunity to glimpse part of that intelligence, perspicacity, and engaged scholarship.

Alphaeus Hunton, ¡presente! Viva!
A Luta Continúa. The Struggle Continues.
A Vitória É Certa. Victory is Certain.

David H Anthony, III
Department of History,
University of California, Santa Cruz

June 2021

REFERENCES

NOTE: *A parenthetical designation following a source, such as (Ref. I, 12), indicates the chapter and item number of the complete reference to the same source.*

CHAPTER 1

1. Robert Benton Seeley, *The Perils of the Nation*, London, 1843, p. 397.
2. Eileen Fletcher, "Kenya's Concentration Camps," an Eyewitness Account," *Peace News* (London), May 4, 1956.
3. *New Age* (Johannesburg), Feb. 16, 1956.
4. Per-Olow Anderson, quoted in *Peace News*, Nov. 30, 1956.
5. *N. Y. Times*, May 15, 1956.
6. K. Onwuka Diké, "African History and Self-Government," *West Africa*, Feb. 28 and March 14, 1953.
7. Jordan K. Ngubane, "Who Are the African Nationalists," *Inkundla Ya Bantu* (Johannesburg), March 12, 1949.
8. Quoted in W. E. B. Du Bois, *The World and Africa*, New York, 1947, 232-235.
9. Eric Williams, *Capitalism and Slavery*, Chapel Hill, 1944, pp. 63-64.
10. Eric Rosenthal, *Stars and Stripes in Africa*, London, 1938, p. 153.
11. Quoted in Eric Williams, *op. cit.*, p. 42.
12. W. E. Burghardt Du Bois, *The Negro*, New York, 1915, pp. 155-156.
13. Geo. C. McGhee, *Dept. of State Bulletin*, June 19, 1950, p. 1002.
14. W. Walton Claridge, *A History of the Gold Coast and Ashanti*, London, 1915, Vol. I, Introduction, pp. x, xii.
15. Quoted in Leonard Barnes, *Empire or Democracy*, London, 1939, p. 188.
16. Parker Thomas Moon, *Imperialism and World Politics*, New York, 1927, pp. 86-87.
17. *East Africa and Rhodesia*, Nov. 3, 1949, p. 268.
18. Rosenthal, *op. cit.*, p. 269.
19. R. L. Buell, *The Native Problem in Africa*, New York, 1928, Vol. II, p. 304.

CHAPTER 2

1. Ewart S. Grogan and Arthur H. Sharp, *From Cape to Cairo*, London, 1902, pp. 365, 367-8, 377-8.
2. W. McGregor Ross, *Kenya from Within*, London, 1927, p. 198.
3. London *Times*, Nov. 27, 1952 and April 30, 1953.
4. Compiled from Hailey, *African Survey*, London, 1938, p. 109, and United Nations and Government reports.

5. G. I. Jones, "Ibo Land Tenure," *Africa*, Vol. XIX (1949), p. 313.
6. *Kenya Colony and Protectorate, 1938*, Colonial Reports–Annual, No. 1920, London, 1939, pp. 14-15.
7. Compiled from periodical sources and government reports.
8. Quoted in Martin L. Kilson, Jr., "Land and the Kikuyu Political Movements," *Journal of Negro History*, April, 1955, p. 136.
9. N. Humphrey, *The Kikuyu Lands*, London, 1945, quoted in *East Africa and Rhodesia*, Sept. 27, 1947, p. 57.
10. Hailey, *op. cit.*, pp. 608-630; and Basil Davidson, *The African Awakening*, London, 1955, Chapt. XIX.
11. East African Protectorate, *Minutes of the Proceedings of the Legislative Council (Second Session) 1920*, Nairobi.
12. W. McGregor Ross, *op. cit.*, pp. 225-227.
13. Jomo Kenyatta, *Kenya: The Land of Conflict*, London, Panaf Service, n.d., p. 11.
14. U.S. Dept. of Commerce, *Investment in Federation of Rhodesia and Nyasaland*, Washington, 1956, pp. 70-71.
15. Quoted in *East Africa and Rhodesia*, Jan. 1, 1943, p. 558.
16. Hailey, *op. cit.*, p. 663, and Ellen Hellman (ed.), *Handbook of Race Relations in South Africa*, Cape Town, 1949, pp. 284-285.
17. United Nations, *Special Study on Economic Conditions in Non-Self-Governing Territories*, New York, 1955, p. 133.
18. United Nations, *Enlargement of the Exchange Economy in Tropical Africa*, New York, 1954, p. 17.
19. *Ibid.*, p. 17, and United Nations, *Scope and Structure of Money Economies in Tropical Africa*, New York, 1955, pp. 9, 18, 19.
20. A. G. Fraser, *Africa and Peace*, Oxford, 1936, pp. 15-16.
21. Gikonyo wa Kiano, "East Africa: The Tug of War Continues," *Africa Is Here*, New York, 1952, pp. 29-32.
22. Quoted in Joseph Okanlawon Balogun, *The Existence of Virtual Monopoly in Nigeria*, Lagos, 1944, p. 1.
23. *Memorandum of Protest Against Government Control of Cocoa in West Africa Submitted by the Delegation of Gold Coast and Nigerian Farmers*, London, Sept. 1945, p. 2.
24. *West African Pilot* (Lagos), Aug. 4, 1950.

CHAPTER 3

1. "Life in the Diamond Fields," *Harper's New Monthly Magazine*, February, 1873, pp. 325-6.
2. *The Mining Industry, Evidence and Report of the Industrial Commission of Enquiry*, Witwatersrand Chamber of Mines, Johannesburg, 1897, p. 44.
3. *Ibid.*, p. 256.
4. *Ibid.*, p. 44.
5. Transvaal Chamber of Mines, *Native Laws Commission of Enquiry*, Johannesburg, April 1947, p. 46.

REFERENCES 261

6. *The Mining Industry, op. cit.*, pp. 22, 85, 375.
7. Union of South Africa, *Report of the Native Economic Commission, 1930-1932* (1933), paragraph 816.
8. Report of the Meeting of the Kimberley Mining Board, December, 1881.
9. *The Mining Industry, op. cit.*, p. 581; and Ray E. Phillips, *The Bantu in the City*, Cape Town, 1937, p. xxi.
10. Compiled from Union of South Africa, *Department of Mines—Annual Report for the Year ended 31st of December, 1953* (U.G. No. 35/1954), Pretoria, pp. 44, 50, 56.
11. *Cape Times* (Cape Town), May 23, 1944.
12. Union of South Africa, *Report of the Native Grievances Inquiry, 1913-1914*, Cape Town, 1914, p. 64.
13. *Ibid.*, pp. 38-39.
14. *Ibid.*, pp. 64-66.
15. *Cape Times*, Oct. 23, 1934. Quoted in Ray E. Phillips, *op. cit.*, p. 371.
16. E. D. Morel, *The Black Man's Burden*, Manchester, 1930, p. 49.
17. *Report of the Commission Appointed to Enquire into the Disturbances in the Copperbelt Northern Rhodesia* (Cmd. 5009), London, 1935, p. 19.
18. *Ibid.*, p. 37.
19. Compiled from *Economic and Statistical Bulletin* (Lusaka), Feb. 1954, p. 20; *East Africa and Rhodesia*, Jan. 18, 1951; and *Department of Mines—Annual Report for 1955* (Lusaka), 1956.

CHAPTER 4

1. United Nations, *Special Study on Social Conditions in Non-Self-Governing Territories*, New York, 1953, pp. 75-76.
2. Union of South Africa, *House of Assembly Debates, Fifth Session—Ninth Parliament*, Cape Town, 1948, p. 130.
3. *East Africa Royal Commission 1953-1955 Report* (Cmd. 9475), London, 1955, p. 207.
4. *African Weekly* (Salisbury), Feb. 16, 1955.
5. *Report of the Commission Appointed to Inquire Into the Operation of Bus Services for Non-Europeans on the Witwatersrand* . . ., 1944, Part IV, p. 10.
6. *Ibid.*, Pt. IV, p. 11.
7. *They Marched to Victory*, Communist Party of South Africa, Cape Town, n.d.
8. *The Friend* (Bloemfontein), Sept. 29, 1937, p. 8.
9. *Ibid.*
10. Ellen Hellman, p. 288 (Ref. II, 16).
11. Compiled from reports of the South African Director of Census and Statistics; Hailey, p. 668 (Ref. II, 4); Phillips, p. 177 (Ref. III, 9), Ellen Hellman, *op. cit.*, p. 290; and H. J. Simons, "Passes and Police," *Africa South* (Cape Town), Oct.-Dec., 1956, p. 52.

12. *Report of the Prisons Department for the Year 1952.* See also United Nations, *Report of the Ad Hoc Committee on Forced Labor*, Geneva, 1953, pp. 77-80.
13. *New Age* (Johannesburg), May 17, 1956.
14. See Kenya Colony and Protectorate, Native Affairs Department, *Annual Report, 1930*, London, 1930, pp. 74, 75, 84; *Kenya Colony and Protectorate, 1938*, Colonial Reports—Annual, No. 1920, London, 1939, pp. 52-53; *Colonial Reports—Kenya 1951*, London, 1952, p. 99.
15. *East Africa and Rhodesia*, Nov. 13, 1952.
16. *Minutes of the All-African Convention*, Dec., 1937. Lovedale Press, n.d., pp. 61-62.

CHAPTER 5

1. *N. Y. Times*, June 1, 1946.
2. *Ibid.*, May 4, 1947.
3. Thomas Hodgkin, "Political Parties in French West Africa," *West Africa*, Feb. 20, 1954, p. 157.
4. Kwame Nkrumah, *What I Mean by Positive Action*, Ghana Pamphlets No. 1, Convention People's Party, Accra, n.d.
5. *Morocco Under the Protectorate*, Istiqlal (Independence) Party of Morocco, New York, 1953, p. 40.
6. *Cape Times*, Nov. 13, 1947.
7. J. B. Danquah, *Friendship and Empire*, Fabian Publications, London, 1949, pp. 16-17.
8. U.K. Inf. Release, *Background to News from the Colonies*, No. 102, Oct. 26, 1946.
9. *Cape Times*, Dec. 18, 1946.
10. *N. Y. Times*, June 29, 1944.
11. *Christian Science Monitor*, Dec. 22, 1942.
12. Mr. Henry S. Villard, Department of State Press Release No. 345, Aug. 19, 1943.
13. *East Africa and Rhodesia*, Oct. 16, 1947, p. 138.

CHAPTER 6

1. Computed from *Department of Mines—1953*, p. 74 (Ref. III, 10), and Press Release of the South African Government Information Office, New York City, June 1, 1956.
2. *Ibid.*, and *Overseas Review*, Barclays Bank (D, C and O), London, June 1955, p. 4.
3. Computed from *East Africa and Rhodesia*, Nov. 16, 1950, and annual production figures, 1950-1955.
4. Computed from *East Africa and Rhodesia*, Feb. 28, 1952, and annual production figures, 1952-1955.
5. *Industrial Review of Africa*, Nov. 1954, pp. 95, 97.

REFERENCES

6. *The African Awakening*, pp. 212-213 (Ref. II, 10).
7. *The Times British Colonies Review*, Summer, 1954, p. 20.
8. *West Africa*, Dec. 31, 1955.
9. "The Hills of Iron," *West Africa*, Nov. 14, 1953.
10. Amanke Okafor, *Nigeria—Why We Fight For Freedom*, London, 1950, p. 24.
11. Hailey, pp. 1512, 1489 (Ref. II, 4), and S. H. Frankel, *Capital Investment in Africa: Its Course and Effects*, London, 1938, pp. 89-92. For the profit-averages of some of the mining companies in South Africa and other areas of the continent, see J. Fred Rippy, "Background for Point Four: Samples of Profitable Investments in the Under-Developed Countries," *The Journal of Business of the University of Chicago*, April 1953.
12. *Weekly Newsletter*, Union of South Africa Bureau of Information, Pretoria, Sept. 30, 1946.
13. "Vers l'Avenir," *Courier d'Afrique* (Leopoldville), June 28, 1946.
14. Frank R. La Macchia, "African Economies: Basic Characteristics and Prospects," *The Annals of the American Academy of Political and Social Science*, March, 1955, p. 49; Harry Bayard Price, *The Marshall Plan and Its Meaning*, Ithaca, N. Y., 1955, p. 150.
15. MSA Bulletin No. 137, Aug. 8, 1952.
16. *Thirteenth Report to Congress of the ECA* for the Quarter ended June 30, 1951, p. 46. For a detailed critique of British economic development schemes in Africa see Chapter X, "Myths of Colonial Development," in R. Palme Dutt, *The Crisis of Britain and the British Empire*, New York, 1953. For an analysis of French schemes see A. L. Dumaine, "La Signification Réale du Second Plan," *Présence Africaine*, April-July, 1955.
17. *Accra Evening News*, Nov. 14, 1950.
18. *Chicago Daily News*, March 18, 1953.

CHAPTER 7

1. *Business Week*, Feb. 10, 1951, p. 141.
2. *Investment in Overseas Territories in Africa, South of the Sahara*, OEEC, Paris, 1951, p. 55.
3. ECA releases No. 1240, Feb. 10, 1950, and No. 1410, April 19, 1950.
4. *Labor Conditions in Northern Rhodesia* (Colonial No. 150), London, 1938, p. 61.
5. U.S. Dept. of State, *Outline of European Recovery Program*, submitted to the Senate Foreign Relations Committee, Dec. 19, 1947, pp. 19, 48.
6. *Report on Progress of the ECA*, U.S. Congress Joint Committee on Foreign Economic Cooperation, 81st Congress, 1st Session, Senate, Report No. 13, Jan. 27, 1949, pp. 46-49, 122, 22.

7. *East Africa and Rhodesia,* April 14, 1949.
8. G. Udegbunem Meniru, *African-American Cooperation,* Glen Garden, N. J., 1954, pp. 91-92.
9. *Industrial Review of Africa,* January, 1955, p. 39.
10. 1936 investments based on Hailey, p. 1319 (Ref. II, 4). Other data compiled from reports of the Export-Import Bank and World Bank and press releases.
11. *East Africa and Rhodesia,* Oct. 22, 1953, p. 192.
12. U.S. Dept. of Commerce, *Kenya, British East Africa—Economic Review, 1953,* Business Information Service, World Trade Series, No. 619, Aug. 1954, p. 13.
13. N. Y. *Times,* May 21, 1953, and *East African Standard,* July 15, 1955.
14. Dr. Mary I. Shannon, "Social Revolution in Kikuyuland," *African World,* Sept. 1955.
15. *East Africa and Rhodesia,* May 28, 1953, and Nov. 11, 1954; *East African Standard,* Jan. 28 and June 17, 1955
16. *Report on Progress of the ECA, op. cit.,* p. 21.
17. Quoted in Edwin S. Munger, "Economics and African Nationalism," *Current History,* July, 1953, p. 11.

CHAPTER 8

1. *The Overseas Territories in the Mutual Security Program,* Mutual Security Agency, Washington, D. C., March 31, 1952, p. 14.
2. Admiral Richard L. Conolly, "Africa's Strategic Significance," *Africa Today,* edited by C. Groves Haines, Baltimore, 1955, p. 56.
3. Hans J. Morgenthau, "United States Policy Toward Africa," *Africa in the Modern World,* edited by Calvin W. Stillman, Chicago, 1955, p. 323.
4. N. Y. *Times,* May 16, 1954.
5. N. Y. *Herald-Tribune,* Nov. 1, 1953.
6. *East Africa and Rhodesia,* Sept. 11, 1952.
7. *West African Pilot,* Feb. 25, 1949.
8. *The Economist,* Nov. 20, 1954, p. 654.

CHAPTER 9

1. Quoted in Nnamdi Azikiwe, *Liberia in World Politics,* London, 1934, p. 146.
2. Raymond Leslie Buell, *Liberia: A Century of Survival, 1847-1947,* University of Pennsylvania Press, 1947, p. 45.
3. Earnest Sevier Cox, *White America,* White America Society, Richmond, Va., 1923, pp. 345-346.
4. *The African Nationalist* (Monrovia), August 21, 1948. The editor was later prosecuted by the Liberian Government and the paper ceased publication.
5. Torkel Holsoe, *Forestry Opportunities in the Republic of Liberia,* Foreign Operations Administration, Washington, 1954, p. 34.

6. Earl Parker Hanson, "The United States Invades Africa," *Harper's*, February, 1947, p. 173.
7. Herbert Solow, "Three-Way Payoff in Liberia," *Fortune*, April, 1953, p. 182.
8. *Liberia Today* (Liberian Embassy, Washington, D. C.), January 1956, p. 4.
9. See *Liberia Today*, February, 1955.
10. Letter of John R. Ross in the New York *Times*, Aug. 12, 1951.
11. Buell, II, 834 (Ref. I, 18).
12. U.S. Dept. of Commerce, *Basic Data on the Economy of Liberia*, World Trade Information Service, Economic Reports Pt. 1, No. 55-8, Washington, 1955, p. 2.
13. *Afro-American* (Baltimore), Feb. 2, 1952.
14. Compiled from reports of the Liberian Government, United States Dept. of Commerce, and Firestone Tire and Rubber Co.
15. *Liberian Age* (Monrovia), June 23, 1952.
16. Henry B. Cole (editor), *The Liberian Yearbook 1956*, London, 1956, p. 117.
17. *The Friend* (Monrovia), April 25, 1958
18. *Afro-American*, Feb. 9, 1952.
19. *African News* (Washington, D. C.), March 1956, p. 2.
20. For the circumstances and aftermath of the last election in Liberia see N. Y. *Times*, Jan. 14, 1956.

CHAPTER 10

1. N. Y. *Times*, July 10, 1956.
2. *Industrial Review of Africa*, May, 1956, p. 36; N. Y. *Times*, Jan. 31, 1954; *South Africa Reports, Economic Review* (Union of South Africa Government Information Office, New York), April 1, 1956.
3. *South Africa Reports*, Oct. 28, 1954.
4. U.S. Dept. of Commerce, *Investment in Union of South Africa*, Washington, 1954, pp. 131-137, gives an incomplete list of 118 United States companies having subsidiary or associated companies operating in South Africa in 1952. It is stated that "several thousand additional American firms are represented in South Africa through sales agents." Fifty-six of those listed, including seven automobile companies, had manufacturing or assembly plants in the Union. *Wall Street Journal*, Oct. 11, 1956, in a detailed article on United States business interests in South Africa, referred to "about 160 American concerns with investments of some type" there.
5. *Barron's*, March 3, 1952.
6. N. Y. *Times*, April 17, 1956.
7. London *Times*, July 16, 1945.
8. *New Age* (Johannesburg), March 22, 1956.

9. *South African-American Survey 1950* (Union of South Africa Government Information Office, New York), p, 25.
10. N. Y. *Times*, Sept. 22, 1949 and Jan. 4, 1950.
11. See C. S. McLean and T. K. Prentice, *The South African Uranium Industry*, United Nations document A/Conf. 8/P/997, June 27, 1955.
12. Mr. Rafford Faulkner, Assistant Director of AEC, quoted in *South Africa Reports, Economic Review*, Nov. 1, 1954.
13. Compiled from periodic mining reports in *Overseas Review, Commonwealth Survey*, and South African Government sources.
14. Computed from *Department of Mines—1953*, pp. 79, 44, 56, 123. (Ref. III, 10); *Mining Survey* (Johannesburg), Aug. 1947, pp. 22, 23.
15. McLean and Prentice, *op. cit.*, p. 22.

CHAPTER 11

1. *East Africa and Rhodesia*, March 6, 1952.
2. *Ibid.*, Dec. 11, 1952.
3. *Ibid.*, Sept. 10, 1953.
4. Y. M. Leonard Chirwa, *Why We Oppose Federation*, Johannesburg, 1952, p. 12.
5. *Investment in Federation* (Ref. II, 14).
6. *East Africa and Rhodesia*, Jan. 13, 1955, p. 614.
7. U.S. Department of Commerce, *Federation of Rhodesia and Nyasaland—Economic Review, 1953*, Business Information Series, WTS, No. 637, Oct., 1954, p. 31.
8. From annual reports of the companies; *Investment in Federation, op. cit.*, p. 23; and Northern Rhodesia official statistics. Figures for Nchanga cover April 1 to March 31 in the years indicated.
9. Rippy, p. 121 (Ref. VI, 11).
10. Federation of Rhodesia and Nyasaland, *Monthly Digest of Statistics* (Salisbury), April, 1935.
11. Compiled from *Report of the Board of Inquiry . . . Into the Advancement of Africans in the Copper Belt Industry in Northern Rhodesia* (Lusaka), 1954, and annual reports of mining companies for 1952-53 and 1953-54.
12. "Kwacha," "We have had enough of save wages!" *World Trade Union Movement*, May, 1955, p. 17. See also R. W. Williams, "Trade Unions in Africa," *African Affairs*, Oct., 1955, pp. 273-274.
13. *Investment in Federation, op. cit.*, pp. 24, 71.
14. N. Y. *Times*, July 8, 1956.
15. Munger, p. 11 (Ref. VII, 17).
16. *East Africa and Rhodesia*, Aug. 26, 1954.

CHAPTER 12

1. Newmont Mining Corporation, Annual Report for 1951.
2. *West African Pilot*, Jan. 28, 1953.

REFERENCES 267

3. *West Africa*, May 5, 1956, p. 242.
4. N. Y. *Herald-Tribune*, Feb. 15, 1953.
5. United Nations, *The International Flow of Private Capital, 1946-1952*, New York, 1954, pp. 24-25.
6. *The Economist*, July 2, 1955, p. 62.
7. For descriptions of the Belgian Congo labor system see *The African Awakening*, pp. 105-129, 148-155 (Ref. II, 10), and James S. Allen, *Atomic Imperialism*, New York, 1952, pp. 202-210.
8. N. Y. *Herald-Tribune*, Feb. 15, 1953.
9. "Industrial Color Bar in Central Africa," *East Africa and Rhodesia*, Dec. 3, 1953, p. 397.
10. *The African Awakening, op. cit.*, p. 151.
11. John Newhouse, "Inga," *Colliers*, Feb. 3, 1956; *Belgian Congo Today*, July, 1955, pp. 123-124.
12. Compiled from: League of Nations, *The Network of World Trade*, Geneva, 1942, p. 126; United Nations, *Statistical Yearbook, 1953*, New York, 1953, pp. 368, 369; United Nations, *Review of Economic Conditions in Africa*, New York, 1951, p. 92; United Nations, *Economic Developments in Africa 1954-1955*, New York, 1956, p. 84; and statistical reports of the United States Dept. of Commerce on trade with Africa.
13. Compiled from: U.S. Treasury Dept., *Census of American-Owned Assets in Foreign Countries*, Washington, 1947; and statistical reports in *Survey of Current Business*, December, 1952; August, 1955; August, 1956.

CHAPTER 13

1. *East Africa and Rhodesia*, Dec. 31, 1953, p. 534.
2. Harry R. Rudin, "Past and Present Role of Africa in World Affairs," *The Annals of the American Academy of Political and Social Science*, March, 1955, p. 38.
3. E. William Moran, Jr., "U.S. Technical and Economic Assistance to Africa," *Africa Today*, Baltimore, 1955, pp. 440-441.
4. *Sunday Times* (London), Oct. 14, 1951. See also Dutt, pp.199, 221-225 (Ref. VI, 16).
5. Julian Friedman, "Empire Building: 1953 Style," *Monthly Review* (New York), October, 1953, p. 285.
6. *New Rhodesia* (Salisbury), Sept. 12, 1947. The same article appeared in the ultra-conservative British *Review of World Affairs*, Dec. 1947.
7. N. Y. *Times*, Jan. 14, 1956.
8. S. H. Frankel, "Investment and Economic Development in Africa," *International Social Science Bulletin*, Vol. III, No. 1.
9. *West Africa*, Sept. 4, 1952, Sept. 26, 1953.
10. "Portuguese Colonial Policy—A Critical View," *African News* (Washington, D. C.), Sept. 1955, p. 2.

11. *East Africa and Rhodesia,* Sept. 1, 1955, p. 1862.
12. Federal Information Department, *Opportunity in Rhodesia and Nyasaland,* Salisbury, n.d., p. 31.
13. Quoted in *Rhodesia-Nyasaland Royal Commission Report,* Cmd. 5949, 1939, p. 70.
14. *Rand Daily Mail,* July 19, 1954.
15. E. A. Vasey, "Economic and Political Trends in Kenya," *African Affairs,* April, 1956, p. 103.
16. Report of the East African Statistical Department, cited in *East African Standard,* Nov. 4, 1955.
17. *Industrial Review of Africa,* April, 1956, p. 52.
18. See United Nations, *Special Study on Social Conditions in Non-Self-Governing Territories,* New York, 1953, pp. 54-57.
19. *East London Daily Dispatch,* Dec. 3, 1953.
20. Quoted in *Concord* (Salisbury), July, 1956, p. 24.
21. *Investment in Federation,* pp. 99-100 (Ref. II, 14).
22. Haines, p. 335 (Ref. VIII, 2).
23. *Commission Report,* p. 430 (Ref. IV, 3).
24. T. Balogh, "Primitive Economies and Primitive Economics," *Venture* (London), January, 1956, p. 9.
25. *N. Y. Times,* May 11, 1954.
26. Haines, p. 201 (Ref. VIII, 2).
27. See Basil Davidson, "The Congo and Angola," *West Africa,* May 22 and 29, 1954.
28. *South Africa Reports,* Jan. 5, 1956.
29. *N. Y. Times,* March 21, 1956.
30. *East Africa and Rhodesia,* Dec. 22, 1955.
31. *South Africa Reports,* July 26, 1956.

CHAPTER 14

1. Harold Callender, "France's Race Problem," *N. Y. Times,* Feb. 14, 1956.
2. For the text of the correspondence see *Spotlight on Africa Newsletter* (Council on African Affairs, New York), March 14, 1952.
3. *East Africa and Rhodesia,* Jan. 20, 1955.
4. *The Sunday Mail,* March 6, 1955.
5. *East Africa and Rhodesia,* April 19, 1956, p. 1162; *Federation Newsletter,* June 11, 1956.
6. Olive Gibson, *The Cost of Living for Africans,* South African Institute of Race Relations, Johannesburg, 1954.
7. Statement by Dr. Olive Robertson, of Salisbury, Southern Rhodesia. Quoted in *East Africa and Rhodesia,* Sept. 29, 1955.
8. *Commission Report,* p. 209 (Ref. IV, 3).

9. *The African Awakening*, p. 151 (Ref. II, 10).
10. "The Labor Code: A Victory for the African Workers," *World Trade Union Movement*, April 16, 1953, p. 21.
11. *East Africa and Rhodesia*, Jan. 15, 1953.
12. *Concord* (Salisbury), December, 1955, p. 25.
13. *East Africa and Rhodesia*, Sept. 18, 1966 *Investment in Federation*, p. 64 (Ref. II, 14).
14. T. L. Hodgkin, "Battle of Schools in the Congo," *West Africa*, Jan. 28, 1956, p. 79.
15. *African Weekly* (Salisbury), Jan. 5, 1955.
16. *East Africa and Rhodesia*, July 30, 1953.
17. Mbiu Koinange, *The People of Kenya Speak for Themselves*, Kenya Publication Fund, Detroit, Michigan, 1955, p. 48.
18. *Ibid.*, p. 62.

CHAPTER 15

1. See V. Larin, "The Cameroons Fight for Unity and Independence," *International* Affairs (Moscow), October, 1955, pp. 90-98.
2. *East Africa and Rhodesia*, Aug. 23, 1956, p. 1821.
3. E. Dumbutshena, "Plain Speaking," *Concord*, December, 1954, p. 36.
4. *East Africa and Rhodesia*, June 21, 1956, pp. 1487, 1508.
5. Chirwa, *Why We Oppose Federation*, p. 5 (Ref. XI, 4).
6. *Bulletin of the Campaign for Defiance of Unjust Laws*, No. 3, July 18, 1952.
7. Alex Hepple, *Trade Unions in Travail*, Johannesburg, 1954, pp. 98-99.
8. "Africans and Non-European Unity," *Inkundla Ya Bantu* (Natal), Oct. 22, 1949.
9. Muhammad el-Farra, "The Algerian Tragedy," *Africa Today* (New York), July-August, 1956, p. 9.
10. *West Africa*, Nov. 5, 1955.
11. *Rhodesia Herald*, Feb. 11, 1956.
12. "Crisis of France in North Africa," *New Statesman and Nation*, April 16, 1955, p. 539.
13. Harold Cooper, "Political Preparedness for Self-Government," *The Annals of the American Academy of Political and Social Science*, July, 1956, pp. 72-74.
14. *Daily Service* (Nigeria), May 13, 1955.
15. *Pittsburgh Courier*, April 14, 1950.
16. Harold Cooper, *African News* (Washington, D. C.), December, 1955, p. 4.
17. Thomas Hodgkin, *Nationalism in Colonial Africa*, London, 1956, p. 162.
18. Quaestor, "The Suez Question," *Labour Monthly* (London), Sept., 1956, p. 414.
19. *Afro-American*, Sept. 15, 1956.

20. Thomas Hodgkin, "Political Parties in French West Africa," *West Africa*, Feb. 20, 1954, p. 159.
21. *West African Pilot*, May 30, 1955.
22. *Industrial Review of Africa*, Oct., 1955, p. 47.
23. F. Oladipo Onipede, "African Nationalism: A Critical Report," *Dissent* (New York), Summer, 1956, p. 282.
24. *West African Pilot*, March 17, 1952.

CHAPTER 16

1. N. Y. *Herald-Tribune*, March 22, 1956.
2. *Indiagram* (Embassy of India, Washington, D. C.), Dec. 27, 1955.
3. *Cape Times*, March 31, 1944.
4. *United Empire* (London), Sept.-Oct., 1945, p. 167. Former Premier Edgar Faure of France, following a four-week trip in 1956 to the same area of the Soviet Union visited by Colonel Ponsonby in 1945, likewise affirmed that the colonial problems inherited from the Czarist regime had been successfully resolved. He contrasted the Soviet's success in such areas as Uzbekistan with French failures in North Africa. (N. Y. *Times*, Oct. 9, 1956.)
5. N. Y. *Herald-Tribune*, Dec. 6, 1955.
6. N. Y. *Times*, May 23, 1956.
7. *Ibid.*, Jan. 7, 1954 .
8. *Ibid.*, April 2, 1956.
9. Scott Long, "African Deadline," N. Y. *Post*, Aug. 16, 1956.
10. The convening powers were Burma, Ceylon, India, Pakistan, and Indonesia. Other participants were China, Japan, Philippines, Afghanistan, Cambodia, Laos, Nepal, Thailand, North Vietnam, and South Vietnam; Iran, Iraq, Jordan, Lebanon, Saudi Arabia, Turkey, Yemen, and Syria; Ethiopia, Gold Coast, Liberia, Libya, Sudan, and Egypt.
11. Jordan K. Ngubane in *Inkundla Ya Bantu*, Aug. 6, 1949.
12. *Ghana Evening News*, Sept. 15, 1955.
13. *Indiagram*, July 18, 1956.
14. *Time*, Aug. 27, 1956, p. 21.

CHAPTER 17

1. New York *Times Magazine*, June 19, 1955, p. 55.
2. "Native Self-Government," *Foreign Affairs*, April, 1944, p. 423.
3. Quoted in Jerome S. Rauch, "Area Institute Programs and African Studies," *Journal of Negro Education*, Fall, 1955, p. 425.
4. N. Y. *Times*, Aug. 23, 1956.
5. N. Y. *Herald-Tribune*, Dec. 29, 1955.

POSTSCRIPT

1. London *Daily Telegraph,* Jan. 14, 1959.
2. Manchester *Guardian,* March 18, 1959.
3. N. Y. *Herald Tribune,* July 10, 1959.
4. Asuquo Ita, "Labor Disunity in Nigeria (3): The Role of Politics and Ideologies," *West African Pilot,* Jan. 23, 1959.
5. Claire François, "Guinée: La décolonisation et ses problemes," *Cahiers Internationaux,* June, 1959, p. 69.
6. *Ibid.,* p. 75.
7. William O. Brown and Hylan Lewis, "Racial Situations and Issues in Africa," in *The United States and Africa,* The American Assembly, Columbia University, New York, 1958, pp. 144-145.

INDEX

Abako (Congo), 156
Action Group, 208-9
Africa, future of, 157-8, 205-6
African Democratic Rally (RDA), 61-62, 215
African history, pre-European, 14-16, 27, 50
African middle class, 170-1, 196-7, 208-10, 225
African National Cong. (S. Africa), 29, 126, 177-9, 199-200.
African National Cong. of N. Rhodesia, 128, 179-81, 198, 202
African Staff Assn. (N. Rhod.), 141
Agricultural production, 32-36, 169, 205, 216
Algeria, 26, 59-60, 172, 175, 176-7, 202; current war, 12, 193; education, 189; farm labor, 33; land expropriation, 28, 206; oil concessions, 95
All-Nigeria T. U. Fed., 216
Aluminium, Ltd., 145-6
American Chemical Corp., 131
American Metal Co., 47, 117-8, 131; investments, 132; profits, 118, 132
American Smelting and Refining Co., 133, 144
Andrews, W. H., 44
Anglo American Corp., 47, 77, 185
Anglo-Transvaal Cons. Investment Co., 124, 133, 145
Angola, 69, 97, 162, 167, 173
Ashanti Goldfields Corp., 70
Asia, 39, 193, 218, 226-7, 230
Awolowo, Obafemi, 208
Azikiwe, Nnamdi, 62, 208, 211, 214

Ball, William H., 129
Banda, T. D. T., 195
Bandung, 214, 226-9
Bases, military, naval, 60, 94, 96-97, 98, 99. *See also* United States, military interests
Beals, Dr. Ralph L., 231
Belgian Congo, 17, 19, 21, 51, 71, 98, 148-52, 162, 173; labor in, 149-51; and *matriculés, évolués,* 189, 196; monopolies in, 148; uranium, 149
Bethlehem Steel Co., 118
Blundell, Michael, 32
Bolton, Frances P., 231
Bourguiba, Habib, 172, 214
Boycotts, 176; in French W. Africa, 61;

Ghana, 62-63; Rhodesias, 53, 179; South Africa, 52-53, 190; by West African farmers, 37
Brazzaville, 184, 221
British Colonial Conference, 64-65
British South Africa Co., 19-20, 72-73, 77
Brown, Dr. William O., 171
Byrnes, James F., 81

Cameroons, 21, 39, 193-4
Capricorn Africa Society, 196-8
Carpenter, Rev. Geo. W., 223-4
Central African Federation, 26, 127-31; opposition to, 30, 127-8, 130
Chaka, 15
Chandos, Lord, 157, 210
China, 219, 222
Chirwa, Y. M. Leonard, 130
Chiume, M. W. K., 194-5, 197
Chou En-lai, 226
Cities, growth of, 50; and black ghettoes, 51-52, 183-4
Clifford, Sir Hugh, 18
Coca Cola, 143
"Collective colonialism," 158-61, 227
Colored, 24; in South Africa, 56, 178, 200
Communism, 46, 61, 173, 198-9, 201, 220, 221, 224-5
Concessionaires, 19, 39, 71-72, 95-97
Congo Free State, 17, 19, 21, 87
Congress of the People, 126
Conorado Petroleum, 95, 96
Convention People's Party (CPP), 63, 209, 211, 212
Cooper, Harold, 207

Dadoo, Dr. Y. M., 198, 200
Danquah, Dr. J. B., 63, 65
D'Arboussier, Gabriel, 61, 191, 215
De Beers syndicate, 20, 66, 73, 119-20; profits, 120; wages, 120
"Development" plans, reaction to, 85, 156-7, 168, 191, 216
Diallo, Abdoulaye, 185
Diamond Co. of Angola, 69; profits, 70; wages, 70
Diké, Dr. K. Onwuka, 14
Doig, Dr. Andrew B., 187, 191
Donges, Dr. T. E., 157
Du Bois, Dr. W. E. B., 9, 17, 67, 224
Dulles, John Foster, 175, 213, 222, 233

273

INDEX

East Africa Royal Commission, 52, 169, 184
Éboué, Felix, 196
Education, 31, 189-90
Egypt, 23, 60, 212-13, 220; aggression against, 12-13, 213, 228; Aswan Dam, 213, 222; oil, 92, 95-96, 143; Suez Canal Control, 96, 212-14, 218
Eisenhower, Dwight D., 86, 116, 129, 228
Embakasi Airport, 89
Ethiopia, 18, 21, 93-94
European common market, 159
European penetration, conquest, 16-21; economic basis of, 18-19; resistance to, 20, 21, 24, 47; and "treaties," 18, 21, 73, 214
Export-Import Bank, 81, 87-88, 103-5, 122-4, 133-4, 151

Ferry, Jules, 19
Firestone Plantations, 18, 100, 101, 103, 107, 109-11; and Firetone profits, 111; wages, 107-8
Flogging, 34, 40, 47, 57, 178-9
Ford Motor Co., 115, 117
Forminière, 87, 148
Franchise, 15, 193-5, 197, 203
Frankel, S. H., 162
Freedom Charter, 126, 195
French Equatorial Africa, 184
French W. Africa, 50, 51, 60-62, 145, 165-6, 193; political parties, 212, 215
Frobisher, Ltd., 148
Funston, G. Keith, 161

General Act of Berlin, 18-19
General Motors, 115, 117
German colonies, division of, 21
Ghana, 13, 14, 18-19, 62-63, 68, 70, 173, 211; agriculture, 33, 35; education, 188-9; oil concession, 97-98; Volta River project, 144-6
Gold Coast, *see* Ghana
Gold Coast T. U. C., 63
Grogan, Ewart S., 22-23, 39
Gulf Oil Corp., 95, 97

Haile Selassie, 18, 88, 93, 94, 225
Havenga, Dr. N. C., 121
Hepple, Alex, 201
Herskovits, Dr. Melville, 230
Hinden, Dr. Rita, 73
Hobson, J. A., 80
Hodgkin, Thomas, 212
Houphouet-Boigny, Felix, 61, 215

Income, per capita or average, in Algeria, 206; Belgian Congo, 164; Ghana, 35; Kenya, 35, 164; Liberia, 109; Nigeria, 35; Uganda, 35
"Independence with interdependence" 171-2, 174-5, 192
Indépendents d'Outre-Mer, 99
India, 218, 219-20, 225
Indians (Asians), 24, 164, 200-1, 208; in South Africa, 56, 178, 200
Int. Basic Commodity Corp., 151
Investments, 19, 87, 172, 210, 211, 219-20; in Congo corporations, 148-9; by European governments, 76, 77, 79, 158, 159; by European finance combinations, 160; in Morocco, 172. *See also* United States investments
Istiqlal Party, 59, 172

Jews, North Africa, 24
Johns-Manville Corp., 131

Katilungu, Lawrence, 142, 181
Kennecott Copper Corp., 124, 144-5
Kenya, 20, 26, 29, 31-33, 57, 88-89, 96-97, 164, 184; agriculture, 36; education, 31, 190; farm labor, 31-33, 182-3, 189; forced labor, 89; land expropriation, 22, 28; Mau Mau uprising, 12, 22-23, 30, 57, 176-7; pass system, 31, 55; White Highlands, 12, 29, 167-8, 206
Kenya African Union, 63, 97, 180, 184, 190, 191, 194
Kenyatta, Jomo, 23, 29, 32, 67, 180
Kikuyu Central Assn., 29, 31, 55
King Ja Ja, 39
Koinange, Mbiu, 190
Kongola, Dixon, 179, 211
Kotane, Moses M., 198
Kreiger, Walter, 115

Labor, and American workers, 235-6; child, 189; convict, 56-57, 89; farm, 31-34, 56-57, 186; forced, 31, 89; and land expropriation, 22, 36, 169; migrant, 33, 42-43, 50, 51, 92, 182, 205; requisitioning of, 30, 43, 107; service contracts, 32-34, 42; and taxes, 29-30, 42; and West African governments, 215
Labor, industrial, color bar, 41-44, 45, 46, 48, 117, 125, 138-42, 163-7 (*see also* Trade unions); in mines, 40-49, 125-6, 137; recruiting system, 42-43; wages, 43-44, 48, 125, 136, 139, 148,

INDEX

150-1, 183, 185 (*see also* Strikes *and* under individual companies)
Land, communal ownership, 18, 27; elimination of, 169-70
Land expropriation, 22, 28-29, 47, 168-71; protests against, 29, 190, 191
Lend-lease, reverse, 65
Leopold II, *see* Congo Free State
Le Tourneau, R. G., 105
Lever Bros., *see* United Africa Co.
Liberia, 18, 21, 100-14, 222, 225; foreign concessions, 104-7, 109-12; labor conditions, 107-9; political climate, 113-14; port agreement, 80-81, 102-3; social conditons, 109-10, 184; taxes, 111, 113
Liberia Co., 81, 102, 103, 105
Liberia Mining Co., 103, 104-6, 111-12, 182; profits, 105, 112; wages, 112
Libya, 21; oil concessions, 94-95; and Wheelus Airfield lease, 99
Living Standards, 51-53, 60-61; deterioration of, 183-4
Lobengula, 20
Logan, Rayford W., 165-6
Luthuli, Albert John, 30, 90, 182, 199

Macaulay, Herbert, 15
Madagascar, 60
Malan, Dr. Daniel F., 120-2, 174
Malvern, Lord, 128, 129, 163, 186, 190, 195
Marketing boards, 35, 37-38
Marquard, Leo, 203
Marshall Plan, 73ff., 81 ff., 96, 120, 133, 144, 160; and support of European economy, 18, 75
Masonite Corp., 117
Matthews, Joseph G., 201
Matthews, Z. K., 182, 199
Mboya, Tom, 194, 202
Military conferences, 92
Minerals extracted, value of, 68-70, 120, 123, 135, 211
Mining, 70, 74; by Africans, 15-16, 71-73; in Angola, 69; Belgian Congo, 69; Ghana, 70, 71, 211; Nigeria, 70, 84; N. Rhodesia Copper-belt, 15, 47-49, 69, 131-2, 135-7; Sierra Leone, 70-72; S. Rhodesia, 47, 69; South Africa, 15, 20, 40-41, 47, 68-69, 118, 123, 126; South West Africa, 15-16, 70
Morgan interests, 48, 87, 100, 116
Morgenthau, Hans J., 92
Morocco, 11-12, 21, 147, 172, 202; and French economy, 64; land expropriation, 28

Moslem belt of Black Africa, 23
Mozambique, 76-77; land alienation, 167, 171; oil concession, 97; uranium, 76
Mutesa II, 147

Nasser, Gamal Abdel, 212-4, 222-3, 228
National Council of Nigeria and Cameroons (NCNC), 63, 208, 211
Nationalism, 15, 65, 191, 201, 227
Negro people in the U.S., 23, 176, 224, 236
Nehru, Jawaharlal, 200, 225, 228
Neo-Destour Party, 172
Neutralism, 222, 228
"New imperialism," 172
Newmont Mining Corp., 81, 115, 117-8, 144; profits, 118 1
Nigeria, 15, 16, 26, 27, 62, 98, 172, 217; agriculture, 33, 35; and columbite, 84, 144-5; foreign concessions, 144, 211, political parties, 208-9
Nixon, Richard M., 13, 222, 223
Nkoloma, M. D., 142
Nkrumah, Kwame, 63, 67, 147-8, 173, 192, 209, 211, 212, 217
Nkumbula, Harry, 179-80, 191
North Atlantic Treaty Org. (NATO), 12, 84, 94, 172, 214
Northern People's Congress, 209
N. Rhod. African Mine Workers Union, 137-42, 181
Nyasaland, 30, 127, 131, 195-6; farm labor, 32
Nyasaland African Congress, 128, 195-6
Nyobe, Ruben Um, 194

Ojukwu, Louis Philip, 208
Okotie-Eboh, Festus Samuel, 208
Olin Mathieson Chemical Corp., 148
O'okiep Copper Co., 117-8; profits, 118
Oppenheimer, Sir Ernest, 47, 119, 140-41

Pacific Iron and Steel Co., 151
Pan-African Congress, 67
Passive resistance, in N. Rhodesia, 179; in South Africa, 34, 177-9
Political control and assimilation policy, 172, 196; forms of, 26, 171-2; and indirect rule, 26, 207; means of, 173. *See also* White settlers
Ponsonby, Sir Charles, 220
Population, in cities, 50; by forms of political control, 26; by territories, 23-24; independent, under African rule, 25; under white rule, 25

INDEX

Portuguese colonies, 26, 167, 171, 227; and *civilizados*, 189, 196; education in, 189. *See also* Angola, Mozambique
Poujadist movement, 202-3
Prain, Sir Ronald L., 129, 139, 141, 150
Présence Francaise, 202-3
Profits, in Belgian Congo, 74, 149; in Copperbelt mines, 135-6; in South Africa, 73-74, 119, 122-3, 125; of Suez Canal Co., 213. *See also* United States investments *and* individual companies

Republic Steel Corp., 105, 112
Resources, and dependent colonial economy, 73, 157-8, 161-2, 186, 205-6, 216; dollar-earnings from, 64-66, 157-8; increased production of, 13, 16, 64, 68, 74-76, 90; power facilities for utilizing, 77, 79, 129, 133-4, 147; search for mineral, 76-77, 92-97, 121; transport facilities for export of, 16, 75, 77, 79, 98, 102-5, 133, 147, 183
Rhodes, Cecil John, 19-20, 41, 80
Rhodesian Anglo American Corp., 132
Rhodesian Selection Trust, 129, 131-2, 139, 140, 150
Rhodesias, 13-14, 47-49, 52, 127-42, 163, 165-6, 168-9, 184; and British South Africa Co., 20, 72; education in, 187-90; "emergency" repression in, 180-1; and Kariba project, 134, 168-9; labor movement in, 49, 137-42, 211; land expropriation in, 28, 134. *See also* Central African Federation
Robeson, Paul, 178, 224
Rockefeller interests, 87, 149, 151
Romulo, Carlos P., 230
Ross, Dr. Emory, 230
Royal Niger Co., 37
Ruanda-Urundi, 15
Rudin, Harry R., 157

Sahara, 23, 95
Sangala, J. S., 195
Searls, Fred, Jr., 81
Self-government, 192, 197, 204, 223-4, 226-9; countries now exercising, 26; and economic emancipation, 204-7, 209-12, 214-7, 226, 231; and national unity, 207-9; and non-African minorities, 202; transition to, 173, 210-12
Self-government demands, 11, 58, 67; in Algeria, 193, 206; Belgian Congo, 194; Cameroons, 193-4; French West Africa, 61, 194; Ghana, 63; Kenya, 194; Morocco, 59, 172; Nigeria, 62; Nyasaland, 194-5; Sierra Leone, 27; South Africa, 195; Tanganyika, 27; Uganda, 194
Senghor, Léopold Sédar, 212
Sierra Leone, 70, 71-2, 186
Sims, Bishop David Henry, 46
Sinclair Oil Corp., 18, 93, 96, 97
Slave trade, 16-17; and the United States, 17
Smuts, Jan C., 220
Société Générale, 148
Soekarno, Achmed, 226
Somali Youth League, 202
Somalia (French), 98
Somalia (Ital. trusteeship), 26, 202; oil concessions in, 96
South Africa, 16, 40-46, 52-57, 115-26, 164-5, 167, 174, 203-4; Bambata's rebellion, 30; Boer War, 21, 41; education, 189-90; farm labor, 33-34, 56-57, 163-4; investment climate, 115; land expropriation, 28, 169; legalized oppression of Africans, 33-34, 42, 54-56, 164, 178-9, 198-9; living standards, 53, 183, 206; pass system, 34, 41, 42, 54-55; persecution of democratic forces, 181-2; police assaults, 12, 54, 178; Suppression of Communism Act, 181, 198; "treason" trial, 182, 198; uranium, 68, 91, 120-6
South African Congress of Trade Unions, 201
South African Indian Congress, 177, 178, 200
South African Institute of Race Relations, 203
Soviet Union, 220-1, 225; cooperation of West and, 221, 232-3; economic aid from, 218-23, 225-6, 231; and Suez issue, 214, 218
Standard Oil (N. J.), 95, 96, 97
Stanley, Henry Morton, 17, 20
Sterling balances, 157-8, 216-7
Stevenson, Adlai, 80
Stettinius, Edw. R., Jr., 80-81, 105
Strijdom, Johannes G., 171, 174
Strikes, 63-64, 184-186; in Ghana, 211; Madagascar, 60; Nigeria, 38, 62; Rhodesias, 47-49, 137-8, 181; South Africa, 45-46; Tunisia, 60
Sudan, Republic of, 213, 214
Swart, Charles Robert, 56, 178

Tanganyika, 15, 36, 77, 169
Tanganyika Concessions, 77, 149

INDEX 277

Thuku, Harry, 32
Todd, R. S. Garfield, 169, 187
Trade Unions, 58, 62, 90, 185-6, 214-6 (*see also* Strikes); non-recognition of, 43, 49, 90; white, 137, 140-1, 201
Trading companies, 37-39, 209
Transvaal Chamber of Mines, 42
Tribalism, 14, 45-46, 208
Tsumeb mines, 15-16, 117; profits, 118; wages, 118
Tubman, William V. S., 88, 106, 107, 109, 112, 113-4
Tunisia, 172, 214-5; land expropriation, 28; oil concessions, 95
Turkson-Ocran, E. C., 173
Twentieth Century-Fox Film Corp., 117

Uganda, 15, 26, 147-8, 156, 191, 216; agriculture, 33, 35, 36
Uganda National Congress, 194, 216
Union Carbide and Carbon Corp., 9c, 131; wages, 131
Union Minière, 148-9; profits, 149, 151; wages, 151
Union of South Africa, see South Africa
United Africa Co., 37-39, 71, 210
United Gold Coast Conv., 63
United States, economic interests, 13, 38, 75, 79, 147; African exports to, 66, 84, 102, 110, 149, 152-3; African imports from, 66, 102, 121, 152-3; competing for control of African markets, 67, 84-85, 114, 117, 153; cooperation with private enterprise, 80-82, 85-86, 104-6, 124; and De Beers monopoly, 119-20; and economic missions to Africa, 66, 75-77, 86, 104, 152; and oil companies in Africa, 93-97, 103, 116, 143; in Ethiopia, 93-94; in Ghana, 83, 90; in Liberia, 100-6; in Rhodesias, 14, 129-35; in South Africa, 40, 41, 115-23, 175
United States Information Service, 224
United States investments, 14, 21, 87, 93, 143-5, 148-9, 151, 153-5; criteria of, 88-90, 129; by oil interests, 95-97, 116, 143; profits on, 154 (*see also* individual companies); in Liberia, 104-7; in Rhodesias, 14, 48, 129-32; in South Africa, 116-8, 124
United States loans, grants, 76, 81, 87-88, 231; as "Cold War" weapon, 222-3, 233-4; through Point Four, 82-83, 85; to Belgian Congo, 151; Ethiopia, 94; Europe, 66-67; French colonies, 76, 82; Ghana, 145; Kenya, 97; Liberia, 103-5; Portuguese colonies, 133; Rhodesias, 129, 131-4; South Africa, 121-3
United States, military interests, 91-92, 94, 98; bases in Africa, 91, 94, 98-99, 103, 215; stock pile program, 83-84, 119, 122, 133
U.S. Plywood Corp., 151
United States policy, on Africa, 157, 174, 224, 230-8; and importance of U.S. role in Africa, 16, 79-80, 159-60, 237; supporting French in North Africa, 13, 15, 91, 175; supporting Kenya settler interests, 88-89; supporting Rhodesia settler interests, 129-30, 175; supporting South African Govt., 91, 115-6, 120-2, 174, 204; on Suez issue, 96, 214; on underdeveloped countries, 86, 109, 161-2
U.S. Steel Corp., 118, 144

Vanadium Corp., 131
Vasey, E. A., 164
Verwoerd, Hendrik F., 163-4, 189-90
Voice of America, 224

Wallace Johnson, I. T. A., 72
Welensky, Roy, 127-8, 161-2, 175
Wheelus Airfield, 94, 99
White settlers, 24, 39, 171; and African-white unity, 197-9, 201; current demands for more, 13-14, 162-3; as dividing factor in Africa, 23, 26-27; land holdings of, 28, 206; land settlement plans for, 167-8; number of, 23-24, 163, 166, 167; political domination by, 26, 27, 54, 127-8, 165, 171, 173-4, 176, 192-3, 195-9, 203; recruitment of, for industrial work, 165-7; and segregation policy, 51, 52, 54-55, 128; subsidies for, 36, 158, 167-8, 187, 206
Williams, Dr. Eric, 16
Women, in Kenya, 12, 31, 89; in South Africa, 34, 50, 53, 178
World Bank, 81, 82, 87-8, 122, 133-4, 151, 219-20, 222
World Trade Union Congress, 67

Young Kikuyu Assn., 31
Youssef, Salah ben, 172

Zik Enterprises, Ltd., 208
Zukas, Simon, 198

www.ingramcontent.com/pod-product-compliance
Lightning Source LLC
Chambersburg PA
CBHW032038150426
43194CB00006B/324